A Walk to the River in Amazonia

A Walk to the River in Amazonia

Ordinary Reality for the Mehinaku Indians

Carla Stang

Berghahn Books
New York • Oxford

First published in 2009 by
Berghahn Books
www.berghahnbooks.com

©2009, 2012 Carla Stang
First paperback edition published in 2012

Library of Congress Cataloging-in-Publication Data
Stang, Carla
  A walk to the river in Amazonia : ordinary reality for the Mehinaku Indians /
Carla Stang.
    p. cm.
  Includes bibliographical references.
  ISBN 978-1-84545-555-2 (hbk) -- ISBN 978-0-85745-155-2 (pbk)
  1. Mehinacu Indians--Psychology. 2. Mehinacu Indians--Attitudes. 3. Mehi-
nacu Indians--Social conditions. I. Title.

  F2520.1.M44S83 2008
  155.8'49839--dc22

                            2008026237

British Library Cataloguing in Publication Data

A catalogue record for this book is available from the British Library

Printed in the United States on acid-free paper.

ISBN 978-0-85745-155-2 (paperback)
ISBN 978-0-85745-449-2 (ebook)

'Examine for a moment an ordinary mind on an ordinary day. The mind receives a myriad impressions – trivial, fantastic, evanescent, or engraved with the sharpness of steel. From all sides they come, an incessant shower of innumerable atoms....'

VIRGINIA WOOLF
The Common Reader

'How strange,' said Bernard, 'the willow looks seen together. I was Byron, and the tree was Byron's tree, lachrymose, down-showering, lamenting. Now that we look at the tree together, it has a combined look, each branch distinct, and I will tell you what I feel, under the compulsion of your clarity.'

VIRGINIA WOOLF
The Waves

Contents

Figures

Plates

Preface

The way of life written about in this book has been under threat for many years. This situation has reached a critical point. In 2007 the Mehinaku, together with the other peoples of the Xingu, declared their concerns to the Brazilian nation and the international community at large.

CARTA ABERTA DOS POVOS XINGUANOS À NAÇÃO BRASILEIRA

Nós, líderes máximos dos povos da civilização xinguana, reunidos na aldeia kuikuro de Ipatse, em 21 de julho de 2007, queremos compartilhar com a nação brasileira a grave situação vivida no Parque Indígena do Xingu (PIX). Nossa civilização milenar vem resistindo há quinhentos anos a guerras de conquista, escravização, epidemias e roubo de terras. Nos últimos anos, a irresponsabilidade social e ambiental na região das cabeceiras dos formadores do rio Xingu coloca em risco a nossa saúde e a continuidade de nossa cultura. O desmatamento acelerado e irracional, a expansão agrícola, o uso desmesurado de agrotóxicos e, agora, a construção de barragens vêm destruindo a própria base de nossa subsistência. A poluição das águas e a contaminação do pescado são uma ameaça para o nosso futuro, não apenas por serem eles condição de nossa reprodução física, mas também de nossa vida cultural. Vivemos milenarmente nesta bacia de forma sustentável e em dependência direta dos recursos aquáticos.

Como representantes legítimos dos povos xinguanos solicitamos o apoio de toda a nação brasileira e da comunidade internacional para resistirmos a mais uma ameaça que nos cerca. Já perdemos boa parte de nossas terras com avanço da fronteira econômica e, agora, a destruição irracional ingressa na terra que nos resta. Exigimos um plano global de gestão da bacia do rio Xingu, não apenas no interior do PIX, mas que abarque toda a região dos formadores. A destruição iminente da bacia atinge a todos nós, índios e não-índios, e em particular às gerações futuras. Não podemos esperar mais 10 anos. O dano ambiental será irreversível. Queremos ações já para preservar um patrimônio que não é só nosso, mas da nação e de toda humanidade.

Em particular, exigimos:

- a imediata paralisação de todas as obras de barragens na região dos formadores;
- uma moratória sobre as licenças para instalação de novas PCHs;
- um estudo detalhado sobre a condição da água e do pescado;
- um plano de reflorestamento das margens dos rios e de seus afluentes;
- a recuperação da posse de áreas tradicionais excluídas da área do PIX;
- o reconhecimento e preservação de nossos locais sagrados, Sagihengu e Kamukwaká, que se encontram fora dos limites do PIX.

AFUKAKA KUIKURO
Afukaká Kuikuro

Aritana Yawalapiti

KUIUSSI SUYA
Kuiusí Kinsêdje

XAMATUÁ MATIPU
Jamatuá Matipu

TAFUKUMA KALAPALO
Tahukumã Kalapalo

MUIN MEHINAKO
Jumuí Mehinaku

KURIKARE KALAPALO
Kugikage Kalapalo

YSAUTAKU VVAURA
Itsautako Waurá

TIRIFE NAFUKUÁ
Tirifé Nahukwá

Awaiatu Aweti
Awaiatu Aweti

OPEN LETTER TO THE BRAZILIAN NATION
FROM THE XINGUANO PEOPLES

We, the principal leaders of the Xinguano civilisation, gathered in the Kuikuro village of Ipatse on the 21st of July 2007, want to share with the Brazilian nation the grave situation in the Indigenous Park of the Xingu (PIX). For five hundred years, our thousands of years old civilization has been resisting subjugation wars, slavery, epidemics and land theft. In the last years, the social and environmental irresponsibility in the region of the headwaters of the Xingu river tributaries has been putting our health and the survival of our culture at risk. The rapid and reckless deforestation, the agricultural development, the excessive use of agro-toxics and, lately, dam-building, have been destroying the very core of our subsistence. Water pollution and fish contamination are a threat to our future, because they are essential not only to our physical reproduction but also to our cultural life. We have lived for thousands of years in this basin in a sustainable way and in direct dependence on its aquatic resources.

As legitimate representatives of the Xinguano people, we seek the support of the whole Brazilian nation and of the international community to fight against this new threat. With the advance of the economic frontier, we have already lost a great part of our territory and now, this careless destruction invades the lands we still have. We demand a global management plan for the river Xingu basin, to cover not only the interior of the PIX, but also the whole region of the headwaters. The impending destruction of the basin affects all of us, Indians and non-Indians, and in particular the future generations. We cannot wait for another ten years. By then, the environmental damage will be irreversible. We want immediate action to preserve a heritage that is not only ours, but also belongs to the nation and the whole of mankind.

We specifically demand:

- the immediate halting of all dam works in the region of the headwaters;
- a moratorium on licences for the installation of new PCHs;
- an in-depth study on the quality of the water and fish;
- a reforestation plan for the banks of the rivers and their tributaries;
- the regaining of the traditional areas excluded from the PIX region;
- the recognition and preservation of our sacred places, Sagihengu and Kamukwaká, which are found outside the PIX limits.

Acknowledgements

My fieldwork in the Mehinaku community was funded by the Cambridge Commonwealth Trust, King's College Cambridge, the Richards Fund and a Worts Travel Grant. My time at the University of Cambridge was supported by King's College, the Cambridge Commonwealth Trust and the Wyse Fund.

I am fortunate to have had Stephen Hugh-Jones as my supervisor, who generous with his incisive, inspiring intelligence and warm and compassionate presence, supported me throughout my research and writing. I am grateful to the Department of Social Anthropology in Cambridge, its staff and students, for the convivial and stimulating environment in which I feel privileged to have been able to pursue this work. I thank King's College for being a haven; the librarians at the college library for gentle help while I set up camp there for months; Professor Macfarlane for the deep love of anthropology he instils.

My deepest gratitude to Jadran Mimica, whose greatness of vision, learning and heart has been from the beginning, and is ever, an inspiration of the best anthropology, not to mention a person, can be. Also, my thanks to Michael Jackson, who during my undergraduate degree at the University of Sydney graced the year that he taught me with the humane and profound insight of his ethnography, which I have aspired to ever since. Also, thank you to Stephen, Jadran and Michael, who were instrumental to getting this book published. I am grateful to the people at Berghahn Books, especially Marion Berghahn for believing in this work and for the insights from conversation with her that have inspired me since, Ann Przyzycki for her warm patience and the intelligent clarity of her comments, and the terrific Melissa Spinelli. In Brazil, the Cohens took me into their family without hesitation; and without Evelyn, *minha mãe Brasileira,* who knows what would have become of me. The people at the Museu Nacional in Rio de Janeiro immediately brought me into their fold and helped me begin the path toward fieldwork, particularly Aparecida

Vilaça, with her practical help and kindnesses, Carlos Fausto, who acted as my Brazilian supervisor, and Cesar Gordon. Also thanks to Cecilia Mc-Callum and Elizabeth Ewart who gave me good and kind pre-fieldwork advice. In the last stage of the preparation of the manuscript I am grateful to the inspirational Michael Taussig, his comments and course, the 'Art of Fieldwork', which together helped me finish this book and made me want to write others.

To those closest to me, thank you for your love and patience. My family, especially my heroic mother and father, always there, every step, nurturing my faint hopes into reality, my sister (the clouds that we see together) and my Supta (the clouds that we paint together). My friends, sources of insight and strength: 'angel' Angelina Kouroubali, lionhearted Erica Packer, Guillermo Olguín, Sheleyah Courtney, Alon Musael and Matthew Tey. Also my friends in Cambridge: Kyle Rand, Andrew Moutu, Keston Sutherland, Martin Holbraad, Federico Williams, Morten Axel Pedersen and Lars Hojer, and for the same and all their substantial help: Alex Regier, Sam Ladkin, Erik Freeman, Ian Houston Shadwell, Alex Wilcox, Howard Collinge and Carlos Viviani.

I dedicate this work to the people of the Mehinaku community who took me in and included me in their wondrous world; for this and for the indelible memories I will be grateful forever. I would particularly like to name Matawarë whose recent death means that a glorious grace and wisdom is gone from this world; also, Takulalu who treated me as a daughter, her daughters Mahí, Kwakani, Kohôlupe, and her son, Maiawai. I try not to miss you too much, as I know you would want it that way.

Pronouncing Mehinaku Words

The following is a guide to pronouncing the way Mehinaku words have been written:

Syllables are to be pronounced with equal stress unless vowel sounds indicate otherwise

Vowels

a, as in b*u*t

ã   as in b*u*t, with vowel nasalation

e, as in r*e*st

é, as in r*e*st, with stress on the syllable it occurs in

ë, as in c*u*rfew, with stress on the syllable it occurs in

i   as in s*i*t

í   as in s*i*t, with stress on the syllable it occurs in

o   as in r*o*ll ('ow' as in c*o*w)

u   as in w*oo*d

Consonants are to be pronounced according to English convention

Glossary

akāi: a kind of tree and its fruit, commonly known as 'pequi', scientific name *Caryocar butyrosum*

amunão: chief(s)

Anapi: the Rainbow Spirit

apapanye: spirit being(s)

Ateshua: a chief of the spirit beings

awëshëpai: well-being of a person or situation

awitsiri: beautiful

branco: a 'white' person (Portuguese)

chuluki: a particular practice of exchanging goods

énéshu: man

Enutsikya: the Thunder/Lightning Spirit

iníya: smell

ipyamawékéhë: sorcerer

Kamë: the Sun Spirit

Kawëka: the Spirit of the Sacred Flutes

Keshë: the Moon Spirit

ketepepei: joyful, gentle behaviour

kupatë: fish

Kwamutë: The Creator Being

pegar: to catch (Portuguese)

shapushë: wild

tinéshu: woman

Umënéshë: the first human women, created by *Kwamutë*

umënupiri: flesh-body

uleitsi: manioc tuber

uwekehë: owner

Washayu: Wild Indians

washë: true

Yakashukuma: the Alligator Spirit

yakulai: soul-body

Yamurikuma: Women Spirit(s) who hunt and fish (also the name of the story of their origin and their music/dance)

yatama: shaman(s)

yerekyuki: the danger of not satisfying hunger

yerepëhë: small humanoid beings of the primordial darkness

yewekui: soul-body of a dead human-being

yeya: an archetypal entity

Introduction

I. The Question

The idea for this book first came to me after watching a spectacular Mehinaku dance called the *Kayapa*. My friend Wanakuwalu and I took up some water containers and began to make our way down the path to the river. As we walked along I thought about the *Kayapa*, its significance and so on, and then watching the forest line felt the stinging heat on my skin from the sun above, smelled the wetness rising from the earth, and looking at Wanakuwalu walking swiftly ahead, suddenly thought: what is all this to her? The earth, the sunshine, the walking along? Why not make this the subject of a study rather than focussing on the events that stand out like dancing, marriage and politics? Instead of studying the *Kayapa* dance, why not investigate the moments after and between, that is, the experience of ordinary reality?

The question of my research thus became: what is the Mehinaku sense of reality like, especially their experience of life when nothing in particular is going on? I see the most obvious significance of such an investigation in the simple fact that most of peoples' lives are, as it happens, constituted by these ordinary moments, and, if only for this reason, are important for an anthropologist to explore. Also, in this anthropology of the ordinary or interstitial that I propose, I hope to show how aspects of the more salient and studied parts of life (such as the dances, marriages, funerary rites) in fact enter into these in-between experiences, as well as how more abstract schemas made by anthropologists, of 'cosmology', 'sociality', 'personhood' etc., are actually lived. It is a common anthropological aim to fulfil, in various ways, Malinowski's 'final goal of anthropology ... to grasp the native's point of view' (1999[1922]: 25); this book however is specifically

concerned with the problematics of studying and the nature of 'the im-
ponderabilia of actual life' (1999[1922]: 18–20).

II. Writing about Lived Experience

My interest then in ordinary reality for the Mehinaku is in terms of it as an
aspect of actual experience. Therefore, before explaining how I will look at
ordinary reality in particular, I will first elucidate this general orientation
towards 'life as lived' (Riesman 1977) and how I will approach writing
about it. Various anthropologists have shared this interest, in fact, as mentioned above, comprehending peoples' 'view of the world' is one of the
most classical anthropological endeavours, Malinowski himself stating:
'[W]hat interests me really in the study of the native is his outlook on life,
… the breath of life and reality which he breathes and by which he lives'
(1999[1922]: 517). Michael Jackson writes of the 'life one wants to understand' (1996: 2), the sense of people's 'being-in-the world' (1996: 1).
Casey maintains that for 'an anthropologist in the field, his task is … to set
forth as accurately as possible what being-in-place means' (1996: 15) to
the people concerned. Similarly, Abu-Lughod looks to 'the lives people see
themselves as living' (*in* Jackson 1996: 7). In regard to Amazonian studies,
Gow has built up a large body of work 'concerned to develop a phenomenological account of the lived world of these people' (2000: 46).[1]
   This concern with 'human consciousness in its lived immediacy' (Jackson 1996: 2) is a phenomenological one and also one of radical empiricism.[2] The pragmatist William James writes that consciousness is 'the immediate flux of life' (1947: 93) and the phenomenologist Merleau-Ponty
describes it as the 'flow of experiences' (1962: 281). This 'stream of pure
experience' (James 1947: 95) must be approached as a totality because
as plain, unqualified actuality it is 'as yet undifferentiated into thing and
thought' (1947: 74). That is to say that in consciousness the subjective and
the objective fuse into a certain continuum as 'human experience vacillates between a sense of ourselves as subjects and objects; in effect, making
us feel sometimes that we are world-makers, sometimes that we are merely
made by the world' (Jackson 1996: 21).
   As this undifferentiated stream of experience is to be the general subject
of this book's enquiry, I shall look more closely at it here. Yet the harder
one attempts to grasp it, the more it evades understanding because it is by
nature 'indeterminate and ambiguous' (Jackson 1996: 14), as well as 'intricate' and 'neverending' (Casey 1996: 19). James writes that in conscious-

ness the world 'comes to us first as a chaos of experiences' (1947: 16) and Merleau-Ponty describes it as a 'play of colours, noises and fleeting tactile sensations' (1962: x). This 'morphological vagueness' (Casey 1996: 27) of experience is a result of the fact that, as Merleau-Ponty puts it, consciousness 'does not give me truth like geometry but presences' (1964: 14 *in* Feld 1996: 91).

Although we cannot hope to transmit the infinite scope of consciousness, I suggest that certain aspects can be discerned in its midst. This implies that experience is constituted by different dimensions, and I believe various theorists have discussed this, albeit in different ways. In his study of Yaka culture, René Devisch (1993) sees these 'levels' as not confined to the human being but as pervading the whole 'spatial layout' as 'fields' of the social, corporeal and cosmic and further elaborated in different 'categories' such as maleness, femaleness, uprightness and concentricity. Likewise, Alfred Schutz discusses existential 'horizons' and 'modalities' (*from* Jackson 1996) and Alfred Gell (1996) writes of Umeda experience in terms of various 'planes'.

These different dimensions of experience are not discrete but relate to each other, correspond with one another. This is possible because they constitute what Gell calls 'a set of paradigmatic equivalents' (1996: 121). Harking back to structuralism, Lévi-Strauss explains how the 'levels' or 'structures' that we have been discussing have 'symbols' that correspond to each other, the symbolic function linking these 'meaningful equivalents' (1963: 203). Devisch writes similarly of 'correlations' between 'categories' (1993: 96), while Jackson discusses how country and person 'coalesce' (1996: 123) in Warlpiri cosmology.

It is important to note here that the nature of these planes and their relations can be extremely culturally specific, as Casey writes: '[E]ven the most primordial level of perceiving is inlaid with cultural categories, in the form of differential patterns of recognition, ways of organising the perceptual field and acting in it and manners of designating and naming items in the field' (1996: 34). Also, this paradigmatic 'pattern' (Gell 1996: 124) that one discerns in the field is not a conceptual model that can simply be 'extracted' from the 'crude ore' of immediate experience (Jackson 1996: 24). That is, it is not a universal abstract waiting to emerge nor is it a group of answers to a universal model imposed from outside. It is quite simply a description of the way immediate experience is working, with the nature of these dimensions and their relations an open empirical question.

Moreover, these patterns of associations are not static but 'activated' in the flow of lived experience. Bachelard calls it the imagination, the flow of consciousness from image to image whereby 'resonances are dispersed on different planes of our life in the world' (1969: xxii). James evokes a similar motion when he compares the way consciousness slips continually from one modality to another 'with the ceaseless movement of a bird between flights and perchings' (*in* Jackson 1996: 26). Merleau-Ponty, employing a Gestalt model, shows us how consciousness continually shifts between figure and ground (*in* Jackson 1996: 14) and Jackson writes about the way human experience vacillates between a sense of ourselves as subject and object (*in* Jackson 1996: 21). What all these theorists are discussing is the dynamic of consciousness, its stream. It is crucial that this flow never be understood as simply a 'thinking' consciousness. Merleau-Ponty writes that consciousness is 'a being towards the thing through the intermediary of the body' (1962: 137), and in Stephen Feld's words it is 'the lived body as an ecstatic/recessive being, engaged in both leaping out and falling back' (1996: 92).

So far, in discussing the nature of consciousness, I have suggested how it is constituted by a paradigmatic network and also by a certain dynamic. However, it is important to emphasise that these never exist independently of one another. So, now I would like to look at how they come indissolubly together, the dynamic activating the levels of associations in a trajectory of lived experience. We have already seen Lévi-Strauss's notion of the 'symbolic function' that mediates the 'different levels of life' via their correspondences. The phenomenological perspective compels us to look at the experience of the structuralists' 'symbolic function', the experience of experience. James describes the flux of pure experience in the following way:

> Far back as we go, the flux, both as a whole and in its parts, ... come as separate in some ways and as continuous in others. Some sensations coalesce with some ideas, and others are irreconcilable. Qualities compenetrate one space, or exclude each other from it. They cling together persistently in groups that move as units, or else they separate. Their changes are abrupt or discontinuous and their kinds resemble or differ; and as they do so, they fall into either even or irregular series ... Prepositions, copulas, and conjunctions, ... flower out of the stream of pure experience, the stream of concretes or the sensational stream, as naturally as nouns and adjectives do, and they melt again as fluidly when we apply them to a new portion of the stream. (1947: 94–95)

So, having begun by referring to the sense of the ambiguousness of experience, we then discerned some of its characteristics and now we focus on how these come together in its 'flux'. James calls this unity of diversity that he described in the quote above, '*concatenated* union', "the world it represents as a collection, some parts of which are conjunctively and others disjunctively related ... [a] determinately various hanging-together" (1996: 107). As a stream of consciousness the 'flux of it tends to fill itself with emphases, and these salient parts become identified and fixed and abstracted; so that experience now flows as if shot through with adjectives and nouns' (James 1996: 94).

Coming back to anthropology, ethnographers before me have indeed set out to describe this concatenated flow of consciousness that moves between correspondences on different planes. In his approach to "taboo" in Umeda culture, Gell portrays a hunter's consciousness in terms of the way certain *tadv* (eating associated) relations 'become salient from moment to moment', in their 'enchainment' in 'the flow of social life' (1996: 122). Devisch writes of the correlations in Yaka culture that emerge and are 'weaved' in the flow of women's dancing (1996: 113). And in a similar way, Feld explores Kaluli consciousness by tracing the 'interiorised macrotour' that a Kaluli person passes along in listening to song (1996: 125). My ethnographic project is an attempt along the general lines of these authors.

III. Writing about Ordinary Reality: from My Walk, through Her World, to Her Walk

Therefore, in this book my general concern is to write about lived experience or consciousness for the Mehinaku, and now I will explain my approach to the specific aspect of this consciousness that is my focus, that is, ordinary reality. At the start of this chapter, I explained that by 'ordinary reality' I mean those parts of life that happen between activities and other discrete events, those moments when one is not concentrating on doing anything in particular: waiting for a bus, pausing during work, lying in a hammock after a meal, or walking along. I am not trying to assert that there is any such cross-cultural 'thing' as ordinary reality. Rather, what I am trying to get at is an understanding of the most general kind of the various flows of a person's consciousness. In using the term 'ordinary', I do not want to imply in any way that these experiences are necessarily mundane or in any way less interesting than others. As I mentioned earlier, I found that this part of life is in fact 'shot through' as it were, with aspects of more salient parts of life, as well as abstract notions like ontological, cosmological conceptualisations; all of these in fact coming into play in this flow of consciousness, while also standing beside and blending with more prosaic moments.

In the previous section, I described how I will write about the flux of experience in terms of a flow of consciousness that moves between correspondences of various levels. The way I will reach an understanding of ordinary reality is by coming to terms with it in one specific incidence of such a flow. I will look at a walk similar to the one with which I began this chapter, another walk to the river with Wanakuwalu that I described in detail in an early journal entry. I will give an excerpt from this journal entry in chapter 1, which will show how I myself experienced the walk, then in chapters 2, 3, 4 and 5 I will explore the various aspects of Mehinaku experience in general, so that in chapter 7 this general knowledge can be used ultimately to come to some comprehension of the way Wanakuwalu,[3] a young woman roughly my own age, experienced the same walk. Therefore the structure of this book has three main parts or stages in which I attempt to guide the reader along what was roughly my own path of understanding: from that walk in the first part of my stay; continuing to live and learn about everything I could with the Mehinaku (including innumerable other walks to the river); to finally, having left the field, turn back, and using the knowledge gained, look differently at that same walk from my journal, attempting to 'imagine' the event through my friend's eyes. Readers thus will make their way along their own journey: from my walk through her world and thus to her walk. There are of course implications for such an approach, which I will consider below.

First of all, the one event that is described is not meant to be representative of all Mehinaku people's experience of ordinary reality. In looking at one 'fragment' of one person's stream of consciousness we can get an exemplary sense of what ordinary reality is like, and how salient and much studied events are lived as part of it, thus fulfilling the aims stated earlier.

Second, besides its own inherent logic, the notion of understanding a part of something according to the principles of the whole, or in this case, one incidence of a person's experience according to the principles of their experience in general, can be related to Malinowski's methods. Malinowski believed that 'finally people's lives do, on the whole, tend to make sense to them' and it was in terms of this 'finally coherent meaningfulness' that he tried to understand any thing in the field (Gow 2001: 25). It is in the Malinowskian tradition then, that in chapters 2, 3, 4 and 5, I will attempt to discern the way Mehinaku lives do 'tend to make sense to them', and with this knowledge then look again at the walk to describe the experience in these terms.

This 'coherent meaningfulness' will be portrayed in terms of the categories, connections and dynamics that I argued earlier are constitutive of human experience. I will write about these somewhat schematically but not in the structuralist sense of their being kinds of conceptual orders that actually exist in themselves, discoverable at the unconscious level (Lévi-Strauss 1963: 229),[4] but rather only as tools, ways into understanding not what is somehow beyond actual lives but the lives themselves as I found them at the time of my fieldwork. Therefore the 'conceptual frameworks' are descriptions of consciousness itself and not something beyond it, and also are not to be thought of as *a priori*. This is again in keeping with James and the phenomenologists who criticise theorists who do not recognise the *post facto* character of their 'abstract and derivative sign-language' (Merleau-Ponty 1962: ix), who take for granted the flux of life their theories are derived from and instead build conceptions on other fetishised conceptions, the theories produced becoming ever more distant from the true foundation of experience (Jackson 1995: 23). Thus phenomenologists and pragmatists/radical empiricists advocate 'returning to the stream of life whence all the meaning of them [words, theories] came' (James 1947: 106); that is recognising that the source of their words is the 'stream of life', and hence seeking to employ words as secondary, descriptive of this primary matrix. As was evident in the previous section, anthropologists have indeed done this in various ways.[5] The manner in which I will do it will be very literal: the 'pure description' of consciousness will be the aim of the book, with the earlier chapters theoretical in a sense (while also descriptive of consciousness), but self-consciously and conspicuously instrumental to the pure description. That is, the body of the text will serve as the framework for understanding the portrayal of Wanakuwalu's experience of the walk that is the final chapter. This relationship between the two kinds of writing will be emphasised by the way the description of the walk will be annotated throughout with references that connect it to the explanations of the previous chapters. Because of this structure, the book might easily be read in reverse, that is, reading the end first, and referring from there to the body of the text for clarification.

IV. Some Methodological Issues to Do with My Approach

I have attempted to justify the way I mean to make the experience of a Mehinaku person's walk comprehensible by referring it to a general outline of Mehinaku experience. This brings up three more issues to do with my approach that relate in turn to certain criticisms that have been levelled at it. First *(i)* whether it is ever really possible to know anything about other peoples' experiences; second *(ii)* that even if it is, how does the fact that these are *my* interpretations affect my findings; and third *(iii)* even if I claim to be able to understand something of others' experience, and maintain that my interpretations are valuable, how can I convey this 'flux of life' in words to the reader.

(i) It is true, one can never know absolutely what is 'going on in someone else's head'. However, I argue that even if it is not possible to know entirely, it is a worthwhile project to come as *close as possible* to understanding others' perspectives. I have already discussed why others, from Malinowski to more contemporary ethnographers, see this as a worthwhile aim, even the heart of anthropological concern. Therefore, even if the knowledge will never be entirely complete[6] and the descriptions secondary to the life they explain, as I said earlier all anthropological approaches are of this nature, even if they do not recognise it, and this should not deter one from the valuable endeavour of understanding others' lives.

I have heard criticisms that this kind of undertaking is exoticising, a case of 'look at how strangely the natives think'. The fact is, that just as one might try to come to terms with an Amazonian person's consciousness, one might just as well do the same with one's neighbour, sibling or even one's own self! In a phenomenological approach one is not attempting to find difference or strangeness but rather simply what *is* for the person or people in question. Therefore, even in the case of working with someone from a very different world, there might be as many similarities as there are differences; what one finds is an open question.[7] Moreover, what one is doing is the very opposite of exoticising: the aim is to draw closer; to understand, not to distance. And as for the differences that one does find, there is nothing wrong with that. The tendency of 'politically correct' approaches to assign human beings universal characteristics is essentialising and in fact involves a homogenisation and distortion of representations of peoples' lives.

If one is to attempt to get to know the details of another's consciousness, how one comes to actually do this as an anthropologist pertains to fieldwork methods and analysis. This is the discovery in the field of the 'coherent meaningfulness' mentioned earlier, perceiving saliences as they arise and the nature of relations between them. This must occur as one goes about the various activities of 'participant observation' as it has been called, that indefinite way that anthropologists come by much of their knowledge. Descola has called this the anthropologist's 'laboratory', 'himself and his relationship with particular people', 'that whole complex mosaic of feelings, qualities and occasions that give our method of enquiry its own particular hue' (1993: 444).

During my own fieldwork I found that there were three main ways I came to understand something of my Mehinaku companions' experiences. The first, which was the most common way at the start, I called in my journal 'Kicking Against the Pricks': learning about the existence of things that had formerly been imperceptible to me, by walking into them unawares and thus coming to know the shape of them by the abrasions they made. This might seem a dramatic way of explaining how I learned things by making mistakes, but the process was in fact often one of palpable and painful discovery. I would walk into a space that was inappropriate for me to be in and feel the unwelcome like walking into a wall. If I was not colliding with aspects of their world I had not been hitherto aware of, I was falling into nothing, to find myself in what felt like a frightening abyss of no meaning at all.[8] This, I think, is a domain of philosophy where the anthropologist holds a privileged position. While Western philosophers have often attempted to find a distance from the conventional meanings of their world, anthropologists in the field may find themselves whether they wish it or not, in such 'existentialist' positions as that of the protagonist of Sartre's *La Nausée,* for whom the meaning of familiar objects and situations shift or even lose their normal signification. I learned after a while that these situations were clues that there was some important difference of understanding. Sometimes, I was able to come to terms with this difference, to comprehend what I had not before, this allowed by what William James has called 'conjunctive relations', the force of which makes it possible even 'for us to reach into experiences as seemingly alien as headhunting' (Jackson 1989: 5). This discovery of commonality occurs more often at a far less radical level, where the ethnographer simply finds what is familiar, which is then noted in itself or becomes the starting point for comprehending the less-familiar.

(ii) I have explained my fieldwork methods in an abstract way but in the chapters to come I will describe in concrete detail how by these methods I came to know about Mehinaku notions. This brings us to the second issue of my approach, that is, the fact that Mehinaku experience is conveyed through my understanding of it. I believe that this is unavoidable and that instead of treating one's own part in the experiences and findings in the field as a 'regrettable disturbance' (Devereux 1967), it is more fruitful to make the interplay between the domains of observer and observed the focus of interest (Jackson 1989: 3). By 'owning up' as it were, to how 'our understanding always emerges out of our interactions and experiences of others in the everyday world' (Jackson 1989: 5), the reader is allowed to see how the findings were made. She or he can then follow along the

path of how the ethnographer came to understand, or else has the choice to diverge at points where she or he believes they would not have made the same conclusions. This is especially important for the description of Wanakuwalu's experience of the walk at the end of the book. This is because the 'imagining', as I put it earlier, of her consciousness, the retrospective reconstruction of the journalised event, is of course my speculation. Which is why it requires such a rigorous delineation of how I came to do it and this in effect is what the whole body of the text constitutes, the explication and justification to the reader for this final interpretation.

The fact that the description is hypothetical, that it is only what Wanakuwalu might have been thinking or feeling, does not detract from its importance. As I argued earlier, to gain even some insight into another's experience is worthwhile, even conjectural is better than nothing at all and is in fact only a form of the way all ethnographies are speculative constructions, either directly of people's experiences (phenomenological approaches) or more theoretical analyses that are based on such constructions although they do not necessarily recognise this.

The above manner of expressing what and how you as ethnographer have comprehended worlds to which there would usually be little or no access, invites the question, *(iii)* how does one use words to do that? As an anthropologist one has only words with which to explain to the reader, and with these one can only play with the categories the reader already has in order to gradually bring the reader to comprehend the categories of others. Therefore, one works with readers' existing conceptions, to gradually build up a picture of very different ones. This occurs step by step, beginning with familiar ideas and then prodding, playing with, reversing and refining these, adding subtlety here, more intensity and colour there, until one gets somewhere closer to conveying something of the others' idea. The sensitive use of language to do this will become especially important in chapter 7, in the description of Wanakuwalu's experience of the walk, where words will be used to represent not analysed conceptions, but a person's consciousness. Before doing this, in chapter 6, issues related to such anthropological writing will be further discussed.

V. Contributions and Limitations of This Book

Ultimately then, the bulk of this book will be comprised of discussions of the general aspects of Mehinaku experience, followed by a description of one 'bit' of ordinary reality, the walk, in which we see how the former actually work. What is the use of these general expositions of the Mehinaku lived world and the description that is an attempt to portray a glimpse of it? So far I have attempted to explain the two central reasons for doing this, that is: what I and others see as the value of studying lived worlds in general, and the main motives for looking at 'ordinary reality' in particular. In regard to the first, I will add here that there is the simple significance that there are not yet any other specifically phenomenological studies about the Mehinaku, nor about any of the other peoples of the Upper Xingu of which the Mehinaku are one.

Thomas Gregor has produced a large body of work in English concerned with the Mehinaku (including the two books: *Mehinaku* [1977] and *Anxious Pleasures* [1985]), showing a special interest in their social relations, myths and rituals, and making a particular contribution to the comparative study of sexuality and 'the Anthropology of Peace'. He has a distinctive approach employing 'dramaturgical metaphor' and also Freudian psychology often in an attempt to show the 'striking similarities' between Mehinaku and Western people 'despite the apparent exoticism'. Gregor's ethnography provides an extensive source about the Mehinaku with which to compare my own findings productively. The difference between his application of analytical models and my phenomenological approach, often results in different interpretations, which, as well as many of our points of agreement, will be apparent at various stages of the book. Maria Heloísa Fénelon Costa has also written a number of articles (1978, 1988, 1997) about the Mehinaku, providing detailed information about their 'aesthetic practices' and 'beliefs'. Hers is also quite different to a phenomenological approach in the sense that she classifies her findings within conventional anthropological categories such as the '*sobrenatural*' (supernatural), the '*sagrado*' (sacred) and the '*quotidiano*' (everyday).

There is a large corpus of work concerning the peoples of the Upper Xingu dating back to the explorers Adalbert Prince of Prussia (1849) and Karl von den Steinen (1888, 1940, 1942). Though none of it is phenomenological *per se,* it forms the solid foundation for any study of a Xinguano people. Apart from Gregor, the other main English component is the work of Ellen Basso. She has written rich ethnographies regarding the Mehinaku's neighbours, the Kalapalo, about such things as their cosmology and narrative discourse; and although these studies are not specifically phenomenological, they are deep with insight into the Kalapalo experience of the world, and I will often refer to them in the chapters to come. There is also Michael Heckenberger whose studies of the Xingu combine archaeology and anthropology and who most recently in his book *Ecology of Power,* writes intriguingly of the long history of the 'Xingu nation'.[9]

The Brazilian research of the Upper Xingu is extensive, some classic works of which are: Galvão's analyses of kinship (1953); Carneiro's ecological studies (from the 1950s onwards); the Villas Boas brothers' *Xingu* (1970); Bastos's *A Musicológica Kamayurá* (1978); Silva's book *Kwarip* (1972). This is only a tiny nod to what is the wealth of research by Brazilian anthropologists[10] that exists about the Upper Xingu, and to which I will refer in the course of this book. Moreover, relatively recently there was the publication of *Os Povos do Alto Xingu* (2000), an edited volume in Portuguese, specifically concerned with the Upper Xingu communities. It compounds what Bruna Franchetto has described as a critical mass that the corpus of ethnographic work on the Upper Xingu region has reached, that 'permits us to delineate the principle contours of the contemporary Xinguano culture' (2000: 9).[11] This means, I believe, that my phenomenological account, distinctive in the difference of its approach, will be a useful contribution to this range in the extant literature, against which it might be fruitfully compared.

In regard to investigating ordinary reality specifically, I have written that the purpose of this would be threefold: to explore that part of life which actually makes up most of human experience; to see how more salient aspects of life come into that experience; and finally, how the abstract schemata and often seemingly bizarre conceptions so often attributed to non-Western and particularly Amazonian worlds, may actually (or not) come into the lives of these people. This aspect of the study is theoretical in nature, suggesting a different domain of study and throwing some light on studied aspects of anthropology by bringing them back into life, while also contributing to the ethnography of the Amazon.

In addition, I believe that the innovative structure of this book might serve as a model for different kinds of anthropological work. This is the methodology I have proposed, of laying out a framework of the 'whole' of a lived world, which is then employed and referenced in the writing of a description of a specific part of experience. In essence, the body of the text forms a kind of *manual* for understanding the depiction of consciousness that is the conclusion. Just as in this book, the approach might be used in other investigations that seek to 'bring to life' a particular experience, and in so doing also 'bring to life' the general theoretical aspects that have been worked out about that world.

To avoid confusion, I would like to point out that in studying what I have called ordinary or interstitial reality, I am studying something different to 'the everyday' in the way that this term has been used in the literature of the social sciences. '[T]he current prominence of the notion of "everyday life"' (Gullestad 1991: 480), that 'has emerged as a domain of significant anthropological attention' (Piot 1993: 95) is concerned with how culture is seen as deriving as much from negotiated, contested everyday practices, as from conventionally defined structures of social reproduction (Bourdieu 1977; Jackson 1989; Rosaldo 1989; Piot 1993; de Certeau 2002; Overing and Passes) Gregor (1977) applies this conception to the Mehinaku calling it the 'drama of daily life'. The differences between the above and what I see as the subject of my own study are in both the domain of investigation itself and also its aim. The 'everyday' is a theoretical conception that refers to a collection of 'practices': 'pragmatic strategies, … informal talk, … small daily struggles and resistances' (Piot 1994), whose prominence is 'tied to a particular stage of modernized secularized society' and is apt to be invested with scholars' own particular experiences and ideologies (Gullestad 1991: 480). The sense of interstitial reality that I am interested in does not refer to a preconceived set of practices but rather to what is between ('interstitial' to) such practices. Also, rather than trying to discern a preconceived set of everyday practices, ordinary reality refers only to where *a short fragment of the flow of a person's experience* has been marked for study, and that is, without preconceptions about the nature of this experience. Nor is the aim of looking to inchoate individual experience concerned with explaining how 'social reproduction is possible' (Bourdieu 1977), nor how 'culture is derived' (Rosaldo 1989); rather, as Jackson writes in his study of the Kuranko: 'It is the character of lived experience I want to explore, not the nature of man' (1989: 2).

I would like to clarify some other limits of this book. In the course of attempting the first and largest part of it – to elucidate the general aspects of the Mehinaku lived world – it touches on many points that invite discussion of various anthropological themes and comparison of ethnographic details. This is due simply to the fact that as a wide-ranging survey it necessarily conjoins with many key points in the literature both regional and general, especially so because of the aforementioned wealth of ethnographic work on the Upper Xingu. I have engaged with various discussions and made comparative notes, but only to a certain extent: where most relevant and mostly in notes. This is because, as my concern is with gradually building up a sense for the reader of the Mehinaku lived world, comparative and thematic points must be made tangentially, as asides as it were, if they are not to interfere with this project. Also, there is simply not space to discuss incidental issues further and, tempting as it was, further exploration of them must be kept for other investigations. Having said all this, I will point out that although I do not focus on these matters, I do see one contribution of this project being these attendant issues that it does raise in relation to the literature of the Upper Xingu, the Amazon, anthropology and even philosophy. The Mehinaku case suggests some interesting, even unusual ideas in regards to such topics as: animism; perspectivism; Amazonian ontology; the nature of Amazonian 'thought' (e.g., 'thought as thing' – ideas and the associations between them as substantial) and its related mythic and ritual logic; shamanism and sorcery; and the Amazonian sense of gender and sociality. As I have said, these digressive discussions will often be made as asides throughout the body of the text, but there will also be some summing up of them in the conclusions drawn in chapter 6.

The following are just a few notes on the presentation of the book. During the year that I spent in the Mehinaku village[12] I spoke mostly in Brazilian Portuguese, although only some of the men – especially the younger men – spoke it well, with many of the old people, women and children knowing only a few words, if any at all. As the year went on I picked up some Mehinaku so that in roughly the second half of my time there I began to get the general gist of the conversations that went on around me and could interact in a basic way in that language. This means that what I would write down of what they told me was usually in Portuguese, interspersed with the Mehinaku words and names that I understood. This is the way that I present this information in the book, with Mehinaku words in italics and Portuguese words in italics and quotes. I do in fact have a substantial amount of material recorded in Mehinaku, particularly traditional stories, various music and shamanic songs. However, as I did not usually understand these word for word, I would often have them translated into Portuguese and these translations appear either verbatim or paraphrased in the text.[13] However much of what I learned, as I discussed in terms of the haziness of the fieldwork process in the section above, was not necessarily verbal, and in fact the richest understandings I felt I came to were with the women with whom I spent most of my time, but with whom I could speak in the least detail. Also, the most interesting and fruitful interactions that I had were almost always in situations where I felt a sound recorder would be an invasive presence[14] or when it simply was not on hand. Consequently, the book will contain a mixture of my personal interpretations of the Mehinaku sense of life and things I was actually told by Mehinaku people, and I will attempt to make it clear when I am doing what.

In the next chapter the 'journey' I have promised the reader, from one walk to another, may begin, but before it does, I will give here a brief overview of what this excursion will look like. Some indication as to its basic shape has already been given, but now I will provide a more detailed outline. It will begin below in this chapter with some preliminary information about the Mehinaku and their world, similar to the knowledge I myself possessed before I began fieldwork. This will serve as a backdrop as it were, putting readers in a similar perspectival situation to my own during my experience of a walk to the river early in my time there. With this background detail and the journal description, readers will see what the walk is like before beginning their understanding of the Mehinaku lived world. In chapter 2 this exploration begins, with various configurations of Mehinaku experience discerned, and in chapter 3 the dynamic aspects of these formations will be explored. After looking to *what* the Mehinaku experience – these being the discernible qualities discussed earlier in phenomenological terms (paradigmatic equivalents, associations etc.) – in chapter 4 there will be a focus on *how* these work as elements of experience or consciousness and how they come together in a particular Mehinaku kind of flow of consciousness. Thus in chapter 4 there will be an exploration of *how* the Mehinaku experience *what* they experience. Although aspects of the social will already have come into the general discussions of the chapters before it, in chapter 5 we will look at major aspects of the Mehinaku social world. Finally, having gained some sense of Mehinaku experience in general, there will be a return to the walk to the river, to see what now can be understood of Wanakuwalu's experience.

VI. Some Background

Close to the geographic centre of Brazil, in the state of Mato Grosso, lie the headwaters of the Rio Xingu, a major northward-flowing tributary of the Amazon. The area in which the headwaters extend forms a basin that is part of a transitional ecological zone between the lowland equatorial forest of southern Amazonia and the tropical scrubland of the Central Brazilian Plateau, while in general having the flora, fauna and sun that is characteristic of the Amazon region.[15] The area that anthropologists refer to as the Upper Xingu refers to a part of this basin that has several communities settled there, known in the anthropological literature as 'the Xinguanos'.[16] These settlements are spatially autonomous and linguistically distinct, the languages spoken constituting three main language groups: one formed by Arawak languages (Waurá, Mehinaku and Yawalapiti), another by Carib (Kuikuro, Kalapalpo, Matiphu and Nahukwa), and another by Tupi languages (Kamayurá and Aweti), as well as an isolated linguistic group called Trumai. Nevertheless, these communities are united in an enduring system by means of social, religious and economic relationships, a kind of society bound together by a tradition of common origin, ties of marriage, ceremonial trade in group-specific artefacts, reciprocal attendance at each other's festivals, traditions of common origin and adherence to a common code of values.[17] Located near the Curisevo River, with a population at the time of my fieldwork in 2001 of 186 people, the Mehinaku comprise one of these communities

The territory where the Xinguanos live constitutes a part of the Xingu National Park (Parque Indígena do Xingu [PIX]), founded in 1961, a large government-administered indigenous reserve[18] that, with its firmly paternalistic protection policy, quickly gained an international reputation as the showcase for Brazil's treatment of its Indian peoples, 'providing an idyllic media image of painted Indians living in a protected wilderness.'[19] This idealised picture of an authentic 'society of nations' of 'peaceful peoples', living in a paradise insulated from the outside world (Villas-Boas and Villas-Boas 1970: 16) is not the entire reality of the situation. First, in actuality, Xingu society is 'characterised by endemic factionalism', and '(P)olitical unity is contextual with competition relating both to indigenous avenues to prestige … [A]nd to their modern extensions" (Hugh-Jones and Hugh-Jones 1996: 14). Also, their history of contact with the outside world has not left the Xinguanos as isolated and unchanged as many accounts suggest, with cultural transformations occurring in various areas of life, such as the use of televisions and two-way radios in many villages and the use, to some extent, of Portuguese as a lingua franca between different language groups and in their ventures outside the reserve.[20]

As their lives are intricately intertwined with their environment, changes are also occurring with the ongoing deterioration of environmental conditions in the Xingu basin. For, far from being the protected paradise the Brazilian government purports it to be, the 'Park' has been subjected to continuous invasions and ongoing destruction, including rapid deforestation (especially for soya production as well as logging, corn farming and cattle ranching), pollution of water and contamination of fish that is a mainstay of the Xinguano diet. Since I was last in the Xingu area, there has been highly contested building work on a hydroelectric dam in the region of the headwaters[21] and there are plans for others. According to the Xinguano peoples themselves, the situation has now become critical, bringing their leaders together in July 2007 to declare the crisis in an open letter to the Brazilian nation.[22]

The changes in the reserve are of quite a different nature to what has gone on in other parts of South America. Unlike other native peoples of the continent, the Xinguano experiences of contact with the outside world have been largely indirect, through contamination by agro-toxins and the like, disease epidemics, the use of manufactured goods and interaction with restricted visitors from outside, rather than by direct day-to-day economic and political subjugation. Because of the types of contact they've experienced, and because of the way the communities have responded to successive crises by reconstitution and integration, in many ways the Xinguanos have been able to continue to live as they have always done to a far greater degree than most other Amazonian peoples.[23]

The Mehinaku, like other Xinguano groups, live in a village with surroundings that are made up of several ecological zones. First there is the tree line that runs along the river, and then inland from the river are floodplains that can extend up to several kilometres in width. Beyond the grassy plains are large areas of forest and it is along the border of the forest and the plains that the Xinguanos settle. The environment of the Xingu transforms dramatically through the year. In late September the rains begin and by December/January the banks of the rivers have overflowed. During this time the plains are so inundated it is possible to canoe across them and even into rivulets that zigzag through the forest. The rainy season is a hungry time; it is difficult to catch fish (that with manioc-bread is the basis of their diet), and there is no more fruit and very little manioc to harvest so that the Mehinaku must depend mostly on the vast amounts of manioc flour they have produced and stored during the dry months, some corn and some Western foods such as rice. Drought begins in May and the manioc orchards are cut. Fishing becomes increasingly productive as water levels drop and in August and September fish are caught en masse with the poison of the 'timbó' vine. Cultivated fruits such as the mangaba, mango and bananas ripen and are eaten with relish. In September, the Mehinaku burn back their orchards and soon the cherished *akãi* fruit[24] ripen and are eaten. When the rains begin in late September, or October, the orchards are planted with manioc and maize and the annual cycle starts again.

At the time of my fieldwork the Mehinaku village was comprised of twelve large elliptical houses that are always set out in the round and facing inwards towards a large well-cleared space (Plates 1 and 2), in the middle of which sits the *kuwékuhë*, the house that contains the 'sacred flutes'. Surrounding the houses are the *akāi* groves and beyond these, close to the forest line, are manioc orchards. The houses are magnificent thatched structures, that can be around 40 feet long and 20 feet high, and in each of

Plate 1. Marikawa leads his grandson into the centre of the village.

Plate 2. The village centre at twilight.

these live extended families of up to fifteen or so people. Nuclear families cluster their hammocks in different parts of each end of the elongated oval of the house, with the areas close to the doors used for work and socialising and the centre of the house for storage of manioc flour, various implements and sometimes (if there is not a separate little house for it out the back) for cooking.

A typical day[25] in the Mehinaku village takes place as follows. People begin to wake a little before sunrise and move around the house. The women with their children eat some cold, leftover *nukaya,* a thick soup of sweet manioc, before heading out to the manioc orchards. There they will work for an hour or so digging up the tubers before carrying it back in great loads on their heads. After this the women and children will usually go off to bathe, and on their return will spend the rest of the morning and sometimes into the afternoon, in the several stages of processing the manioc that produces its edible flour. This work, like what generally goes on in the Mehinaku village, takes place in an atmosphere of calm and cheerful banter. After work on the manioc is finished for the day, they will usually bathe once again, though they may go at other times during the day, always returning with a large container of water for the use of their family. Once they return, the rest of the afternoon is spent at the back of the house, twirling cotton, nitpicking other women and children of the household (Plate 3), making *nukaya* and often grooming themselves and each other. Both men and women may also spend this time making various traditional objects either for their own use or as 'artesenatos', which are taken periodically by individuals to cities to sell to 'Brancos' (the Portuguese for 'White people'). Very often such a daytime activity or even the middle of the night is punctuated by the spectacle or involvement in various music making and dance.

The men's day is usually rather different to the women and children's. They also wake around dawn and after eating a little, go to bathe while it is still early. After this they might: work on their orchards; go hunting or fishing, make things such as arrows, benches or body ornaments; play the flutes in the men's house (the House of Flutes), or lie around in their hammocks. If they have been hunting or fishing and bring back meat or fish, whenever that may be will be mealtime for the members of the household (Plate 4). In the afternoon, apart from bathing again, the men will often wrestle in front of the House of Flutes (Plate 5), with women watching from inside the front door. Before the sun sets, men, women and children go to bathe once more, married couples often making this trip together during which they will also often have sexual relations in the forest or the

Plate 3. Nitpicking hair in the afternoon.

Plate 4. Eating smoked fish and manioc water (*uwitsakyuwi*).

Plate 5. Men's wrestling.

orchards. Just before sunset the women of each house will often go to sit just outside their front door, gossiping and watching the young men who usually play football at this time, the shamans smoking in a huddled group before the House of Flutes. Just before the sun drops below the horizon, people move back into their houses and begin to settle for the night, families taking refuge in their hammocks, often by a little fire, as they sip sweet hot *nukaya,* and then lying back to talk and sometimes tell stories in the darkness before sleep.

Notes

1. For just one example, see Gow's critique of ethnographic analyses of history in the Amazon which he sees as employing reified 'schemata'. He looks instead to what history and kinship are for the people themselves, revealing historical change as interior to the ongoing creation of kinship (1991: 15).
2. A term William James coined to encourage us to recover a lost sense of the immediate, active, ambiguous 'plenum of experiences' in which all ideas and intellectual constructions are grounded (Jackson 1989: 3).
3. I have not given Wanakuwalu's real name nor biographical details out of respect for her privacy.
4. Ethnography of indigenous Amazonia is pervaded by this kind of structuralist analysis (for examples see S. Hugh-Jones (1979); C. Hugh-Jones (1979); Basso (1973); Seeger (1981); Descola (1994, 1996); Viveiros de Castro (1992).
5. For work specifically employing this kind of approach, see also the edited volume: Michael Jackson, ed., *Things As They Are: New Directions in Phenomenological Anthropology,* (Bloomington and Indianapolis, 1996).
6. Tormaid Campbell writes: 'the job of learning about the people is like a journey without end. There is never a point when you can pack up and say "That's it, done." All you can ask is: "How far will I get in the time?"' (1999: 1)
7. As Gow has written, "[T]he analytical concept of the lived world stresses an ethnographic project of elucidation of a found situation, over against any preconceived ideas of what form that lived world must necessarily take" (2001: 26).
8. For example, often a few men would enter the house and hang around darting looks at me. I did not understand why they were there, and there were long uncomfortable moments of staring and looking away. I could feel their expectations tugging at me, but I did not know what these were and felt deeply 'at a loss'. Other such situations will be described in the body of the text to explain how I came to understand certain things.
9. That they 'are an exception in this part of the world, as a living cultural tradition that extends back in time ... over centuries and even millennia' (2004: 3).
10. For example, the work of Barcelos Neto; Carneiro da Cunha; Carneiro; Fausto; Fénelon Costa; Franchetto; Galvão; Lima; Menezes; Ribeiro; Viveiros de Castro.

There is also the work of the legendary brothers Claudio and Orlando Villas-Boas. Of course there has also been research conducted in other languages apart from Portuguese and English, such as that by Lévi-Strauss and Monod-Becquelin. See Bibliography for details.

11. *'[N]os permite delinear os principais contornos da cultura xinguana contemporânea'* (2000: 9).
12. My fieldwork was conducted through 2001, with two short breaks during that time.
13. Verbatim communications appear in inverted commas.
14. See Gow (2001: 28) for a discussion of similar feelings on this aspect of fieldwork technique.
15. (Heckenberger 2000: 28)
16. (Basso 1973; Heckenberger 2000)
17. (Hugh-Jones and Hugh-Jones 1996: 13)
18. For a history of the Park, see Pires Menezes (2000).
19. (Hugh-Jones and Hugh-Jones 1996: 13)
20. For detailed discussions about these changes see Franchetto (2000); Heckenberger (2000); Menezes (2000).
21. The Paranatinga II on the Culuene River.
22. This 'open letter' has been reproduced in the Preface of this book in the original Portuguese and in English translation.
23. (Ireland 1988; Franchetto 2000)
24. Commonly known as 'pequi', scientific name *Caryocar butyrosum.*
25. This day is more usual of the dry season, with those of the rainy season basically the same but with more time indoors, making things and telling stories.

Plate 6. The path from the back of a house, through an *akāi* grove towards the river.

1

My Walk

Here I will give the portrayal of my experience of a trip to a river in Amazonia. It was one of countless such walks I made during my time with the Mehinaku and one of the first I happened to write down in my journal in some detail. Everyone, if they are able, makes this trip about three times a day to bathe, and for the women also to bring water. Throughout my time there, I walked to the river with the women of the house I lived in (just as I did almost everything in their company), sometimes with just a few little girls but most often with my friend of my own age, Wanakuwalu. I suggest that my experience of that trip with her nearer the beginning of my fieldwork, which I will describe below, might be similar to how the reader, who has not spent time with the Mehinaku, would experience such a walk. After reading this depiction, this first stroll through the Mehinaku world, I hope that you the reader, will gradually explore in the chapters to come what it is to be Mehinaku, so that at the conclusion of the book, we can go on that walk again, but this time as Wanakuwalu.

The sun is now visible above the horizon but the early morning air is still chill, the sky grey, and the little plants along the dirt path wet our legs with dew. Our feet are black, dirt-encrusted from our dawn-work in the orchard, knees and fingernails also dark from the kneeling and digging in the earth for manioc. So I am already quite tired from this toil as I follow Wanakuwalu, who shows no sign of fatigue, down the path towards the river. The large steel pail for water swinging in one hand, her step is rhythmic and brisk, a kind of trot, and I fall in behind her at more or less the same pace. And it is to this steady beat that I watch the landscape, first the close green of the *akāi* groves behind our house, the fluting birdcalls, and then across the boggy plain of high grasses where the sky is very wide. It takes about fifteen minutes to cross this meadow. Far off to the left and right rise up the forest edges, behind is the village, and in front there are the trees before the river. Gazing at the forest line, I remember the sound of a jaguar during our work this morning that had come from somewhere within the green tangle, so that we women froze in our positions in the earth, and I felt my heart pounding, not knowing what would happen. Nothing happened. To be safe, we waited for some minutes, tense, listening, then took what we had already dug up and returned to the village.

We continue on along the grassland. A cool mist still clings to the land, but just above, the sky is already brightening. Later, it will be like a perfect blue bowl, the sun beating down from its top. I look forward to this burning sun, which not only buoys my spirits now that the rains have ended but feels also somehow to clean the mustiness from the ground, the houses, the residue of mild poison in the bites that cover my legs and arms. There is the warm smell of the earth carried up by water as the sun evaporates it, mixed with the dark scent of the gold-green grass, sweet as though it is being caramelised by the heat. Thump, thump, thump sound my own feet through my body and I watch Wanakuwalu's feet moving to the same time. My gaze ranges over the monotonous grassland, curious as usual about what new thing I might see. A large bird is flying overhead. *'Urubu!'* Wanakuwalu exclaims, turning to point towards it with her chin without breaking her stride. I admire its broad wing-span, wondering what it last fed upon, where it is going. On and on we walk. The vulture makes me think of hunger and I worry about the current state of satisfaction of various members of the village. I check through them: did I give Kamaluku all the things I said I would in exchange for the story she told me yesterday? Today I am due to cook something for the family; it's two days now that I haven't. It is of vital impor- tance that I do the constant work of maintaining the balance of give-and–take if I am to avoid the exclusion I felt in my first weeks, when, unaware of their expectations I caused their collective displeasure. *'Anapi,'* Wanakuwalu is pointing at a rainbow that is faintly arcing the sky above the forest to our right. I realise that while worrying I have been blind to the world around me, missing, I reproach myself, brief visions of beauty such as rainbows, and I stare in wonder at the colours in the air. Wanakuwalu has dropped back to walk alongside me, so that she can tell me the story of *Anapi,* the Rainbow, the great serpent in the sky. I stop walking and listen carefully, trying to imagine the rainbow not simply as a marvel of nature but as a serpent; how does she see it this way? I make a mental note to ask others about this story. *'Ayí!,'* 'Let's go!' says Wanakuwalu and we continue. There are some plants growing between the grasses that I recognise from a herb-lore lesson a few days before, *tërtu* and another whose name I don't remember, the roots of which the Mehinaku use as a herbal po- tion for beautifying and growth. The earth rises now as we approach the band of trees that runs before the river.

As we enter the cool beneath the great trees, a few of the little black *tzipinyu* birds are heard and then swoop above our heads across the path. I peer into the green spaces between trees, mystified by the immense richness of the forest beyond and look up at the delicate interlacing of branches high above. Some bright blue but- terflies flutter across the path and around Wanakuwalu who pays them no attention. We are almost there now, the tan-coloured swirls of the River Curisevo glints ahead of us. It is so wide and completely opaque. I think of anaconda and fish with huge teeth. Up surges the dread I always feel at the idea of getting in. Wanakuwalu casually drops her pail and in the same movement begins her descent of the steep clay bank. I watch her gracefulness, feeling ungainly as I try to follow, slipping here and there down to the water. . . .

2

Configurations in Mehinaku Experience

For our final purpose, after many chapters to come, of comprehending Wanakuwalu's walk to the river, an experience of Mehinaku ordinary reality, here we begin the exploration of Mehinaku reality in general. In this chapter we will look at the various formations in their lived experience.

I. Substance

During the first weeks with the Mehinaku what struck me most was how material their sense of existence seemed to be. This appeared to contradict the elaborate cosmologies that are written about Xinguano and other Amazonian peoples, of animal and tree spirits, shamans and soul journeys. During this time I was told many narratives by women, men and children about human, bird, animal and tree spirits *('espiritos')*. Yet whenever I asked if these entities still existed, people invariably said that what I was being told were stories *'historias'*, and that they occurred *'antigamente'*, 'a long time ago'. Contrary to my expectations it appeared that the Mehinaku relegated such aspects of existence simply and firmly to the past, in much the same way Europeans do with the personages and events of the Bible, and yet with more general assurance of their verity, a kind of ancient history. When I asked one young man, Kemenyá, why the men were doing the *Kayapa* dance, if the *Kayapa* being no longer existed, he gave me the answer I always received for this question in those weeks when I did not know how to ask better. He answered that Mehinaku people dance for the joy *('alegria')* of it. No mention was ever made to me about a *Kayapa* being, nor any other such entity as existing in the world the Mehinaku presently lived in.

For these reasons at first it seemed to me that life for the Mehinaku was lived in purely materialist terms. In this first section I will explain how this is in fact so, that is, how the Mehinaku do indeed apprehend all aspects of existence as substantial. The rest of this chapter is concerned with how my initial understanding of a material world, though correct, is complicated by more subtle Mehinaku notions about the nature of substance, of which I only learned later on. The exploration of these conceptions will lead to some engagement with the subjects of 'animism' and 'cosmology' and related anthropological ideas. Before this exposition however, I should point out that the Mehinaku themselves do not have a word for 'substance', each material has its own proper name. However the Mehinaku *do* apprehend all these different materials as having the quality of what we would call 'substance', although for them it is assumed and there is no need to distinguish this. On the other hand for the outsider trying to understand Mehinaku experience from first principles, there is such a need, and hence the exposition that follows.

In the Mehinaku world of substances, there is an evident emphasis on the human body. The tangible human form, the *umé,* is understood to be constructed very literally by a 'building up' of materials. Occasionally I would casually compliment a mother or father on how beautiful, tall or strong their baby was going to grow up to be. These comments, so normal to me, were invariably received in silence, bringing whatever conversation we were having to a sudden halt. This is because for the Mehinaku, what I was saying very simply did not make sense. In the West it is generally assumed that although growth is influenced by environmental factors, still, a child's body contains in some way the adult form it will take, into which it gradually develops. For the Mehinaku this is not at all the case. For them the body only grows because it is *made,* and one is constantly involved in the 'building'[1] of this substantial self.

This process starts with the building of the foetus, which involves the gathering up of paternal semen.[2] Since the mother may have sex with a number of men during her pregnancy, the semen can come from a number of male sources so that a baby is often said to resemble one man a little, another man a lot and yet another even more. From birth these body-building activities involve food and other substances administered to build up the physique of the baby and then the child, including a most elaborate couvade.[3] Another practice that begins during childhood and onwards for the majority of one's life is the use of the *imya,* an instrument made with tree thorns. With it, the skin is scraped over most of the body yielding light scratches into which a certain root potion *(tërtu)* is rubbed. One submits to this procedure, usually performed by a close family member, every few weeks.[4] This becomes most intensive during the period of puberty seclusion, and it is supposed to cause one's flesh to swell into the desired rounded forms of the Mehinaku bodily aesthetic. The period of puberty seclusion for boys and girls is primarily about this body-making process, with a whole range of practices by which the *painyawalatai* (girl in seclusion) and *painyakwa* (boy in seclusion) are literally *made* into Mehinaku adults.[5]

In the practice of using the *imya*, it is evident that this 'body-making' is not simply a different concept of growth, that is, it does not stop when one becomes an adult. For the entirety of a person's life, she or he is always involved in a maintenance *(papapiritsa* – 'taking care of') of the bodily form, which is understood to require a constant process of 'body-building' up. This substantiality of the Mehinaku sense of the body is evident in their stories[6] about the creation of human beings.

The first people in the world were five women, made by *Kwamutë,* the 'Grandfather Creator' as copies of his five 'spirit'[7] daughters, the *Apapanyëshë*.[8] He constructs them in a mechanical process of trial and error, by putting together different things or substances. First he makes their bodies from trunks of the *umé* tree. He then adds fibres from pineapple plants for hair, but his real daughters say it is too light and ugly for hair. Instead, he adds the nest of the little bird, *ëshëmatëshë,* which is black and the daughters approve of as beautiful. 'Now they need vaginas', the *Apapanyëshë* women say, and so *Kwamutë* makes for the *umënëshë,* 'women of wood', vaginas from the fragrant fruit of the *wapëshë* plant. After these are experimented on by the armadillo and the sloth, it is decided that the scent of these vaginas, though delicious, is so strong that men would always know who the women had sex with. They decide to use the *ulu* shell instead, which is found to be perfect (the *ulu* shell was traditionally used to scrape manioc tubers, that for the Mehinaku are associated with penises). *Kwamutë* then adds the buriti palm fibre belt, the *uluri,* around the hips and between the legs, which is still worn by women today. Finally he puts in stones for teeth and these are considered too black, so he replaces them with the white seeds of the *ketula* (mangaba[9]) fruit.

This sense of the human body as being built up out of substances or things is also evident in the story of the creation of the first men. It features the Sun *(Kamë)* and the Moon *(Keshë),* twin children of one of the human *Umënëshë* women and the Jaguar Spirit. With the instruction of their grandfather *Kwamutë,* the two make men from *uku,* the long arrows traditionally used for fishing and hunting.[10] They do this at *Kwamutë's* village *Yëpunatë,* making the men in different colours. They then set these out in groups in the central circular space of the village, to give each of them their own particular kind of food, drink, language and weaponry, while also appointing each group the place where they will live in the world.[11] Although this story is more concerned with the distribution of characteristics to the different groups of humans in the world (the Indians, the *Washayu* or Wild Indians and the Whites or *'Brancos'*), like the tale of the creation of women, it also portrays the emphasis on the human-being as a body substantially built up. This sense of a body created or constructed mostly of wood (either the *uku* arrow, or the *umé* log) is not simply story, it is inherent in the very word for 'body' used in everyday life, *umé-nupiri,* meaning '*umé* (tree trunk) – mine'.

So for the Mehinaku the human body is understood as made and in a constant process of being made in a material way. As *Kwamutë* and his grandsons created the first people by putting together different materials, humans take over this process to do this themselves: parents build up their babies, adolescents are made into adults and all these bodily forms are maintained by the regular use of the *imya* scraper and root potions. It is important to note that the bodies are not simply built up with uniform stuff; substances are always particular, and are used in particular ways. As in the first creation myth, the making of bodies for the Mehinaku is an intricate, gendered and aesthetically nuanced process wherein the better this process proceeds, the better the body created. And cultivating this superior kind of body, what the Mehinaku call *awisitiri-pai,* is of the utmost importance in these people's lives.

Awisitiri-pai is the very particular Mehinaku sense of 'beauty'. It refers to things and people that are physically young, clean and new, whole and perfectly formed, strong and not vulnerable. 'Beautiful like a fresh page of your book' is the way chief Marikawa[12] explained it to me, pointing at my fieldwork journal. That which is '*aitsa awitsiri-pai',* or 'ugly', is physically old, dirty, broken, weak and vulnerable. Beauty, or *awitsiri* is a great preoccupation for all the Mehinaku, in every sphere of life, in the content of mythical stories, in ordinary conversations and as the object of multitudes of practices. Most *ownaki,* or mythical[13] stories begin 'I am going to tell you a story *(n-ownaki-tsala-pitsu)* about a young man/woman, very beautiful!' – followed by an extolling of the various beautiful attributes of the main character. In ordinary conversation, whether with the family at the hearth or bathing with friends, the quality of peoples' physical characteristics is the principal means by which they are discussed. When a person is not working during the day, both men and women spend most of this relaxing time, in or at the back of the house, scrutinising, discussing and attending to the quality of one another's skin and hair, painting, plucking, cutting, or preening themselves with a mirror (a valuable *'branco'* commodity).

We shall see that this preoccupation with beautiful appearance is different to ideas and issues of beauty that exist in the West. I will discuss later in this chapter and in those to come, how for the Mehinaku physical appearance is bound up with a whole complex of ideas about the nature of substance, so that, for example, morality and beauty are inextricably related. At this point however, let me simply emphasise how significant beauty is for the Mehinaku and outline some of their practices of beautification. While the word *awitsiri* always implies youthful perfection and strength, men and women also each have their own very specific beauty ideals within that category.

For women, the archetype of beauty to be strived for is embodied in *Shapushënéshë,* translated literally as the 'Wild Woman'. She is one of the *apapanyéshë,* the five daughters of *Kwamutë* in the tale of creation I recounted. From the period of the puberty seclusion, women, their mothers and grandmothers use various techniques in striving to attain a likeness of this mythical woman's natural form, painting their feet and brow with the orangey-red tint of the *epitsiri* seed, black *ulutaki* and the blue-black stains of genipapo (for *Shapushënéshë* the designs are part of her skin), depriving their skin of sunlight to make it pale, and drinking particular root potions that are then vomited up over and over again to make their calves and thighs swell into roundness (see Plates 7 and 8).[14]

Men have their own special practices concentrated during puberty while the adult form is being produced, and these are also concerned with attaining the form of the men and the 'spirits'[15] (the *apapanye*) of mythical stories. Some of these practices can be very dangerous and are only used depending on how much the man is willing to risk attaining the body he wants. For example, the oil of the anaconda snake may bestow great muscles and strength for wrestling, but if the Anaconda Spirit is offended by a smell he doesn't like, he can hurt or even kill the man. Many practices are risky in a similar way for both men and women, though few so deadly. Still, to make sure there are no disturbances, these practices are conducted in secret. It is always up to the individual what techniques they employ (even for adolescents, who can end seclusion whenever they choose), so that these practices are employed piecemeal throughout people's lives, depending on the effect they would like to achieve.

Plate 7. Takulalu produces dye from *epitsiri* pods.

Plate 8. Young women dressed according to the women's ideal of beauty, with *epitsiri* band across the brow.

The Mehinaku are always striving then to make themselves, as *Kwa-mutë*, the Sun and the Moon, once made them, using various materials in the world, in imitation of the form of First Beings. This is the most important, the overarching framework if you will, but not the only way the Mehinaku understand the materiality of their bodies. Others are more metaphorical, whereby the body and/or its parts are associated with other things in the world. Such a relation is made between the human body and the monolithic solidity of the *uleitsi,* the manioc tuber that is the staple of the Mehinaku diet. Like the *uleitsi,* the human body is understood to shrivel in the sun, and like the tuber growing well in the cool darkness of the earth, the limbs of the secluded adolescent will grow fat, rounded and white in the cool darkness of the house. The tuber is also associated with the aroused penis. The *walu* aforementioned in the story of creation, used to make the vaginas of women, are employed by women to scrape the skin from the *uleitsi,* like the movement of the corresponding body parts in sexual intercourse.

Another way the Mehinaku understand the materiality of their bodies is by associating themselves with fish. The *Kuarup,* an inter-village fune-real gathering that still occurs today among the Alto-Xinguano groups, took place first in myth for the human mother of the Sun *(Kamë)* and the Moon *(Keshë).* The two main groups participating in the *kuarup* were the 'folk' *(yënewnewnew)* of the Sun and the Moon who were the animals of the forests (the jaguar, the wolf, the snake and the sloth etc.), and the fish 'folk'. The first main event was the *huka-huka* wrestling and one by one different opponents from each group wrestled one another, the fish ultimately the winners of the contest.

It is the brave and strong fish the Mehinaku (and the other Xinguano peoples) identify with and not the wild and angry *(shapushë)* animals, whom they relate to their traditional tribal enemies and these days also to White people. The Mehinaku believe that one becomes imbued with the qualities of what one eats. Therefore, the Mehinaku relate the violence of their enemies, whom they call *Washayu,* to the fact that these people eat forest animals that have fur, are understood to be dirty[16] and have anger-inflaming blood. The Mehinaku, who deplore anger and violence,[17] will not for this reason eat most animals[18] and consume almost nothing but fish *(kupatë),* which they perceive as being beautiful, clean and strong. This bodily association with fish is taken further by physically emulating the smoothness of fish skin through the removal of bodily hair, including eyebrows and pubic hair. Also, most designs on skin *(yana)* are repetitive shapes based on fish, either on their whole bodies, their bones, or fish scales (Plate 9).[19] Also, as fish are seen to be clean and cool because of their immersion in water, so too the Mehinaku keep themselves clean and cool by bathing many times during the day.

Therefore, apart from the Mehinaku understanding of their bodies as built according to the form of the image of the spirits, they also substantially associate their bodies with each of the constituents of their staple diet, the manioc tuber and fish *(uleitse* and *kupatë).*[20] I have said that these associations are 'metaphorical', but the exact 'how' of the way these people experience their bodies as 'like' fish or manioc or anything else for that matter, is a crucial subject of this book that will be discussed later (chapter 4). Nevertheless, it is important to note at this point that the different ways of understanding the body materially are not discrete in consciousness; rather, they blend so that at different moments one might understand oneself more in one way, then in another and later as a mixture of these.[21] Furthermore, it must be emphasised that whether the body is materially experienced in terms of fish, manioc, as pieced together in the form of the spirits, or as some combination thereof, these kinds of bodily understanding are always about substances, and moreover substances that are profoundly particular.

The reason I have gone into detail about the body as substance, particularly the Mehinaku preoccupation with the material making of their bodies, and the making of them into beautiful bodies, is that this is in fact a general focus of their lives, what people, for a large part, think and talk about and do.[22] Also, as I wrote at the start of the chapter, the importance of the body as substance is part of an understanding of the way the whole world works in terms of materials. Substances, I will explain, constitute not only the body itself, but emanate out from the body, are between bodies, and are between all things in the world.

Not only, as I have explained, are bodies made up of certain substances, these substances are also understood to radiate from the body. This is mostly perceived to be happening in terms of *iníya,* 'smells' (*'cheiro'* in Portuguese).[23] The highly differentiated substances of male and female bodies discussed earlier are thus also emitted from the body as invisible odours, just as the different Xinguano tribes, *washayu* ('wild') Indians, and 'White people', understood to have materially different bodies, therefore exude different scents. Apart from the smells of one's basic bodily constituents (which includes what one eats), one may also pick up smells, so that for the Mehinaku, a person goes about in the world surrounded by something like an invisible 'cloud' of composite odours, depending on who they are and what they have been doing. Also, smells flow out from animals and

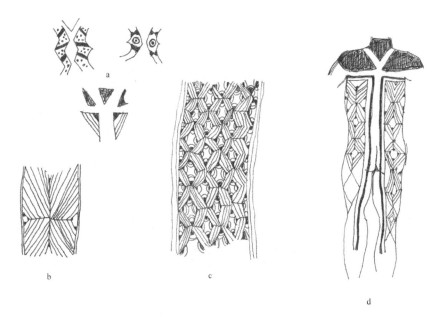

a

b

c

d

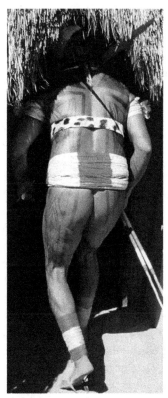

Plate 9. Fish designs for body paintings.

things, not only from people. When these different bodies near one another, even at some distance, the smell-substances exuded by each interact and may affect the substances of the body of the other. For example, a menstruating women is thought to affect the growth of a secluded youth, because of the odour, the *iníya,* of her blood. In some cases, simply her 'woman smell', which is thought to be very strong and reminiscent of fish, will do the same. Maiawai, a young man, once told me that grappling with an anaconda snake, the bad and strong smell *('cheiro ruím, forte')* of the animal entered his body (he tapped on his chest to indicate this) and made him nauseous when he ate honey later on (the good scent of which is incompatible with that of the snake). One may rid oneself of certain smells by bathing and by spitting. Once walking with a number of Mehinaku men in Rio de Janeiro, they all suddenly began to spit on the ground. One man explained to me that this was because the place was 'bad' *('ruím'),* and the 'badness' of the place had entered their bodies as smell, which they had to spit out to get rid of.

This Mehinaku sense of scent[24] then, is the main way they understand the potency of all things, and the way these potencies are transferred and interact.[25] Basso, in her excellent analysis of Kalapalo myth and ritual performance, found that for this neighbouring community, it is in fact sound which is most existentially crucial, with a 'hierarchy of animacy' determined by 'successively encompassing levels of sound productivity' (1985: 70). I also found sound to be of great significance to the Mehinaku, however not with exactly the same meaning and emphasis as Basso did with the Kalapalo, a fact that will be discussed later in this book in regard to the nature of the manifestation of realities (section V. of this chapter) and the consequent effectiveness of ritual (chapter 4).

At this point let us say that apart from scent, other ways that interactions in the world are understood in substantial terms do indeed include sound. Sound works as a material interplay. The words and names sung by the shaman have a materially causal effect on the patient, so that if what is sung is incorrect, it will cause the patient to ail further.[26] Similarly, in a story I was told, a man lost in the forest not many years ago, calls and calls but is not found and dies there. Afterwards a shaman finds him by following the calling. The dead man's soul has gone to the sky but his voice has actually remained there as a material 'thing' *(chawaka)* in the air, like a recording on tape *('um gravação'),* as the storyteller explained it in Portuguese.

'Seeing' also works substantially: simply looking at men dressed as the *apapanye* spirits, will make a woman fall ill, or even die; shamans plant their special tobacco, *hëka,* deep in the forest because if ordinary people look at it the plant's growth will be stunted. Touching is of course a blatant interaction of visible substances but it also involves a material transmission of invisible substance. Again, substances might interact unfavourably between people and/or objects, so physical contact of all kinds is kept to the minimum necessary: family members and friends rarely touch each other out of affection and even babies, who are held and soothed if upset, are generally not often caressed; sexual intercourse is a quick and anxious affair.[27] The milk of the woman's breasts which is understood to weaken the strength of men, enters the man's chest, precluding languorous embraces and necessitating bathing afterwards. In fact both men and women bathe after sex so that all 'other-gendered' substances are washed away.

Not only are what we would classify in the West as 'the senses' understood materially by the Mehinaku. Even thought and emotion (that for them are not distinct from each other) are apprehended in substantial terms: sadness and longing palpably attract illnesses[28] (on many occasions people made statements to the effect of 'do not be sad, do not miss home, you will get sick'); the emotional shock of Yahatí (his *'tristessa e soffremento'*) after being pecked by an eagle kept by the chief, Marikawa, is compensated as for a physical loss, with payments *('pagamentos')* in fish; the only word for love is the physical glance "*nututaí*" – 'my eye' and even thinking is a material act of the body, with the word for 'to think' – *naóntëkanatër,* defined for me in Portuguese as *'todo corpo vai pensar o que fazer'* – 'all the body is going to think what to do'. Thoughts of others can enter and affect one as substances,[29] which is how others' feelings are understood to affect one's own.

Not only individual experience but also sociality[30] on all levels, from the family, to the village, to between villages, is also understood substantially. In the centre of each house is always kept a large container of what is called *uwitsakyuwi,* a mixture of water and thin manioc wafer bread that is slightly fermented, which all members of the household drink from throughout the day. Imbibing the same white watery substance joins the separate individuals as a certain kind of whole which is the household unit: when someone wishes to indicate hospitality they offer *uwitsakyuwi,* a temporary absorption into the material totality/aggregate of the household; the people of my house would indicate their relationship to me by saying that I drank their *uwitsakyuwi* and ate with them. The village is joined in a similar way by *wakula,* a fish stew offered to the spirits that is shared out to every person in every house in the village (see Plate 15). Similarly, one village may show 'solidarity' with another by sending a huge

amount of *akãipé,* a sticky sweet orange paste made from the treasured
akãi fruit, to be distributed to all members of the other village. In each
case, the substance shared is viscous and homogenous, working like a 'social glue', doled out from a single vessel to make singular social wholes.[31]

We have seen how the Mehinaku understand not only their bodies in
particular substantial ways, but also the manner in which these bodies
interact in the world. In terms of the latter concern, that is 'the world as
substances', it is significant that whether it be sense perception, thoughts
and feelings, or notions of social solidarity, all of these are understood
somehow as 'things'[32] that can have independent causal efficacy distinct
from the personal body. In other words, senses and feelings can be experienced as 'forces' or 'things' separate from people or the individual person,
for example, emotion can separate from one person, come to another from
without, and the latter person can choose to let the 'emotional-stuff' into
her or his body or not. For that is what is involved here: for the Mehinaku
there are bodies, themselves substantial, and between these flow different
kinds of visible and invisible substances, sometimes transmitted sometimes received, so that hearing is a taking in of substance, and looking is
an exertion of a kind of substance that can transform what is looked at.[33]

I have not yet discussed aspects of the non-human world, such as sunshine, rain, fire and stars, as well as plants and animals. These too are apprehended by the Mehinaku in material terms. Like human beings, these
features of the non-human landscape were created in a process of substantial rendering. They were made during that time of creation when humans
were made, *hekwimyanão* – 'a very long time ago', and like humans, they
were also made mostly by *Kwamutë* and his grandsons *Kamë* and *Keshë*.
For example, sunshine is a kind of luminous stuff that *Kamë* produced
gradually by mechanically rubbing ('like one sharpens a knife') one of the
two heads of the Vulture Spirit against a flint rock, releasing the great light
that shone from his four eyes.

Material too are the forms of the stars, that are the whole bodies or eyes
of various beings such as the Jaguar Spirit *(Yanamaka)* and the Black Bee
Spirit *(Alama),* who after creation were sent or went voluntarily to live
in the sky. Each of these 'star-spirits' live up in the sky with their respec-
tive spouses, so that for the Mehinaku each star in the sky is paired with
another. Rain is very literally water-substance thrown down *('eles jogam o
agua')* by these 'star couples'.[34] All the water on the ground was once held
in huge clay vessels by a certain bird spirit called *Yanamaka,* who would
share only a tiny bit of it with others. Out of pity for a little *wapu* bird
('bobinha' in Portuguese) crying from thirst, *Kamë* smashed these vessels

with an arrow, releasing the water (and also the fish and snakes that were held inside), which flowed out to form the rivers of the world.

Therefore, both human and non-human parts of the world are substantial to the Mehinaku. Further, several aspects of this 'substantialist' view of the world may be discerned: First, substances were not created from nothingness. The story of creation is not a beginning of all existence, rather it is only the start of the world that humans know. *Kwamutë* and the *apapanye* are already existent when the creation stories begin, and when *Kwamutë* and later his grandsons make humans and the features of the landscape, they do so from materials that are already lying about. Second, the way these substances are used in the creative process is in a very literal, material way, by building-up and fashioning, first by the creators of the world, and then by humans in the process of making and maintaining their own bodies. Third, the interaction between these discrete forms or bodies is also understood substantially, involving the movement of visible and invisible substances each with their own independent causal efficacy. These interactions as movements of substances, do not only occur between human bodies, but between all entities in the world, so rain is water substance physically thrown down by star-entities onto the land below and sunlight is a material literally squeezed out by a mechanical process from the body of a great Vulture that then passes down onto the skin of human beings.

The plants and animals that also make up the Mehinaku world have not yet been accounted for. This is because they are related inextricably to the *apapanye,* and the explications of the nature of these latter entities and their substantiality is complicated, requiring a whole section of their own.

II. Who Are the *Apapanye?*: the Substantiality of Spirits

As a start to the exploration of the general formations of Mehinaku experience, I have explained so far how everything is substantial – bodies and objects and also the interactions between them. But what of the *apapanye,* those beings from the stories, *Shapushënéshë* the 'Wild Woman' and *Yanumaka* the 'Jaguar Spirit' among a myriad of others, all of whom I was told throughout my first phase of fieldwork, no longer existed? The answer to this question came literally as a lightening bolt, or rather the thunder that comes after it. Once, I was sitting with my 'mother'[35] Takulalu in the cooking hut (the *mehehe*) behind the main house, the rain pouring down outside. Suddenly a great rumbling of thunder could be heard. *"O! ...*

Enutsikya! … shapushapai … agora ele é brabo, muito brabo!" – 'Listen! … *Enutsikya!* … he is wild and angry … now he is mad, very mad!', Takulalu exclaimed, pointing in the direction of the low, booming sound and looking at me seriously to see whether I understood. 'He is there now?' I asked, 'Yes . . . very mad', she answered. I had been told the story of the *apapanye-Enutsikya* before, who in a rage had made the sound of thunder with a club as he chased the little bird *Terem* who had tricked him. I had thought that he had created thunder and lightening in the past and was now gone, but now Takulalu was making it clear to me that this *Enutsikya*-being was still rampaging in the sky.

As I have said, I had been under the impression that these creatures in the *ownaki* stories had done their deeds, created various things in some hazy time of beginnings and now no longer existed or at most had gone to live in the sky. No one had ever mentioned or made it known to me otherwise (at least in a way that I understood) that these beings were still in any way around. Whenever I had directly questioned a storyteller about whether the *apapanye* in the story still existed, the answer had always been a categorical no. This then, was the first indication that I had misunderstood, had perhaps asked the wrong questions. In any case, it was clear to me now that at least one *apapanye* and perhaps others, were still in some way at large in the Mehinaku world.

After this revelation, the outline of how the *apapanye* exist for the Mehinaku began to be clearer to me, this first happening in relation to issues of illness. Sickness is the most salient way in which the Mehinaku as a community relate to these beings because relationships with them become crucial when they go wrong, causing a person or a number of people to become ill. At the start of this chapter I wrote that when I asked Kemenyá why the men were doing the *Kayapa* dance, he replied that it was for the 'joy' of it. What I began to discover was that the *Kayapa* and other forms of music are made principally because the *apapanye* called *Kayapa*, has made an individual sick. This person becomes the *uwekehë* or 'dono' (Portuguese for 'owner') of the *Kayapa*, the person responsible for placating and keeping this *apapanye* content so that it no longer inflicts harm on that person nor on anyone else.[36] The relationship between the 'dono' and her/his *apapanye* is characterised by the Mehinaku as being like parent to child; that the 'dono' 'cria', 'brings up' the invisible spirit. I will go into the details of this complex relationship (which I will call the '*uwekehë* complex') in the next chapter. However, what I want to stress at this point is their belief that the *Kayapa* being is present in their midst during the dancing, that the food eaten by the dancers and others is believed to also be eaten by and make happy *Kayapa* himself.[37]

Gradually I discovered that it is not only on such special occasions that the *apapanye* are felt to be near. Though invisible, they are understood to be very substantially present, potentially anywhere and everywhere. Sitting chatting in the house, a friend once said to me of them: 'They are probably all around us now only we can't see them.' The many people I asked said that they did not usually feel this closeness of the *apapanye* in any palpable way during the dancing/singing nor during regular everyday activities. However almost every day some one of my household did in fact come into sensible contact with one of these beings and the stories of such everyday encounters are countless. So, while taking a dip in a lake with little ten-year-old Kohôlupe what sounded to me like a breeze starting up was heard by her as the terrifying *Owtu* boar-beast who lives in the water deeps (we ended up a tree where she forced me to wait out the danger). Another day, my friend Mahí left the path where we were walking to go to relieve herself, coming back to tell me excitedly how as she crouched down, a loud sound like the whirring of bicycle wheels alerted her to the presence of an *apapanye*. Mahí said that the *apapanye* was there because of the big trees in that place, large trees being one of the many markers of possible *apapanye* presence that make the landscape for the Mehinaku a labyrinth of dangers that must be navigated. The men will not fish in a certain place for the giant piranha known to live there. Most men will also tell you how walking alone in the forest they have heard the whistle of *Shapushënéshë*, whom I mentioned earlier as the daughter of the creator *Kwamutë*. As I have described, she has the appearance of an extremely beautiful woman; however simply the sight of her will kill a man, particularly to see her eyes that are said to be like *'estrellas'* – 'stars'. I was told by a number of men how the sound of her whistle gives one the shivering, almost painful sensation of an electric shock, although it has no effect on women.

Day by day then, I began to comprehend how the *apapanye* were understood to be omnipresent, and that one might encounter them at any time. However I wanted to understand what exactly these creatures are to the Mehinaku, what precisely is the nature of their existence. What I found was that, like other aspects of their lives, the *apapanye* are understood to be constituted by substances in the same way as other things. Though the Mehinaku use the term *'espirito'* in Portuguese in an attempt to translate, the *apapanye* are not vague, hazily numinous presences in the way the Portuguese word can imply. Rather, these 'spirits' are as materially 'real' as everything else the Mehinaku engage with in their world, so that both young and old share a rich and detailed knowledge of their material nature[38] (see Plates 10, 11, 12). Below I attempt to sketch some of the characteristics of these entities that constitute a most significant aspect of the substantiality of the Mehinaku world.

An *apapanye* spirit has a body that is basically human in form, similar in appearance to a Mehinaku person when she or he is dressed to dance and make music. However, the designs on an *apapanye*'s skin, the cloth ties on the knees, elbows and arms, and the necklaces and belts, are not adornments but part of his or her actual body (humans 'dress up' then, to simulate the superior bodies of the *apapanye*). In addition, they are extraordinarily beautiful.[39] The different *apapanye* have added to this basic human form their own particular characteristics that echo the animal form they will sometimes take, so that the *Awayulukuma* (the Forest Fox-*apapanye*) looks like a man but also has the pungent odour and devious temperament of the fox, and *Uikyuma* (the Snake-*apapanye*) is strong and slippery-skinned. For this reason the *apapanye* are often explained in Portuguese to be '*gente-bichos*' – 'people-animals'. In this human-like form the *apapanye* are usually invisible to normal Mehinaku human beings. However they can be visible to ordinary people in their dreams; and can also appear in this quasi-human bodily form, as well as grotesque guises to Mehinaku shamans *(yatama)*, and also people who will be, or are already ill. Apart from this, the *apapanye* can be visible as unusually large and beautiful animals; that is why they will often be referred to as their specific name followed by the suffix *kuma* meaning great or large. Also, ordinary people can perceive them by other senses (usually sound), as we have seen with the not uncommon encounters experienced by Mahí and Kohôlupe.

Many of the *apapanye* make creatures in their own images, and these are the 'ordinary' plants and animals the Mehinaku usually encounter in their world.[40] The question of the nature of these 'copies' *(ënai* or *matapu)* and their making, will be discussed in detail later in this chapter. At this point let it simply be said that the relationship between the *apapanye* and these imitation copies of themselves, is one of caring, in the same way as a mother takes care of her children. It is out of this parental protectiveness then, that an *apapanye* will punish (by making ill) a Mehinaku person who kills too many of the animals or plants the *apapanye* has made.

Other *apapanye* do not have animal or plant characteristics in their human-shaped form, nor do they make animal or plant copies of themselves. Their usual, default form, is basically human but the distinctive

▲ *Plate 10.* The *apapanye Yewekwikyuma.*

◄ *Plate 11.* The *apapanye Ateshua.*

▼ *Plate 12.* The *apapanye Arakuni.*

features that differentiate them are peculiar only to them. For example *Shapakuyawa* has the legs of a bird, huge teeth and a beard, is very childish and is especially known for playfully insulting people. A *'cacique'* or chief of the *apapanye* is *Ateshua,* who has a large disc-like form (much like a satellite dish) with *miyoka* snakes on the surface and snakes and sorcerers' charms *('feitiços')* inside it (see Plate 11). His very dangerous presence is portended by the high-pitched whistling sound he makes, unusual fires on the horizon, or by whirlwinds that suddenly descend from the sky (one such wind caused havoc in our 'backyard', and as we women ran about trying to control the damage, the other women saw Mahí lifted off her feet. It was *Ateshua* attempting to snatch her up and take her into the forest!).

More difficult to comprehend are the *apapanye* of certain musical forms, who simply look like Mehinaku people dressed and with special instruments, dancing and playing the *apapanye's* music. Therefore *Kayapa,* whom I have mentioned earlier, actually has the same appearance and sound as when the Mehinaku make his music. The differences are that the ornamentation and the instruments the Mehinaku use, are for *Kayapa* parts of his body. It is the same for the *Takwara* and for the *Kawëka,* each of whom play their own special type of flute. The latter, the *Kawëka,* is by far the most powerful of the *apapanye,* 'chief' *('cacique'* or *'amunão')* even to the chief *Ateshua,* and is so dangerous that women may never look at his music being played, nor even the man-made instruments that play it, as his presence is understood to be always near those flutes. The *Kawëka* is in fact the most important of the *apapanye* to Mehinaku life. The other *apapanye* are only sometimes in the midst of the community, at which times their different musics are played. The *Kawëka,* on the other hand, are always there in the village, in the very centre of the circular ring of houses, in the place understood to be their 'house', the *kuwekehë* where their flutes are kept. In addition, *Kwamutë* (the creator of humans), his daughters and grandsons *Kamë* and *Keshë,* are also *apapanye* although they now mostly live in the sky (except *Shapushënëshë* the 'Wild Woman') and do not interact directly with the Mehinaku as often as the other *apapanye.*

There are several other attributes helpful to comprehending the nature of the *apapanye.* The entities are understood to 'know everything' *('eles sabem tudo')* and can also be in more than one place at once. We shall see in chapter 5 how this exerts a kind of behavioural surveillance on the Mehinaku community: 'If someone murders someone or steals something, the *apapanye* know.' They are also able to travel great distances through the air at incredible speeds, even as far as and into 'White peoples' cities. They prefer to go about at night, 'for them it is not dark'. They live together in villages that look just like the Mehinaku's own, and they walk around their villages looking like Mehinaku people, though more beautiful and always dressed up *('enfeitado')*. They are all friends with one another, and although each *apapanye* speaks a different language, they understand each other and when they speak to humans they speak in whatever language the person understands. Smoke is their food and they are always smoking, even the ones who appear to be children, and they often smoke by bringing the cigar up to breathe the smoke in through the nose (the cigars of wild forest tobacco are the same as those used by the *yatama,* the 'shamans', though the latter only ever smoke with their mouths).

My initial impression of the *apapanye,* when I had at first understood that they did in fact exist for the Mehinkau, was that they were malevolent forces that occasionally impinged on people's lives, making them ill and so requiring assuagement. *Apapanye* do cause illness, however, as I will discuss in the next chapter, this pertains only to the particular complex of human-*apapanye* relations (the *uwekehë* complex) related to excesses of 'emotionality'. Once a fuller picture of the *apapanye* emerged, described to some extent above, I realised that the *apapanye* are not only the abrupt and occasional intrusions of sickness into the world of the Mehinaku. To a great extent the *apapanye are* this world. Apart from the impersonal substances of the world, the *apapanye* and their creations are, put most simply, what make up most of the landscape for the Mehinaku, apart from the Mehinaku themselves.

Therefore, the *apapanye* are not contingent forces the Mehinaku must sometimes fight against but the most important aspects of the world they live *with* in leading their lives. I have said that all of the plants and animals that the Mehinaku use for food, to make their houses and other smaller objects, as well as all of the other creatures they simply come into contact with throughout their day, are 'imitations' that the *apapanye* have made of themselves, or are even sometimes *apapanye* themselves in their plant or animal form. As we shall see in the next chapter, when in good relations with humans, the *apapanye* will give of themselves in this way. Moreover, the *apapanye* do not only produce these copies and protect them, groups of *apapanye* also nurture the fruitfulness of certain plants, most importantly the two most significant to the Mehinaku, that is the *uleitsi* (manioc tubers) and the *akãi* (pequi fruit trees).[41] The particular *apapanye* who together look after a certain plant, live together in one of the *apapanye* villages mentioned earlier. This village exists invisibly in the very same place as the plant's orchard, so that, as one man told me, when one walks into the *akãi* grove for example, one might at any moment be walking into one of the *apapanye*'s houses.

I have attempted to explain to what extent and in what myriad ways the Mehinaku understand the *apapanye* to be substantial. What I hope to have ultimately conveyed is that the Mehinaku are constantly relating in one way or another to these substantial entities that are the *apapanye*. This is not only because out of misfortune they are sometimes forced to but because the *apapanye* generates the world in which the Mehinaku live. That is, they are the entities that make, protect and nurture the growth of the crucial aspects of the materialistic Mehinaku world.

III. The Deception of Substance: All about 'Skins'

Thus far, I have described those aspects of the radical materialism of the Mehinaku worldview that first became apparent. To my Western sensibility, these people's apprehension of their world seemed remarkably similar to the philosophical perspective of Western physicalism, which holds that there are no things other than physical things.[42] There are indeed similarities between the metaphysical points of view of these two cultures. However, the Mehinaku conceptions of an utterly material world that I recognised first, because they in some way corresponded to my own culture's ideas, are in fact parts of understandings of the world that are extremely different to our own Western conceptual/experiential foundations. Coming back to the methodology outlined in the introduction, I suggest that this is an example of how one can come to comprehend worlds to which there would otherwise be little or no access. That is, one starts at the points where there is even minimally some convergence of understanding (where else could one start?) and then explains from there. As I wrote in the introduction, as an anthropologist I have only words with which to explain to my reader, and with these I can only play with the conceptions/categories the reader already has to gradually bring the reader to comprehending others.

Therefore, I would now like to build upon that starting-point for understanding, the description of the Mehinaku world of materials, to begin to show its more subtle aspects. Because for these people, although all is substance, this substance is not the abject matter-substrate of the Western physicalists, nor is it the raw stuff that simply and objectively makes up the world in the 'common sense' Western worldview. For the Mehinaku, all the things/beings of the world are not what they seem, in a sense they are in fact shells. The world then is only one of surfaces understood in terms of masks *('mascaras'/shepeku)*, houses *('casa'/pāi)*, skins *(umay)* and most importantly clothing/covering *(ënai)*. As Viveiros de Castro has stated, "'(T)he notion of the body as "clothing"... is very likely pan-American (1998: 484, n.1), and has already been remarked upon in regard to the Mehinaku by Gregor who mentions a class of spirits whose 'skins are garments *(ñai)* ... that can open' (1972: 322). However, this discussion has been in terms of bodies only and not for the nature of all entities in existence as I propose is the case for the Mehinaku.

My first sense of the surface-like nature of things was in hearing the myth of *Kamakuwaka*, a beautiful young man who avoids the attention of females by covering himself in the *'capa'* or cape of an old man. The women do not want to feed him because he looks so ugly and old, until a young girl who is hiding sees him take off the old cape to have his skin beneath bathed and scraped by his grandfather at the river, after which she pursues and marries him. In the storytelling this body-skin was referred to as *ënai,* a covering, which is the same word the Mehinaku use to call the Western clothing that they themselves sometimes wear, and this body-skin is literally pulled on just like any other clothing, from feet usually to the top of the head. However, once such an *ënai* is put on the body, it transforms it into an utterly new body. This was my first glimpse of how the world that I had learned to be material all around, was indeed substantial but not as dense and fixed as I had assumed.

The changing of *ënai* body-skins is not usually done by ordinary people but rather by the *apapanye* and the human sorcerers *(ipyamawékéhë)* to whom certain of the former *apapanye (Ateshua, Kamë* etc.) gave this ability. As described earlier, the 'bare' form of the *apapanye* is quasi-human, however when they appear to human-beings they often put on the *ënai*-clothing of various animals, trees or other natural phenomena. They do this depending on the circumstances. For example, chasing a human victim *Ateshua* might change from a whirlwind, to a raging fire-ball to a patch of deadly quicksand. When an *apapanye* falls in love with a human it will often change its form to that of a human person, such as *Yakashukuma* who steps out of a coat of the great Alligator (that he 'unzips' like any other clothing, I was told) as a beautiful man in order to have sex with two young sisters sitting on the riverbank. Likewise a love affair begins between the little bird *Yatërërë* and a girl who falls in love with the bird's sweet song, the *apapanye* then secretly appearing to her as a man playing a small flute *(kawëkatāi)*. The *apapanye* also put on different forms amongst each other, chiefly to trick one another, such as when *Kamë* (the Sun) changed into a fish in order to steal *Keshë's* (the Moon's) beautiful red-feathered arrows, *Keshë* shooting the arrows to catch the huge fish, not knowing it was his own brother who was happily swimming away with the arrows in his back.

Human sorcerers, like *apapanye,* also have the ability to change their 'body-clothing' easily. It is said varyingly, that *Kamë, Enutsikya, Ateshua* or the *Yerepëhë* gave sorcerers their special sorcerers' things. The sorcerer keeps all of these, as well as body wraps, jewellery, powerful bones, and various skins of jaguars – yellow, spotted and black – hidden in a cave-like hole deep in the forest. He goes down into this place under the earth, usually at night, chooses one of the skins, puts it on and goes out to roam the forest. Sorcerers in the guise of jaguars will attempt to attack and kill people. In a story told to me about the neighbouring Waurá village, a mother and a daughter set out in a canoe to gather wild cotton, setting up camp when it became dark. In the night the low grunting of jaguars woke the daughter. She whispered to her mother and they hid, and watched with fright as two jaguars entered the circle of firelight. The beasts took off their skins to reveal two Waurá men – they were sorcerers! 'Where are the women who were here?' they exclaimed to one another and when they could not find the women, went to sleep in the women's hammocks. Quickly, the women put on the jaguar skins and killed the sorcerers. They went out into the forest and never returned to their village. Even now, if you are in the forest near the Waurá circle of houses, you may hear the mother and daughter, the grunt of jaguars.

Although it is uncommon for anyone but *apapanye* and sorcerers to change skins at will while awake, all human beings do so whenever they dream. When a person sleeps, the *yakulai,* a kind of soul-body, leaves the *umënupiri* flesh body, and moves around having experiences, these experiences being one's dreams *(shepuni).* The *yakulai* does not contradict the purported materialism of the Mehinaku world because as shall be discussed shortly, it too is material.

I have described how substantial bodies are in fact transposable capes or skins, so that the stolid, solid world of material things that I perceived first, and described in the previous section, is in fact one of dynamic shifting surfaces of swapping, changing, revealing and hiding in skins of things. In the next section we shall see how not just bodies but all things in the Mehinaku landscape are shells, masks or clothing (except for the souls that use them). It has been this way since sunshine first made the world appear in light, and the *Yerepëhë,* the child-like beings that had lived in the landscape in darkness, escaped into the water and 'into the masks' – *'dentro as mascaras'* – that are still encountered in the world.

IV. Eternal Archetypes and the Generation of Skins

In this section I will explain how not only bodies but all objects in the landscape are shells or 'capes', and that furthermore these capes are copies generated from 'originals' called the *yeya,* a concept that might be peculiar to the Mehinaku both in the Upper Xingu and the Amazon.

These *yeya* are the masks wherein the *Yerepëhë* took refuge from the sunshine, and which still exist at the bottom of waters and in the forest. I was told that there is literally a *yeya* for every single thing that exists, including even the things of 'White people' such as cars and watches! There are *yeyas* for the birds and fish, ceramic pots and houses, jaguars and feather headdresses. It was first explained to me that a *yeya* is an exact, true-to-colour miniature version of its copies, from palm-size to forearm length. One of my informants, Arako, told me that his uncle Sepai, who is known as a very powerful shaman of the Yawalapiti community, kept two *yeyas* of an armadillo *(ukalu)* secretly hidden in his house. When they were children, Arako's cousin showed these to him. Inside Sepai's shamanic straw mat-roll for tobacco and other shamans' things, Arako saw the *yeya.* It looked exactly like an armadillo, except it was very tiny, the size of his hand, extremely delicate but moving, shivering and alive.

These *yeya* are the immortal, 'true' versions of all things that surround human beings in their world. They have existed since the very first light of the sun. Before the dawn of the first day, the beings that existed were the wildly passionate *apapanye* as well as the gentle and human-child formed *yerepëhë.*[43] It was the latter, who when the first light came, made the forms of the world – masks – so as to hide. These masks, or 'First-Forms' as they might be called, are the *yeya* and are understood to exist now as the proper bodily forms of the *apapanye.*

These *yeya* of the *apapanye*[44] are the archetypal forms from which inferior copies are issued. The way the Mehinaku express this 'firstness' is with the Portuguese word for 'true' – *'verdadeiro',* as a translation of the Mehinaku *washë.* For example, a fish *yeya* is called *Kupatë-washë,* which means 'Fish-true', distinct from an ordinary fish, which is called a *Kupatë-ënai,* 'fish-cape/clothing'. These 'True-Fish', the *Kupatëwashë,* live in the deeps of the waters and are the stars in the 'shining river' *('o rio fica brillhante')* in the sky, the Milky Way. They are the 'chiefs' *('chefes' – amunão),* making regular fish, *Kupatë-ënai,* for people to catch and eat. These 'fish-copies', the superficial replicas of the 'first', or 'chief' fish, were explained to me as 'fish-shirts' *('camisas de peixe').* They have an ordinary, not particularly satisfying taste and are harder. On the other hand, on the rare occasion that a

'True-Fish' is caught, these are found to be fatter and softer, with a flavour that is extraordinarily tasty. These special fish can only be captured using White peoples' poison, not with an arrow or hook as they know to avoid these. Arako explained to me that this is in fact why the number of fish are decreasing: that is, White peoples' poison has killed too many 'True Fish' and those that are left angrily cease to make their replica-fish and do not allow themselves to be caught.

The *yeya* of the *apapanye,* both in its form of the 'first' or 'true being' or as a miniature, is the body from which its' copies issue. How the replica-skins actually come forth from the *yeya* is unclear, but there is definitely some sense of organic reproduction, with the *apapanye-yeya* understood to relate to its *ënai*-copies 'as mother to children' (as mentioned in the last section), with an *apapanye-yeya* often referred to as, for example, 'Mother of the Fish'. In all of this there is a sense of material connection between the *yeya* and their *ënai,* the latter derived from and thus containing a trace of the former's body, and associated with this, an emotional relationship of the caring parental kind.

Therefore the concept of 'Masters of the Animals' common to much of Amazonia has a particular take in the Mehinaku case wherein these entities constitute archetypes, a conception in many ways closer to that of Plato's "Forms' of Ancient Greece[45] than notions that have been written about the Amazon. The idea that the 'inhabitants of the forest are created and controlled by their *dueños, "owners",*[46] and by their *madres,* "mothers"' is, as Viveiros de Castro has said, one of the 'classical themes of Amazonian culture' (1992: 345). The Mehinaku sense that 'the "mother" looks after her species' (Gow 1991: 79) is identical to other groups like the Piro for example. However, the Mehinaku sense of the species as imitations that issue substantially from a substantial archetype is slightly different.[47] Interestingly, in the literature of the Xingu, I have not found mention of a special relationship between 'powerful beings' and 'regular' plants and animals. The Kalapalo, distinguish the *itseke* as simply separate from *ago,* 'living things', different 'categories' of a 'paradigmatic set' (1973: 17), and also as part of a 'hierarchy of animacy' (1985: 70). Gregor's interpretation of the Mehinaku found the *apapãyei,* as he refers to them, to be simply distinct from 'humans and fauna' (1977: 322), that is, not distinguished by any particular relationship, neither the notions I found of humans as built up in imitation of the *apapanye,*[48] nor that of all other entities generated as imitations from a mother-archetype.

To come into contact with an *apapanye's yeya* is extremely dangerous. To see or even dream of one will cause an ordinary person to become very ill and eventually die unless a *yatama*-shaman succeeds in healing the victim.[49] Even *yatama* themselves must be extremely careful in handling the *yeyas;* in fact even Monaím, considered one of the greatest shamans in the Alto-Xingu, admits to being unable to deal directly with *yeya*. However, it is said to be possible to find and work with a *yeya* to one's own advantage. With the required strength and knowledge, one can hide and keep a *yeya,* attending to it with certain ceremonial preparations (paint and songs, building it a little house). Then one places it somewhere, to which it gathers great numbers of its copies. This occurs because of the parental relationship between *yeya* and their replicas, the *ënai* understood as moving near to the *yeya* naturally, as children do to their mother. There are numerous stories past and present about this occurring, most commonly with great numbers of fish being attracted by the use of Fish-*yeya,* placed by a shaman in water for the good of the whole community. Sorcerers, as we shall see, can also use them but do so for their own selfish and malevolent purposes.

There is another way that the *yeya* are conceived, apart from the notion of them as 'true fish/animals' or as miniature archetypes observable in the landscape. It is the notion of the *yeya* as a beautiful little stone or ceramic piece *('pedrinho bontinho')* that has the image or 'drawing' *('desenho')* of its entity upon it. These work in the same way as the miniature type *yeyas,* and are basically another kind of *yeya* manifestation of the *apapanye*. It should be noted that there can be a number of each kind of *apapanye* and each of these may have a number of *yeya*.[50]

At the end of the last section, the idea was introduced that for the Mehinaku everything is an outer shell or mask, not only their own bodies and those in which the *apapanye* usually appear, but every single thing in their world. This section has been an attempt to come to terms with how this is so by looking closely at the concept crucial to the problem, that of the *yeya*. In coming to understand the phenomenon, its various aspects have been explored, its origin, nature and various types. The *yeya* of 'true' forms, the stones with figures and the archetypal miniatures have been described, all of these essential to comprehending the Mehinaku 'world of skins', a conception I have found to be somewhat unique in the literature. The outer layers or skins that constitute most of the way the world appears, emerge from these original eternal things, which, having been formed at the first dawn of the world, can still be found in the landscape. Before the sun there had been darkness. The coming of light caused the first definition, the differentiating of things into the 'First Forms', from which further definition occurs as they continue to proliferate their skin-replicas, which we shall see are in turn perceived as different realities.

V. The Lake of Butterflies: an Amazonian Metaphysics

After describing the substantiality of Mehinaku existence, we have seen that it is not however, as prosaically solid as this would seem to imply, but rather that the landscapes that the *apapanye* and human souls inhabit are in fact constituted by interchangeable skins – the *yeya* and their copies. I will now attempt to explain a further and the most difficult complication to this 'picture' thus far. That is, that these 'skins of the world' do not straightforwardly exist as such as an 'out there', objective reality. The nature of the forms and copies entirely depends on how they are perceived by the human souls and *apapanye*, that is, the reality of skins perceived is the consequence of the kind of soul perceiving, with groups of different kinds of soul together perceiving different realities. These ideas will be explored in their relevance to issues of personhood and the nature of reality (particularly the conception of animism) in the anthropology of the Amazon.

The first hint for me that for the Mehinaku the world around us was not necessarily as it appeared, was in a story told to me by Kohôlupe, an eleven-year-old friend, as she and I and two younger girls made our way down a path to fetch water. It was noon and we walked on a path between gold-coloured grasses that stood hip-high, and stretched away in all directions across a floodplain. Rounding a corner of the path we suddenly came upon a multitude of fluttering butterflies, a living cloud of blue and green, through which the children ran happily, barely taking notice. Walking through the flickering colours, I made some exclamation and then Kohô-lupe began to tell me a story as we continued along our way. She told of how once a Mehinaku man had been walking a long a path as we were, on his way to the river, when suddenly he had come upon just such a gathering of butterflies. However, instead of seeing butterflies in the air, the man saw a lake moving with many fish. He hurried back to tell others of his discovery, of a place full of fish they might catch. But when the other men went with him to the spot, though the man again saw water swirling with fish, the others saw only butterflies quivering in the air.

The explanation Kohôlupe and later others gave for the reason the man saw what he saw, was that he was ill, his soul had been stolen, and because of this in the end of the story the man dies. After much questioning about this explanation, I understood that it was not that illness had confused the man into seeing what was not there. He was not mistaken that the butterflies were fish, they *were* fish for him, just as they *were* butterflies for the other men. These *ënai*-skins being perceived as either fish or butterflies, are not 'really' one nor the other, their nature is always relative to whom

they are perceived by. The dead apprehend things in a completely different way to the living (as shall soon be explained in detail); the reason then
why the sick man of the story saw differently to his healthy companions
was that a part of him was already detached and seeing as the dead do,
sharing in the collective sense of the reality of the dead. For there is no
one 'real' reality, rather there are a number of shared senses of world that
I will refer to using the term *'consensus realities'*. In other words, the skins
of things in existence have no ultimate nature (at least the Mehinaku do
not speculate about what it might be). They are seen in different ways by
different groups,[51] if they are seen at all (some things are simply insensible
to certain perspectives). These are the worlds of living human beings, of
the human dead, of the *apapanye,* as well as that of dreams.

The best way to describe the way these 'consensus realities' work is in
terms of shared domains of seeing. This is because this issue of being in a
world is for the most part understood and discussed in terms of the modality of 'seeing' or vision. To see the skins of the world a certain way is
to enter into a reality where others see it in the same way that you do. For
example, the living human world is what exists for you as long as you see
as a living human.

The fact that it is one's vision of things that is understood to be what
determines the reality one takes part in, is evident in the name the *apapanye* beings give to humans to distinguish them from themselves. They
call living humans *ipyama nututai* meaning 'two eyes' (though many of
them have forms with two eyes) referring to the human body's two eyes
with the consequent manifest world humans share. That is why if a living
human 'lays eyes' on an *apapanye,* it means that she or he will then enter
the reality of the *apapanye.* Simply seeing one thing that is part of another
consensus reality, will enter you into that world, so that in the case of the
last example, a 'change of eyes' occurs, whereby the human body gradually dies and all other aspects of that world of seeing disappears for that
person, while a new world of skins, that of the *apapanye* will open up to
her or him. The *yatama,* the Mehinaku shamans, are able to see and so
take part in both the worlds of the *apapanye* and that of the human living
and once again this is understood as a shift in the capacity of the eyes, so
that her grandson describes the start of the *yatama* Kaiti's shamanising by
saying: 'her eyes began to dream of *apapanye*'.

How one sees and the resultant world of skins one lives in, relates to
one's state of being or consciousness. Different entities living in different
realities have their different constitutions of consciousness. The *apapanye,*
as was discussed in the previous section, are understood to perceive in

their fundamental humanoid forms but sometimes choose to inhabit their *yeya* forms or other skins. For living humans, consciousness comprises two parts blended together, the intentionality of the 'flesh-body', the *umën-upiri,* and that of the 'soul-body', the *yakulai,* which is an immortal part of the Mehinaku person that in life informs the waking consciousness.[52] In sleep the *yakulai* attains a separate state of consciousness as it separates from the *umënupiri* body to travel in dreams, and at death the *yakulai* forms a different state of consciousness again, as it separates permanently from the flesh body to become the *yewekui.*

The flesh *umënupiri* body, the material physique discussed in detail at the start of this chapter, is also understood to play a part in seeing and all perceiving and intentionally responding to the world, so that even thinking is understood to be an exercise of the whole body: the word for 'to think' – *naôntëkanutër* – means 'all the body is going to think what to do'. This flesh-body perception as something in itself, is proven by the fact that when the illness of soul-loss is experienced, a subject to be discussed in some detail in the chapters to come, the body that remains is still able to remain awake and function, although the person appears listless. However, the perception of the *umënupiri* cannot survive long without the animation of the *yakulai,* the flesh weakening to death without it – as with the man who saw the lake of butterflies – and its existence can even be immediately extinguished as occurs in another story where a scorned *apapanye* kills her human lover by stamping on his shadow (a form of the *yakulai*). Normal waking consciousness is constituted by the *yakulai* and the *umënupiri* perceiving together, the two parts infusing one another. In coming together each of the two parts are understood to affect the state of the other. The quality of the state of the *yakulai* is given physical manifestation in the *umënupiri,* so that *yakulai* anger for example results in an ugly appearance, and mild contentment in a pleasing and attractive appearance. On the other hand, things done to the *umënupiri* can affect the *yakulai,* for example by eating meat the consumption of blood into the flesh-body agitates the soul-body with violence.

It is important to emphasise that the notions of *yakulai* and *umën-upiri* do not contradict the idea maintained from the start, that for the Mehinaku all the world is substance. It might appear that these entities do negate this central proposition of the chapter, in that I have used the words 'body' and 'soul' that historically have denoted aspects of being that are both split and opposed, wherein body is substance separate to soul which is its opposite, 'a thin insubstantial human image' (Tylor 1958: 11). Employing these terms can be misleading, for in the Mehinaku case, both the *yakulai* and the *umënupiri,* albeit different in the ways previously de-scribed, are both material and both intentional. Not only is the latter, the solid flesh-body, substantial, so too is the *yakulai* that has its own substan-tial bodily form, that eats, and talks and walks in dream, and is able to be destroyed as was mentioned, by being physically stamped upon. On the other hand, the body is not just pure, unreflecting matter as the conven-tional dichotomy maintains. As we have said, for the Mehinaku the *umën-upiri* body is also understood to be reflectively, intentionally responding to the world, the whole body a thinking, perceiving entity. Therefore the notions of the *yakulai* and the *umënupiri* do not inhere in the usual op-position of body and soul but rather each possesses qualities of both sides of this traditional opposition.

Having said that the Mehinaku believe different realities exist, seen by different consensus perceptions and that these different kinds of perceiv-ing are done by different states of consciousness, we have looked at what the states of consciousness are comprised of for humans. There are the two parts, *yakulai* and the *umënupiri,* infusing one another in waking con-sciousness, each with different qualities but both substantial. These are separable in sleep creating a different state of consciousness, that of dream-ing (the *yakulai* perceiving alone) . Finally, there is the consciousness of the dead that occurs when the *yakulai* permanently separates to become the *yewekui.* All states of consciousness then, not just that of the *apapanye* as we saw earlier, but also that of human waking consciousness, that of dreaming and that of the dead, are different kinds of substantial soul, sometimes perceiving through substantial flesh-bodies, sometimes with-out, and in their different kinds of substantiality perceiving different kinds of substantial worlds, the various natures of which will be described later in this chapter.

But first it must be seen how these souls differ in their substance and hence the consensus reality apprehended. The different perspectives of waking *(umënupiri + yakulai),* that of dreaming *(yakulai)* and that of death *(yakulai > yewekui)* are different orders so to speak of human soul, varia-tions that share a common human quality[53]. The crucial difference of soul substance is between what is seen to be this essential humanity and that of the *apapanye.* This difference is an *emotional* quality, where the *apapanye* are distinguished by extreme emotion whereas the three kinds of human-soul-perspective all possess emotional restraint, a kind of gentleness that is understood as characteristically human. These crucial traits form two principles, as it were, *shapushapai* (wildness) and *aitsá-shapushapai* ('not-wildness'), both of which have been present since the very beginning of existence. As described earlier, in the myths of the very beginnings of things there existed four kinds of beings: the *apapanye,* the *yerepëhë, Kwamutë* (who with his daughters can sometimes be thought of as *yerepëhë,* sometimes *apapanye*) and finally human souls. The *apapanye* were then in their fundamental nature exactly as they are now, the souls of the animals, trees and other entities, living in villages in their humanoid soul-forms, differentiated by attributes of their individual types but sharing the quality of volatile passion, and other associated features that were described earlier. On the other hand, the little *yerepëhë* were very gentle and were the prey of the *apapanye. Kwamutë,* the Creator-being and his daughters are set apart in a sense, but at least in the first stories of creation, they are identified with the *yerepëhë.*[54] Thus when *Kwamutë* makes the first human women in the image of his daughters, they are made calm and sweet-natured. The reason the first human women were made by *Kwamutë* was to give them to the Jaguar-*apapanye* to assuage his desire to eat *Kwamutë* himself. After the human women have married the Jaguar-*apapanye,* one day they find that he is still hunting and eating *yerepëhë.* They cry to him that he should not be doing this, as stopping him and other *apapanye* from this behaviour was the very reason they were married to him in the first place and he agrees that the *apapanye* will from that point on cease to kill the *yerepëhë.* Therefore the two primordial states of being were wildness and gentleness, with the latter ever victim of the former. This then changes with the creation of humans, where in the mythical marriage between the Jaguar *apapanye* and the first human women, peaceful beings are able to form relationships with wild ones in a way that curbs the latter's violence so as to be mutually beneficial, this relationship becoming the prototype for human-nonhuman relations to the present.

The difference between the gentleness of human souls and the fierceness of the *apapanye* is, however, not absolute but rather they are different ends of one kind of continuum. All souls are made of desire, the difference being *how much*[55] care or restraint placed on desire is also in the soul. In other words, each soul has as its possibilities for consciousness, a continuum of desire. How much control the individual soul imposes on its own continuum of desire, determines the kind of soul/perspective/subjectivity it is (Figure 1). *Apapanye* are at the unrestrained end of each of their continua and humans[56] are at the most restrained,[57] and because it is a continuum it is possible to be in between (for example sorcerers, *Washayu* Indians and White people) and also to change, so that a human who is quite *apapanye*-like, can gradually even transform all the way to the other side to become an *apapanye.* This notion that desire (more or

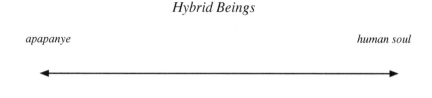

Figure 1. The Soul Continuum: each soul's possibilities for consciousness.

less restrained) is the basic stuff of the state of the soul will be discussed in detail in the next chapter that is devoted to exploring how the Mehinaku understand all existence in terms of various articulations of this dynamic of life.

This Mehinaku sense of worlds constituted by different kinds of souls perceiving different realities, relates to the contentious subject of 'animism' in the study of the Amazon and the related issues of personhood. In Descola's more recent version of animism, the relation between society and nature is interpreted as the projection of human sociality onto 'natural beings' (1996: 87–88). As Viveiros de Castro points out, the problems of this 'socio-centric model' is that if animals are attributed the same form of subjectivity, 'then what in the end is the difference between humans and animals?' (1998: 474). The way Viveiros de Castro answers this question is by saying that indeed all humans, animals and all other subjectivities that inhabit the world have as their internal form or 'soul' human consciousness and what differentiates them and their perspectives of the world are the bodies that 'clothe' them (1998: 470–1), the body as 'the great differentiator in Amazonian cosmologies' (1998: 479). And yet, it has been evident in the Mehinaku case that the intentionalities, or souls, of the various beings in the world are *not* all human in quality but rather have always been differentiated in kind[58] by the defining qualities of wildness and gentleness as well, as we have seen, by other particularities. For the Mehinaku there are the wild souls of animals and trees *(apapanye),* the 'unwild' souls of humans, as well as the souls of the human dead that are 'unwild' but different again and so on. Mehinaku corporeality (skins and flesh bodies) as it has been described above, does indeed fit with Viveiros de Castro's idea of the particularity of substances and the Amerindian model of the body as clothing, 'mere envelope' (1998: 471), and also the idea that this body-clothing can affect the soul within it *(umënupiri >*

yakulai).[59] However for the Mehinaku, the main determining factor for one's perspective is the quality and thus kind of soul, which thus perceives with the rest of its soul-kind a world of particular substances. Therefore one might say that the Mehinaku represent an Amazonian conception not of 'a spiritual unity and a corporeal diversity' (Viveiros de Castro 1998: 470) but of both a spiritual diversity and a corporeal diversity with a causal link between them, where not only the corporeal/skin affects the state of the spirit/soul but also visa versa. In a way this is a combination of Tylor's animism with the 'perspectivism' discussed by Viveiros de Castro; there is Tylor's classical notion of different kinds of 'Spiritual Beings' (1958: 9) but instead of these existing in a simple objective reality, they create their material reality through their perspective, and at the same time 'perspectivism' is at work as this material reality can also impact on the quality of these 'spiritual beings' or souls. This view contributes to Rivière's general notion of the 'highly transformational world' (1994: 256) of the Amazon, as here not only is there the shifting of surfaces, bodies, skin-envelopes but also fluctuations and sometimes transformations of states and identities of souls.

For the sake of clarification let me sum up the preceding ideas in terms of the notion of substance I began the chapter with. There are two main orders of substance that have always been in existence, the desire-stuff of souls and the stuff that was simply lying about from which the first skins of things, and all the replicas since have been created. The latter kind of substance has no knowable ultimate qualities, or at least the Mehinaku do not try to find out what they are, the qualities of these subordinate substances always being determined by the perspective of the former soul kind of substance. Conversely, soul-substance is able to be affected by the subordinate skin/replica substance, although this process is less determinative.

At the start of this section I argued that how one sees determines the world of skins one perceives, and now I have described how this depends for the most part on one's general state of consciousness which is the quality of one's soul. Let us see then how by changing the quality of one's soul in a number of ways, one may change the world one lives in. The crucial transformation of vision and hence of reality by a change in emotional register, the definitive characteristic of the soul, has already been discussed. A shift in the restraint of a living human's desires towards the *apapanyes'* state of consciousness – of uncontrolled emotion, hunger, greed, anger etc – if reaching great enough proportions, may move one's soul over to the *apapanyes'* world and in the most extreme cases, the person can completely transform into an *apapanye*. This occurs in the incest myth of *Arakuni* who in his uncontrolled desire for his sister ultimately transforms into a great snake, as well as in the story of the *Yamurikuma* women, who are abandoned by their husbands, fathers and sons. While away together on a fishing trip the men-folk decide in their greed they would rather keep the fish for themselves, than return and share it with the women, and soon hair grows over their bodies, their teeth become pointed and their eyes huge and shining as they become *apapanye*.

The conversion of one's world, including one's body, as a result of a change in emotional consciousness can also occur to a lesser extent. This is in fact true of all the shifts of consciousness/world that have been described and that will be described below. Because differences in the states of one's being are along a continuum of desire, the change from one perception and world to another perception and world does not necessarily have to be a complete change from one to another. As discussed earlier, there can be a partial or gradual shift of consciousness so that there is a blurring overlap of worlds, which is in fact usually the case in illness (such as in the first story of the man and the lake of butterflies) where the person has only partially gone over to another world and therefore sees sometimes as a living person and at other times as the dead. Also, even within a consensus reality there is a more subtle level of differentiation of states of consciousness or individual experiences of reality and hence individual effects on one's own body and consensus reality manifestation. The most obvious evidence of this are peoples' bodies, each of which is understood to be an expression or symptom of the person's vision of the world. In turn, the state of one's body, its beauty or ugliness, either bolsters or is destructive to the consensus reality shared by the community.[60]

There are other ways that a change in a state of consciousness and hence reality may occur. I have mentioned already that simply seeing an aspect of another reality may enter one into that world, as in the case of a person's soul splitting from the body simply with a glimpse of an *apapanye*'s form. Another way this kind of shift can occur is with cigar smoke *('hëka')*. The state of consciousness that one assumes when smoking is that of the *apapanye*.[61] As I have already mentioned, the *apapanye*, even the child-like ones, are understood to be always smoking in their world. Shamans are able then to enter the material reality of the *apapanye* by smoking copious amounts of *hëka*, sometimes with the *yakulai* soul separating and travelling in that other world while the body lies prone on the ground, or while having a waking vision, with the *yatama* having the unique capacity (unlike other humans) to remain in both realities at once, the flesh-body awake and moving in the world of the living, and at the same time seeing and interacting in the world of the *apapanye*.

VI. Mirroring and Parallel Configurations of Different Soul-worlds

Having explored how different realities of skins manifest for different kinds of consciousness, including individual variation and straddling of worlds, I would now like to come back to the basic wholes of the shared worlds, to describe the two main ways these realities are arranged. The first configuration is the vertical mirroring of the world of the human living on earth and the world of the birds and the dead in the sky. The Mehinaku will tell you that the way they know about the villages in the sky is because of the man Yapikyeku. Long ago Yapikyeku went fishing at night with his four brothers. On the way they stopped their canoe at a Waurá village where they drank sweet *nukaya* soup and made a *buriti* palm torch to illuminate the sleeping fish in the water. Soon after setting off, while his brothers slept, Yapikyeku spotted an enormous *'pintado'* fish, and shooting an arrow at it, only managed to hit the base of its neck. Waking his brothers, together they made chase of the fish, Yapikyeku shooting arrow after arrow without ever succeeding in stopping the *pintado*. Without their realising it the brothers followed their quarry up into the sky, as the fish continued from the river on earth into the river in the sky, *Irapuéné*, the Milky Way. Suddenly the men realised where they were and began to shout 'Oh look where we are! We are up above!' and with sadness they continued to row along until the *pintado* finally brought them to the village of the birds. There in the bird village in the sky the men found many of the inhabitants frightening and dangerous but they were protected and fed by *Tëyu,* a little arara bird. Finally, the Great Vulture brought the men back one by one to the earth. But when the Vulture landed, each of the men were killed on his shoulder spines, all except Yapikyeku who survived to tell what he saw during the journey into the sky.

As well as the village of bird-*apapanye* up above, there are also the various villages of the dead, the realities of whom are diametrically opposed to the world below of the living Mehinaku. One particular story portrays in detail the mirroring of the vertically opposed worlds. It tells of the youth Alatapuwana, who is so grief-stricken when his best friend dies that he barely ceases to think about his loss. At dawn one day after bathing, he is sitting by a fire he has made on the riverbank thinking about his friend when he hears the cry of a maned-fox. He goes to investigate but he sees not a fox but his friend, now a soul of the dead (*yewekui*), come to visit him. 'Don't be sad that I am dead', he said, 'I do not suffer. I live in a village in the sky that is just like a village of the living only even more joyous. There is always fish and festivities. Come with me and you will see. But before we go I warn you that it is a dangerous path to the villages of the dead in the sky.' Together then the two companions, Alatapuwana and his dead friend set out into the forest.

Going along the path, the dead friend suddenly stops. Crouching away in a panic he whispers that there is a wild Indian *(washayu)* up ahead, 'very dangerous!' Alatapuwana tries to comfort him, 'Oh no, it is only a little crab', but his friend will not listen. 'Don't you remember crabs, look …' says Alatapuwana and steps on it, 'See, it is not dangerous'. They continue on and again the dead friend stops, frightened, pointing ahead at the path. 'But they are only *shatoba* leaves lying on the ground', Alatapuwana says. 'No, they are enormous butterflies, they will fly up when you step there!' his dead friend whispers. Alatapuwana leads his terrified friend across the path and after walking together for a long while they finally arrive in the sky.

First they come across the village of all those who died of disease. The inhabitants offer the travellers the milky manioc drink, *uwitzikyuwi,* but the dead friend warns his companion that in this village the drink is made of the white pus of disease and so neither accept it. They continue on and come to another village, which is inhabited by those who died of murder and violent accidents. Again the pair is offered *uwitzikyuwi* but again it is not made of manioc but this time of blood and so neither accepts. Finally they arrive at the dead friend's village. There are great houses and everything is decorated for a celebration and the many people there offer him lots of fish. But this fish is not fish for Alatapuwana; he sees cockroaches instead and refuses the food. 'Tonight', his dead friend says 'we will sleep together in a hammock and I warn you now, in the dark at night all of us here turn into beasts. If you wake in the night I will be a snake beside you'. Alatapuwana does wake and with fright he sees a snake beside him in the hammock. 'No, I am your friend', his dead friend in snake form tries to comfort him but before he can go on, a great disturbance can be heard outside. The dead are being attacked by their enemies, the birds. Fighting ensues but the strength of the living Alatapuwana helps expel the attackers. After this Alatapuwana returns down from the sky to the land of the living, and tells of what he saw above in the world of the dead.

In this story it becomes evident that the two realities, that of the dead and that of the living, are configured in a specific relation to one another whereby the two worlds are vertically opposed (above and below) and have realities of skins that are the mirrored opposites of one another. From earlier discussion of states of consciousness and their manifestations, we can understand that in dying, the friend's consciousness has changed to another kind and so manifests a different reality that is shared by others of that same kind of (dead) consciousness. This reality is the mirrored opposite of his former consciousness so that for this dead friend, in the land of the living, what is safe to the living appears as dangerous to him. Also, visa-versa, for Alatapuwana the food of the dead is inedible, and the dead themselves may appear as beasts. It is important that the sense of what is 'normal' is the same for each of the friends: to have human form, to eat *uwitzikyuwi* and fish, to live in houses and villages. However what one sees as normal the other sees as abnormal, denizens of two worlds, above and below, mirrored opposites of each other.[62]

Apart from the arrangement of two realities as vertical, reverse reflections, the other way realities are arranged for the Mehinaku is as horizontal and in certain places superimposed. 'Superimposed' not in the sense of different things overlaid but rather, as has been described earlier, the same things seen from different perspectives. The worlds of the living (*nëëwnëëwnëëw*), dreams (*shepuni*), the *apapanye* and the forest (*atataku*)[63] exist along the same horizontal plane on which the Mehinaku understand the terrestrial world to extend indefinitely.[64] For the most part, the realm of the living is constituted by the circle of the village (*ahápëna*) and the orchards that surround it. The further one goes from the centre circle, however, the more one enters into the realities of dreams and the spirits, so that there one may encounter that fatally seductive being, *Shapushënéshë* – the Wild Woman, daughter of *Kwamutë* the Creator – and other roaming *apapanye*. In the deepest forest there are whole villages of *apapanye* such as the village of 'Amazon women' from the *Yamurikuma* story,[65] as well as souls kidnapped by the *apapanye* and the roving souls of the dreaming.

The worlds of the *apapanye* and of dreams are distinct from each other, although they are overlaid and seep into one another. Various characteristics of the *apapanye* have been described earlier in this chapter, how their forms and life-style are much like living humans but with plant/animal exaggerations of form and passionate temperament, as well as omniscience, omnipresence and the ability to change form at will. These beings, very different from the fearful and fragile souls of the dead, live in villages much like those of living humans but with particular habits such as the constant smoking of cigars. The world of dreaming souls is a different one again, where the dreaming bodies, the wandering[66] *yakulai* that often encounter one another, have more or less the same human appearance as their *umé* flesh-body, but the landscape, though having many features in common with the waking-world, is constituted by portentous entities that transform in its yellow half-light.

The main regions of these two worlds superimpose in what waking-human eyes see as the forest and they also often blend into one another. The reason for this is a fundamental similarity between the *apapanye* and dreaming *yakulai* and the realities they thus manifest, which in fact includes the souls of the dead as well. When a person dreams, it is said that their *yakulai*-soul *'inyeweku'*-dreams, which is also a word that is used for one state of being of the *apapanye,* and that is also the root of the word for the dead: *'yewekui'.* This certain likeness between the dead, the dreaming and the *apapanye* allows a certain overlap of their seeing and hence realities (a case of partial 'consensus reality'), an intersection and blending of worlds that may sometimes afford, to varying degrees, mutual visibility. It is because of this that in dreams the *yakulai*-soul of the living may encounter the dead and the *apapanye.* This association between the world of dreaming and that of the *apapanye* is why Maiawai said that his grandmother's eyes began to 'dream' rather than simply to 'see' *apapanye* and why people will describe *apapanye* 'like people you see in dreams', or 'spirit-dreams', *sonhos espiritual'.* Not only is there a blending of the two superimposed worlds of the forest (that of the dreaming and that of the *apapanye*), there is also some overlapping of the horizontally distanced regions of the Mehinaku village and the forest worlds. Between the circular zone of the village and the actual forest edge, the orchards and *'campo'* floodplains form a type of blended border-zone where *apapanye,* dreaming souls and waking-humans all move. Although the *apapanye* can watch the humans in their midst, they themselves are usually invisible to waking-human eyes. Apart from this blended area, there are also forays from each world right into the very centre of the other. It is not their usual place, but the *apapanye* may enter the circle of the Mehinaku village, or right into the very houses. The human inhabitants will not see them, except for the shamans who may, with their ability to occasionally see the reality of *apapanye.* Similarly, when people fall asleep, their *yakulai*-souls move through the Mehinaku village on their way to the forest realm.

Just as the *yakulai* and the *apapanye* can move right through or into the *ahápëna,* the circular realm of the living that is the village, so too do the living Mehinaku enter the forest. This overlap of neighbouring realities occurs when Mehinaku families make camp away on fishing expeditions, in the hunting and fishing trips the men go on every day, and more rarely when women make short trips together into the forest to collect bananas and other foods that do not grow in the orchards. The material world that manifests there to the human interlopers is simply one of birds and animals and the dense growth of various plants. As in the story of Alatapu-wana visiting his dead friend's village in the sky, the intruder experiences a completely different reality to that of the native inhabitants of the place. The dissimilar realities are not however, mirrored like those of the dead and the living. Rather, they are simply unlike one another, so that for the dreaming-*yakulai* and the *apapanye* there are paths that lead to villages and all their denizens and objects therein, while the Mehinaku see only trees and animals.

As part of our general investigation of the Mehinaku lived world, in this chapter I have concentrated on elucidating the main configurations in Mehinaku experience. I started by explaining how from the start of my fieldwork I was struck by how for the Mehinaku everything in the world is understood in terms of substance, the world around and its creation, the human body and its senses, the *apapanye* spirits and even the stars, rain and sunshine. This 'Mehinaku substantialism' seemed to me to have much in common with the physicalism of Western philosophy and even the common-sense worldview held by many people in the West. However, it gradually became apparent that the Mehinaku understanding of an utterly material world had fundamentally different experiential/conceptual foundations that are also somewhat different from extant Amazonian models and accounts. The Mehinaku world of substances which I had at first assumed fixed and dense as in my own cultural point of view, was in fact a world of skins, constantly shifting, generated by eternal archetypes that have existed from the time of creation and that still exist in the landscape. Finally it became clear that not only is the world of substances one where souls inhabit a constantly changing world of originals and their body-copies or shells; there is also no sense of it having a 'final' objective reality. Far from the traditional anthropological representation of '"primitive society" as a closed system', the social 'coextensive with the cosmos' (Viveiros de Castro 1992: 3–4), for the Mehinaku there are in fact a number of such shifting worlds, each of which have material qualities determined by collectives of different kinds of material souls (as forms of desire). These realities configure in particular ways in relation to one another. Those of the dead and the living mirror each other as opposites, and the world of the living, the *apapanye* and the dreaming lie beside one another on the horizontal expanse of the earth, superimposing in places and occasionally interpenetrating.

Notes

1. See similar finding for the Yawalapiti by Viveiros de Castro (1987).
2. Like for the Araweté (Viveiros de Castro 1992: 179). For the Barasana the foetus is built up not only from semen but also from menstrual blood (C. Hugh-Jones 1979: 221).
3. For more detail on this, see Gregor (1977: 279–73).
4. Many of the elder adults said that in the past, people submitted themselves to this procedure every five days or so, and that they themselves did as children.
5. The puberty seclusion practice lasts from one or two and up to four years during which the young man and woman remains hidden from view, and apart from their bodies being constantly worked upon, they are instructed in various ways by parents and grandparents in the skills and knowledge deemed necessary for life as a Mehinaku adult.
6. The exact relation for the Mehinaku between their stories/myths and the sense of their own lives will be explored in chapter 4, sec. II.
7. I use the word 'spirit' to translate at this point the Mehinaku word *apapanye*, as it is commonly used to denote such entities in the Amazonian context, and it is also how the Mehinaku themselves translated it to me in the Portuguese *('espirito')*. However it is important to note that in the Mehinaku case, the connotations of insubstantiality of this word are misleading. As we shall find later in this chapter, these 'Spirits', the *apapanye,* are in their own way, in fact very substantial indeed.
8. See Basso (1985: 10–12) for the very similar story the Kalapalo tell about the creation of the first women.
9. Latin name: Hancornia speciosa Gomes.
10. Presently, the Mehinaku use mostly rifles for hunting and hook and line for fishing, although the *uku* are still in use.
11. The Kalapalo story of the creation of men described by Basso (1985: 12) shares the arrow motif, and the differentiation of Xinguanos, other Indians and non-Indians, but among other differences, does not contain the notion of the Sun and the Moon building up the bodies of men from the wood of arrows. Rather they are born from the womb of their Aunt who is made to step over an arrow.
12. Who has appeared in documents previously as Yumuin. The Mehinaku have a number of names during their lives. At any given time a person is called by two names, one by their maternal and the other by their paternal side, both of these names changing at different life stages (see also Gregor 1977).
13. As we shall see in chapter 4, the Mehinaku do not have a special word to distinguish different kinds of stories. When I write 'mythical' it is to refer to those stories the Mehinaku tell that together form a 'canon', told and retold, even owned

as 'things', usually featuring *apapanye* spirit-beings and most often describing the creation of things and the establishment of certain important relationships.

14. Many Mehinaku people have also begun to wear some Western clothes. It is mostly young and middle-aged men and women who use them, shorts for the men and smocked dresses (made on foot treadle sewing machines with fabric brought from outside the preserve) by the women. These clothes are worn as people feel like it, connoting a certain fashionableness and prestige.

15. The nature of these *apapanye* will be discussed in the next section.

16. Marikawa explained this 'dirtiness' *(ketekepei)* by saying: 'their bellies touch the ground as they walk through the forest.'

17. This will be discussed in detail in chapter 5.

18. Exceptions to this are certain birds, turtles and their eggs and also *pahër,* the howler monkey. The reason for eating monkey is in fact because they are like baby humans; hence they are not 'wild' and can be eaten.

19. Although predominantly of fish, elements of other animals, like the jaguar, can also be mixed into the designs.

20. The symbolic meanings of the main foods used by peoples of the Amazon is a much discussed topic, for example starch representing semen, and pepper hot female sexuality as among the Barasana (Christine Hugh-Jones 1979), to cite one of numerous discussions.

21. For example, eating might be experienced in some moments as a creative 'building up' and at other moments (or even mixed in at the same time) as a rounding out of their body to be like the manioc tuber. A few minutes later the same person might pluck her or his eyebrows thinking to emulate the *Umënéshë* woman, as well as the smoothness of the fish skin.

22. Even in the case of old and sick people, where the focus is perhaps less on beauty (although it is still always a concern – old people are teased for being ugly!), there is still an emphasis on body substance, in building it back up to the proper form. This maintaining of the body will be discussed as part of the issue of the holding up of form in general, in chapter 3.

23. The sense of taste is included in the Mehinaku notion of *iníya.*

24. The key importance of 'odours' as a way of classifying the world has been found for other Amazonian groups (Classen 1990), such as the Suyá (Seeger 1981), the Bororo (Crocker 1985) and the Mehinaku by Gregor (1985), but not in the same terms as the above and Gregor found more of an emphasis on taste alone.

25. It will be seen in the next section, how it is mostly to the smell of humans that the *apapanye* beings react and how these interactions are focal in daily life.

26. The causal efficacy of sound in ritual will be discussed in chapter 4, and also its specific role in shamanic rituals (in chapter 5).

27. Thomas Gregor has written in detail on the subject of Mehinaku sexual anxiety, in his book *Anxious Pleasures: the Sexual Lives of an Amazonian People* (1977), and I will also discuss this further in an investigation of issues of gender in chapter 5.

28. How this exactly occurs will be explained at the end of this chapter and throughout the next one, in terms of the *apapanye* and the concept of *yerekyuki.*

29. The consequent need for practices of maintaining integrity of self will be discussed in section VI. of the next chapter.

30. Sociality as a theme will be addressed in chapter 5, sec.III.

31. Similarly, the 'liquidity' of the hallucinogen *yagé* substantially connects the present-day Barasana with their ancestors (C. Hugh-Jones 1979: 230). More generally, the sense of community bound together by substances occurs also among the Piro in the 'idiom of "blood"' (Gow 1991: 263) being 'life itself' (264), 'as a substantial link between generations' (263).

32. The tendency of the Mehinaku to conceptualise in terms of 'things' will be discussed in section I of chapter 4.

33. It is important to note that these impersonal substances are not intentional themselves; their particular qualities are given form by the persons who receive and transmit them.

34. The seasons are defined by the appearance of these stars on the horizon, with different star-pairs 'throwing down' rain at different seasons.

35. I will refer to members of the household in which I lived with kinship terms as I became a kind of foster member of its core nuclear family.

36. Other writers on the Xinguanos have written about such people as 'sponsors' with rather a different sense of the notion to the one I will describe in section III.

37. The dancers do not feel themselves to be or become the entity they represent in the dancing. The human and the *apapanye* are understood to remain distinct, although a certain kind of relationship is formed in the dancing. How exactly this occurs will be explored further in the explanation of the *uwekehë* complex in the next chapter, and also in a discussion of the workings of ritual in chapter 4.

38. Gregor found differently to myself that these beings were immaterial, purporting '"non-substantial being" as a gloss for *apapãyei'* (1972: 321), upholding the binarism between spirit and substance characteristic to the classical anthropological notion of animism that will be discussed in the last section of this chapter. Gregor also gives a rather different picture of 'spirits' (322–323) than what I found obtained for the Mehinaku and described in the text.

39. Similar to the Araweté's conception of their 'god' as having a 'splendid appearance, elegantly painted and seductively perfumed that is far superior to the blotchy, incompleteness of the appearance of humans' (Viveiros de Castro 1992: 40).

40. This calls to mind the much discussed notion of the 'Master of the Animals' in Amazonia. The *apapanye* do possess certain of these qualities, but are more like what exists for the Wayãpi people, beings that possess specific entities or domains of the cosmos, than they are like the *nã* of the *Araweté* who control in a more general way (Viveiros de Castro 1992: 345) or similarly the 'spirit owners of the forest and river' of the Piro (Gow 1991: 242). The *apapanye* seem unique in that apart from being anthropomorphic entities responsible for aspects of the cosmos, the domains in the possession of the *apapanye* are owned by them in the sense that they are *made of* the *apapanye* as imitations of them, and thus their relation is one of being materially linked, as we shall see in section III of this chapter.

41. For example, the most important of the *apapanye* who look after the *akái* are: *Ahira* the Humming-bird, *Tsiritsitsi* the Wild Honey Bee and *Alukaka* the Caterpillar.

42. For a brief and definitive description of physicalism, see the introduction to D. M. Armstrong's book *A World of States of Affairs* (1997).

43. During the primordial darkness, the *apapanye* and the *yerepëhë* are understood to have been distinctly different kinds of beings, however after the creation of the 'first light', they are either mutually identified or the *yerepëhë* are understood to have ceased to exist.

44. The *apapanye* and its *yeya* are not understood as separately the inside and outside of the same being, in a neat, objectified way. Also, the *yeya* is a manifestation of the *apapanye's* presence, and therefore always implies its presence. This kind of blending, overlapping and merging of categories in Mehinaku experience will be explored in detail in chapter 4.

45. Wherein the objects or forms that humans see around them are the replicas of 'real forms'. Like the Mehinaku's *apapanye* compared to humans and their other copies, Plato's real forms are more beautiful and perfect than their copies; and like we will see in chapter 4 for the Mehinaku, in Plato's conception there is the sense that humans should strive to make and nurture things in the likeness of the superior original archetypes. And as we shall see later in this chapter, akin to Plato's description of the realm of forms ('the true earth'), *apapanye* do also inhabit their own world.

46. The Mehinaku notion of *'donos' (uwekehë)*, though similar in some ways to concepts found elsewhere in the Amazon, is differentiated in other ways that will be discussed in section VI of the next chapter.

47. The most similar notion to that of *ënai* copies is the Barasana conception of *wuho*, '"imprint" or "residue" – something made by the original being or object, but which is not actually that being or object itself. If a mythical character transformed himself into a bird, examples of that species of bird which exist today are his *wuho*.' (C. Hugh-Jones 1979: 113) Therefore, the basic concept of 'imitation' is similar, although for the Barasana there is not the sense of the original still in existence, of a living archetype. Also, for the Barasana conception, it has not been specified exactly how the *wuho* 'imprints' are made from the 'first being'.

48. As discussed previously in the first section.

49. The way the *yatama* effects such healing will be discussed in chapter 5.

50. It should be mentioned, though they do not play a role in the generation of skins, that the Mehinaku also use the word *'yeya'* to refer to the temporary outer form or skin that the *apapanye* can choose to take. These *yeya* of fluid, shifting, material form are usually observed during terrifying encounters Mehinaku people have with *apapanye*. The *apapanye* may also give one such *yeya* skin, or part of it, to sorcerers to use, such as the jaguar skins kept in sorcerers' caves described earlier. The Mehinaku say that the tempestuous lightning *apapanye*, *Enutsikya*, gave a large number of such things to members of the neighbouring communities, the Kuikuro and the Kalapalo.

51. Drawing from Århem (1993), Viveiros de Castro describes the basic sense of this notion as 'that aspect of Amerindian thought which has been called its "perspectival quality"' (198: 469). However, we will see below how the way the Mehinaku understand this to work is quite different to what has been previously written.

52. It is understood to be visible as the 'shadow' of a person, as well as an entity in the eyes that may be seen by another as a minute version of the person's bodily form.

53. Therefore, the Mehinaku dead remain vulnerably human in some basic way, which we shall see makes them vulnerable even to birds. They do not become immortal, like the souls of the Araweté dead, who become as their 'gods' (Viveiros de Castro 1989: 1).

54. *Kwamuté*'s daughters later themselves become *apapanye* and *Kwamuté* remains an ambiguously unique figure defined by his creative powers but associated qualitatively with and sometimes directly implied as being a *yerepëhë*.

55. This sense of things in terms of 'how much' is in keeping with what others have called the 'anti-essentialist philosophy of being' that is 'a marker of Xinguano culture' where 'the nature of things is a matter of degree not of absolute opposition' (McCallum 1994: 93). Basso (1973) writes about this in relation to kinship and Viveiros de Castro in terms of cosmology and personhood (from McCallum 1994).

56. Including all three kinds of human consciousness, the living (*yakulai* + *umënu-piri*), the dreaming (*yakulai*) and the dead (*yewekui*).

57. With a principle of care, '*paparitsa*', as shall be seen in the next chapter.

58. See Guss (1989: 49–52) for another Amazonian example of a diversity of souls. Among the Yekuana there is even a multiplicity of souls for the one human being, each person possessing six.

59. As in the story of the mother and daughter who become *apapanye* upon putting on the skins of a jaguar.

60. This shall be discussed in chapter 3.

61. Perhaps because of its heating effect, heat being associated with the wildness of these beings.

62. The conception of the perspectives and worlds of the living and dead as diametrically opposed also occurs amongst the Barasana, except that rather than the sky, 'the Underworld is a reversal of life on earth'. (C. Hugh-Jones 1979: 111)

63. In the forest there are also the *Washayu* (the 'Wild Indians') and beyond the forest are the cities of '*Brancos*' (White people). Although each of these groups are understood to be different from the Xinguanos, the differences are only a matter of degree (they are still humans) so that their domains are not understood as completely distinct from the reality of the living-Mehinaku, in the way that those discussed above are.

64. The Mehinaku do not share the Western understanding of the Earth as a globe.

65. For the story in detail see section II of chapter 5.

66. See Gregor's articles (1981a; 1981b) on Mehinaku dreaming and Basso (1987).

3
Dynamic Aspects in
Mehinaku Experience

In this chapter we continue with our journey through Mehinaku experience toward an understanding of the particular experience of a walk to the river. Here I will discuss what are the specifically dynamic aspects in Mehinaku experience, as well as related categories and connections. We will begin by looking at how the universal dynamic of human existence, the 'ongoingness' of life, has particular qualities in the Mehinaku context, one of flowing continuity and particular rhythmic and substantial attributes. As the chapter goes on it will be seen what these flows have to do with the different kinds of 'souls of desire' and the 'worlds of substance' they perceive, described previously. It will become evident that life for the Mehinaku is understood in terms of how this desire as a dynamic flow courses through and between the worlds and must be modulated in particular ways to sustain these worlds.

I. The Constant Movement of Mehinaku Existence

A certain 'flowingness' of movement generally pervades everyday life in the Mehinaku community. Before discussing this at length, I will say that 'flow' as such, is not a marked category for these people. I am not however, suggesting an abstract concept that is somehow beyond Mehinaku lived experience. As with other notions discussed throughout the book, in keeping with my intention to 'come to terms' with the often amorphous aspects of life as they are for the Mehinaku, I will discuss below how 'flow' is a discernible quality of their lives whether or not they have an actual term for it. I noticed this quality first one cool dawn as I tried to keep up behind the steady trot of the women down the path to the orchard. The women's walk from one place to another, or even from one spot to another in the house, is a rhythmic step, which at its most pronounced, echoes certain dance movements.[1] Walking then behind my foster-mother Takulalu, was to fall into step with this steady, continuous motion, her regular inhalations and exhalations often accompanied by a whistling out-breath. Other activities also have regular, repetitive movement, from the grating of manioc, to the washing of implements and the twirling of cotton on a spindle.

What is more, the transition between activities is also one of flowing continuity. This is also true of the men whose gait and activities are not as markedly rhythmic as the women's but still have a fluid motion about them, evident in the smooth actions of making a feather headdress, or binding an arrow tip. For both men and women, the movement from one activity to another flows so continuously that the movements appear almost dance-like. For example, a woman will go from the regular motions of straining water through manioc pulp, to attend to a fire, with a movement that seamlessly joins the two actions so there is no clear stopping of one and beginning of the other. In a similar way the beginning and end of ritual activities are not marked from what occurs before and after them. Any kind of dancing will begin with people gradually coming to join, and then splintering off little by little as people choose to stop. Likewise, in a shamanising event, after one *yatama* begins, others may join him at any time and as they choose to finish and leave, they simply walk away.

This flowing cadence that characterizes Mehinaku life is strikingly embodied in the qualities of certain dances themselves. This is especially so in the *Takwára,* which involves five men elaborately painted and decorated, each playing a long wooden flute, with each possibly accompanied by one or two women who dance behind holding the man's shoulder. The *Takwára* is a colourful spectacle of vigorously rhythmic, flowing motion. The men dance in line, one behind the other, into and then out of each house in the village circle, the sound and movement continuous, the melody of the music changing gradually, the participants only pausing occasionally to rest for a few moments during the many hours that the *Takwára* goes on. This dance also highlights the way this dynamic of flow works on a general social level and the architectural structure that allows it. The doors of every Mehinaku house are open all day and people from different houses can enter and exit with little ceremony. The *Takwára* constantly reminds one of this fact in the most exaggerated way, the boisterous display entering someone's house every twenty minutes or so, for hours on end sometimes day after day.

The smooth onward motion is also evident in Mehinaku language or *yaka*. The sound of the words is a lilting flow and the talk streams along with the continuous movement of Mehinaku activities that has been described. The rhythm of the language that continues along with the cadenced actions is such that one does not necessarily stop what one is doing to face another to speak, nor even do people look up as a new person enters into a conversation. For example in the case of a group of women washing things in the river, new women arrive at the neighbouring washing-logs and the women who are already there simply recognize the voices of the newcomers as they join in the ongoing banter, without anyone looking up from their work. It (and in fact all conversation) is an unbroken stream of discussion, where no one talks over another person's voice, so that the very expressive, onomatopoeic talk flows from voice to voice, joined together with '*Áha*' (the first syllable extending in length for emphasis), the acknowledgement that someone is listening, approving. Ongoing flow is also apparent in the content of the words. One does not say 'good-bye' and hence end an interaction, rather in coming to an end of an activity, and moving off, one says '*ayí!*' ('let's go!'), urging further movement. Another word, *kalahã*, has no meaning in itself; it is merely what one says instead of pausing, so that the flow of a person's speech continues uninterruptedly.[2]

The various substances of the world, particularly liquids, described at length in the last chapter, are also understood to be in continuous flow. It was discussed how *uwitzikyuwi*, the manioc-water beverage, is drunk from a single container at the centre of the house by all of its members, and how in a similar way, *akãipé*, the pequi fruit stew, is given out to members of other villages. In both cases it was described how the sharing of each of the liquid substances acts as a social cohesive that forms particular social-wholes. Here it is important to emphasise that this sharing of substance is a dynamic process, a movement or flow of material between people.[3] Another stream of substance of great significance in Mehinaku experience is the constant flow of water both inside and on the outside of the body. Every Mehinaku person bathes about three times a day, in springs, lakes or rivers (or from water containers inside the house if ill or elderly), very early in the morning, around midday and before sunset in the evening, and sometimes more often if necessary after particular activities. The point of the bathing is not only about the removal of dirt (one very often goes straight back to working with earth-encrusted manioc etc.), but also about being regularly sluiced with a flow of water. In a similar way, after puberty people use the various root potions *('raiz')*, the huge amounts of liquid drunk and then vomited up. These are experienced as a regular cleansing wash of water internally, apart from imbuing the body with the specific properties of the root.[4] The same principle of the necessity of maintaining flow or continuity is at work in the scraping of skin with the *imya*. The movement of blood out of the scratches is understood to keep the blood clean by keeping it flowing, which otherwise would stagnate in stillness and become dirty.

The steady 'flowingness' of movement within and between activities, with breath and words moving along with it and substances also in motion within and without, are aspects of a very general sense of living as part of the flow of the ongoing cycles of the world. The Mehinaku live, constantly responding to the myriad cycles of the various aspects of their landscape. Different flowers bloom, fruits ripen and they are associated with the appearance of certain animals, such as insects and the movement of flocks of birds. These events are understood as regular reoccurrences linked with the anticipated 'seasonal' rise and fall of river water levels and the periods (often estimated by the waxing and waning of the moon) of rain and dryness. All of these repetitive, successive events are in turn heralded for the Mehinaku by the regular appearance of certain of the ever-wheeling stars.[5] Often in order to explain to me when and how a certain seasonal event would begin or end, an individual would point her or his finger at a star in the sky, and explain that it was with the appearance or disappearance of this star that the event concerned would occur.

The motions of Mehinaku experience that have been described thus far are not however about passively flowing along, simply carried by the greater forces of the landscape. The experience of ongoing continuity in all areas of life is consciously valued, encouraged and worked for by the Mehinaku. This is apparent in the activities already discussed, such as the cleansing of the body inside and out with water and by bleeding, as well as the admonishments in language to always keep going. The sense of danger here in stopping is in going against the very nature of existence, understood as the incessant flow of all parts of the world. Sometimes though, even the most significant features of the landscape cease moving as they are meant to, so that humans must help maintain the very forces of the worlds, as in the case of a solar eclipse.

Understood as a halt in the regular path of the Sun *(Kamë)*, this being is thought to be menstruating, something he never need do. The pause in the course of things is a dangerous state of affairs where the darkness is understood to be *Kamë*'s menstrual blood, which is harmful to human bodies. Apart from taking various actions to protect themselves from this and other harms threatened during the hiatus, the Mehinaku are very concerned to start the flow going again when the eclipse is ended. The most obvious way they do this is by conducting a *chuluki,* another type of movement of materials, in this case the exchange of goods between members of the community. Depending on whether it is a men's or a woman's *chuluki,* either all of the men or all of the women move in a group from house to house around the circle of the village. In each house, the members of the household of the gender participating bring things out to the circle of the group, who then offers things in exchange for the item. Although many enjoy this trading, it is not necessary as bartering is normally conducted in an ad-hoc way between individuals. Rather, the most important sense of this practice, especially in the context of the eclipse, is that it is trade for trade's sake. An eclipse occurred while I was there and after the darkness, when the *chuluki* began, I asked a man named Kemenya why it was occurring just then. He answered that it was because of the eclipse, that otherwise people would become stingy *('kainumairi').*[6] Through the *chuluki,* the Mehinaku were consciously and actively promoting the flow of things between people to make up for the break in continuity that had occurred with the eclipse.

Whereas the problem of an interruption like an eclipse is dealt with by dynamic stimulation of the continuity of life, other halts and obstacles to the flow of things are often actively absorbed into the flow. Socially, any faltering in the smooth and steady way things are supposed to progress, from the most minor things to the very grave are to be absorbed. When a girl accidentally drops the manioc bread *(uleiki)* she is making onto the ground, the women watching say nothing, waiting for her to continue as though nothing had happened, and similarly a conversation will continue even if one of the parties slips in the middle of it and falls into mud (something I personally came to know quite well). Aggression, which also threatens to disturb the normal gentle flow of social interaction, is also absorbed into the acceptable social state of being.[7] This is often achieved using language, for example by enquiring *'awëshëpai?'* or *'pawëshëtsai?'* – 'Is everything fine?' As there is no other possible answer, the angry person must answer with the same word in response, that everything is 'fine', even though it is not. Absorption even occurs with death. Five or so days afterwards, everyone in the village is expected to 'forget quickly' I was told by one informant, so that death is absorbed as quickly as possible into the normal run of day-to-day life.

In addition, obvious differences in cultural practices do not interrupt the flowing Mehinaku way of doing things, rather they are enclosed into or dissolved if possible into, what is often a self-conscious conceptualisation of a Mehinaku 'way of life', or *anaka.*[8] The Mehinaku have few

qualms about involving outsiders in their own practices, something I experienced daily in their encouragement of my involvement in all of their
activities. In joining an activity – for example, peeling manioc – there was
always minimum to no instruction; the activity of the others would go on
around me until I learned by participating to do it along with them. Any
mistakes I made, or differences to the way I did the activity were ignored
with the expectation that I would eventually 'cotton on' and do it the way
they did. Utterly new practices that are introduced by White people for
example, may be adopted but only insofar as they are judged by individuals to fit into the Mehinaku *anaka*,[9] and if a practice is found to be utterly
incongruous, it is simply tolerated in others.[10] This absorptive tendency is
evident also in the effect of the Xinguano groups meeting their non-Xinguano indigenous neighbours. The literature[11] has described how contact
between these groups has most often resulted in the non-Xinguanos taking up the Alto-Xinguano ways of doing things, from the way the women
do their hair to whole rituals. This is also evident on the level of whole
populaces in the peculiar history of the Alto-Xingu, where completely different ethnic/language groups absorbed each others' differences to live in
what they recognise as generally the same ways.[12]

The most obvious and everyday way that a flow is encouraged by the
Mehinaku is in work *(ukatumalapai)*. This term for 'work' is the same
word as for 'generally doing things', and there is no real difference between
these two as a person is almost always meant to be involved in productively
doing things. This is their definition of work: there is literally meant to be
no cease of industrious pursuit during the day, the person going from one
activity to the next.[13] Even if relaxing after strenuous actions, one will still
do something quiet such as sitting and weaving mats or preparing arrow-
tips. There is no notion as in the West of 'time off', a break during the day,
let alone a day-off, weekend or holidays. I learned that even the children
have a strong sense of this. One day I was taken by some girls to bathe and
was astonished at the beauty of a lake I had never before seen. Wanting to
luxuriate for a time in the cool water, I suggested to my companions that
we stay a while. A child can play for a short time or an adult can gossip,
but this is done *during* an activity and once it is finished one must keep on
going, it makes no sense to stay, thus I was urged by my young companions to leave the water and return to the village.

Even in death there is no ending of the flow of this daily activity. For
the dead person's *yewekui,* all features of the life one lives on earth – the
village, relatives, work – all of it continues on in the sky-village.[14] Unlike
in transcendental worldviews, where one anticipates in death a radically

different mode of existence,[15] for example in eschatologies of hell and heaven, for the Mehinaku there is never a ceasing of their village way of being; existence is all there is, and it flows on in death as it does in life.

Sobo (1993) has found that notions of flow or 'flow models' as she calls them, are evident in many different cultures: in New Guinea and Mexico, in the ideas of Western biomedical scientists, and in the health traditions of African Americans and Caribbean Islanders of African descent, in which notions of flow are invoked in native theories of menstruation, contraception, abortion and fertility enhancement. In the above we have seen how the Mehinaku also experience things in terms of flow, in fact all the worlds and their lives in terms of flowing, streaming and measured motions, within activities and between them. Breath and word, dance and all substances move with this cadenced continuity, and all are lived as part of the larger flow of the cycles of the landscape. Continuity of movement is consciously cultivated, breaks in it are compensated for, obstacles to it absorbed, even passing to the village of the dead is a flow, from earth to sky along the water of the *Itapuéné* River, the Milky Way, and even there existence goes on an on.

II. 'Star Birds': Movement between Different Dimensions of Reality

The dynamics of ongoing flow I have been discussing are the motions of and within the structures of experience discussed in the preceding chapter. There are however motions between these structures, the rogue motions of individuals between dimensions. This is the cross-over of worlds which can happen for just a moment as in the glimpse of an *apapanye* while walking in the orchards, or it can be heard each night in the hooting of owls on the roofs, understood to be the laments of the dead. Harking back to the notion introduced previously of the existence of a number of 'consensus realities', according to the sense of this conception, the visitor from another world is an interloper, whose sounds and appearance are not in keeping with the shared sense of the world he or she visits. This kind of trespassing movement can take place across the two main configurations of realities that were discussed in the last chapter. It can occur vertically between the worlds of the earth and the sky or horizontally between the world of the village and the world of the forest.[16]

From the heavens to the earth, the birds who are always at war with the human-dead in the sky descend from that world and fly in flocks overhead, perching in the orchards of the living Mehinaku. My foster-sister Mahí would often point out the *tsipinyu,* small birds whose sleek blackness is made from the hair of the Mehinaku dead that the birds pluck from these souls in battle. 'They do not have feathers do you see, it is hair!' Mahí would say. These birds are visible as stars in the night-sky and their appearance at certain times as birds in the sky heralds seasonal changes such as the onset of the rainy season. Maiawai, Mahí's brother, indicated a *tsipinyu*-bird perched on a branch and said, 'it has come from the sky! … the rest of the time it is a star in the sky'.[17] Apart from the 'Star Birds', certain *apapanye* also move vertically between the worlds of the sky and the earth and most commonly spoken of in this regard are *Anapi* and *Ateshua.*[18] *Anapi* is the rainbow that arches in the sky, and it is understood to be a great snake that poses no danger while up there but which may descend and cause mass destruction. There is a story commonly told in which *'hekwimyanão'* 'long ago' (four or more generations back), a community called the Kutanapu, who like the Waurá basically spoke the same language as the Mehinaku, were all but wiped out by *Anapi.* Alternatively, this incident is attributed to *Ateshua,* who with his huge disc-like head was seen very white and spiraling slowly down, before landing on the ground.

The infringement of one realm into another does not only occur vertically between the sky and the earth. This kind of encroachment also transpires horizontally when the denizens of the forest, the *apapanye* spirits and dreaming souls, intrude into the reality of the Mehinaku village, and occasionally when living-waking Mehinaku find their way into the world of the *apapanye,* as well as when sorcerers move back and forth between these worlds. It should be clarified how the kind of movement I am discussing in this section is not simply a visit but a true intrusion. As mentioned in the last chapter, overlaps can occur between domains but these are not penetrations into the reality of the inhabitants of the domain: for example when living humans walk through the forest, they do not usually participate in the reality of the denizens of the forest and likewise the *apapanye* are often insensibly present in the Mehinaku village. The intrusive dynamic we are discussing here pertains to the encroachment of a being from one reality into another, wherein the intruder interacts with the members of the other reality whilst retaining her or his other-worldly characteristics.[19]

The trespassing of *apapanye* and dreaming souls into the realm of the Mehinaku village most often occurs at night. The Mehinaku would often talk to me about being visited in the darkness whilst sleeping in their hammocks. Once, pointing at a large bruise on my leg, a young girlfriend of mine asked me what I had dreamt of the night before. I dreamt of a friend in Mexico I told her. She responded that I was given that bruise on the calf by the dreaming soul of that friend who had journeyed from his home to where I slept. And it is not only roaming souls that enter and interact with the sleeping members of the Mehinaku village, more dangerously certain *apapanye* will do this, most commonly the *apapanye* of the *sheboya* snake. The spirit-snake has been known to enter the house to come to make love with a sleeping woman, who is then usually woken in fright by a shaking of her hammock in the middle of the night. The *apapanye* can also perilously intrude into waking daily life, as shown by a story told to me about a man of the Kamayurá community who was walking in the orchards when he saw *Kamë* the Sun in the guise of a *'caraíba'*, a white man. The Sun-*apapanye* who appeared suddenly between the trees as a *'branco'* wearing trousers and a tie, said to the man, 'you will not live any longer, because you have killed too many *arara* birds', and the man died five days later.

The intrusion of one reality into another also takes place in the other direction, when people find their way into the realm of the *apapanye*. The Mehinaku tell the story of one such individual, who entered from the human reality of the forest, of trees and animals into the parallel world of the *apapanye,* with its paths and villages. He was a young man who, though strong, was not very good at wrestling *(hukahuka)* and it was for this reason that when walking in the forest one day he stopped before a *mawaya* tree. This is because the root of the *mawaya* tree is boiled into a brew *(atatapa)* made to strengthen young wrestlers for the fight, and the youth had decided to ask the *apapanye* of the tree for help. "What should I do?" he beseeched the spirit of the tree and suddenly the *apapanye* appeared to him in the form of a man. "Follow me!" the spirit bade him and right before the young man was a path that had not been there before. It was a spirit-path, the landscape had changed because he was now in the spirit-realm and everywhere around him were paths he had not seen earlier. Following the *apapanye* down one of these paths, he arrived at the village of the tree spirits where he was taught to be the greatest wrestler of them all. Similarly, Kaití the oldest of my foster-sisters, met an anaconda-*apapanye* in the pequi groves and made love with him in his world. The anaconda had tricked her by disguising himself in the form of her husband, who was away and whom she was missing terribly. The consequence of this encounter was typical, her *yewekui* soul-body split from her flesh-body, and was taken to live with him in his house in his world, and her flesh-body ailed without its counterpart until her uncle the shaman Monaím brought it back.

Unlike ordinary Mehinaku people, shamans *(yatama)* frequently interact with the *apapanye,* moving back and forth between the different realities.

The initial movement into the *apapanye* world is usually brought on by intoxication with cigar smoke *(hëka)*, after which the *yatama* is usually met by his particular *apapanye* spirit-helper, who escorts and helps him in that other world he is visiting. Sorcerers (the *ipyamawëkéhë*) likewise can shift between the realms of the village and the *apapanye*, although not to retrieve stolen souls or to find lost things, but rather to gather allies and weapons from the *apapanye*, for theft and murder in the land of the living.[20]

Apart from the random intrusive movements between the sky and the earth and the forest and the village, there is a place where this kind of shift is especially prone to occur in either of the two directions. This is *Morena* as it is commonly known in the Xingu, *Mushuna* to the Mehinaku. It is the site of the creation of the first people, the 'women of wood' (the *umënéshë*), where once was the village of their creator *Kwamutë*, and also that of the Jaguar-*apapanye* and his children the Sun and the Moon. Although these beings are said to no longer live there, the site is understood to be dangerous with the things they left behind and their presence that is still felt to be near.

This place where not only the *apapanye* but also the dead are believed to constantly come and go is not understood to exist vaguely, mystically somewhere beyond the tree-line. Morena – this intersection point of realities – is an actual area that can and has been clearly pointed out to me a number of times on a map, a region that is located very near to the present settlement of the Kamyurá community. The Mehinaku also lived in the area, moved there by the Villas-Boas brothers in the 1960s as part of the establishment of the Xingu National Park. The Mehinaku were not content living near *Morena*, for all the dangers of the different worlds that overlap there. Apart from the *apapanye* and the dead one may encounter, there are such terrors as 'bellies of earth' *('barrigas da terra')* that open up and swallow unsuspecting hunters, as well as the many *'coisas do Sol'*, 'things of the Sun', the *apapanye Kamë* is understood to have left around the region, perilous fish, animals, poisons and sorcerers' things. They say that the people of the Kamayurá will eventually be wiped out if they continue to live there. The Mehinaku say that living near this place of perilous beings and their things has made many Kamayurá people sorcerers.

III. The Impetus of Movement: the Dynamic of Desire

As part of the general picture of Mehinaku experience we are building up in these chapters, we have seen then that apart from the motions of the structures of the Mehinaku worlds, there are also the intrusive movements of individuals between them. I have discussed how this breach of realities can occur in two directions, contravening the two main configurations of worlds for the Mehinaku. They are vertically between the sky and earth, and 'on the ground' between the dream and spirit realms and that of the village. But what makes the star come down to the earth as a bird, and why does the Snake-*apapanye* appear to women in the orchards behind the houses? Why are beings not content to simply continue living in their own worlds; what makes them leave their own realities to interfere in others?

The answer to this question is desire. The impetus for the intrusive and often forceful movement between realities is the desire[21] that occurs between the living, the dead, dreaming-souls and spirits. In the last chapter it was explained how the basic stuff of the soul is desire and indeed the Mehinaku believe that the dreaming soul of a lover comes from far away to the hammock of his or her sleeping beloved drawn by desire, and likewise it is out of desire, a hunger for knowledge and for ability in wrestling, that the living man of the story of the *Mawaya* tree[22] entered the world of the tree *apapanye*. The living who greatly long for the dead may follow them to the village in the sky, as in the story of *Alatapuwana* recounted in the previous chapter. And similarly it is out of yearning for his living friend that at the end of the story[23] the dead friend appears in the land of the living as a snake in the manioc orchards, as he misses his living friend so much he would bite and kill him, thus bringing him to his own world.

In the same way, the desire between the *apapanye* and humans often moves one into the other's world. The Mehinaku will tell you that when illness occurs because a person's soul has been taken by an *apapanye*, it is not from spite but from love that the *apapanye* does this; the *apapanye* brings the human soul back to its home because it desires to live with it there. Such 'soul-theft' occurs all the time in the Mehinaku community, understood as it is to be the most common cause of illness. It has been mentioned how Kaití was sick in this way after her amorous encounter with a snake-*apapanye* disguised as her husband. Mahí, Kaití's sister, was almost carried off by another *apapanye*, the powerful chief of the spirits *Ateshua*.[24] This occurred one afternoon as the women of the household, including myself, sat in the cooking house by the fire waiting for a whole turtle that was cooking in it to be ready. A large whirlwind suddenly blew up the dust just outside the door and the women rushed out screaming and running to secure the things that had been tossed about in the dusty darkness. When the wind finally ceased there was an uproar about what had happened and all agreed it had been *Ateshua*. I was surprised by the shouting of these women whom I had never seen show emotion in excess of their normally calm modulated manner, and I was shocked by the fear I had seen in my foster-mother Takulalu's face in the fray. A very frightened Mahí then recounted how she had been lifted off the ground and that it must have been *Ateshua* trying to take her away. It was *Ateshua*'s sexual desire for Mahí that was emphasised. She told of how her dress hem had been lifted by Him and Kwakani her younger sister joked to Mahí's husband, that he had almost lost his wife to the *apapanye*. During the event, what was most striking was the Mehinaku's palpable dread of the desirous *apapanye* and how much this real fear impinged on daily life.

The desire for the living that moves the *apapanye* into the world of the living is reciprocal. As was explained in chapter 2, the *apapanye* are basically human in form but of extraordinary beauty and this beauty proves extremely attractive to living human beings. The *apapanye* called *Shapushënéshë*, the 'Wild Woman', is the most obvious example of the allure of the *apapanye*. She was mentioned in the last chapter as the daughter of the creator *Kwamutë* and it was said that she is very lovely, in fact literally the ideal of female beauty. She is extremely desirable to human men but to encounter her is to risk moving with her into her *apapanye* reality. There is a well-known story of such a relationship between a human man and *Shapushënéshë*. His name was Kapukwa and he was a young man in seclusion who met the *apapanye*-woman bathing at twilight at the forest edge. He was immediately enamoured by her and wanted to have sex with her. She warned him that it would be deadly for him because of the dangerous creatures, small snakes, biting ants and piranha fish, that live in her belly but he convinced her to remove them, helped her do so and they made love. For five days or so she came to his house at night and he left with her into the forest. Finally however he became afraid of her and rejected her but she became angry at this and took his soul. Initially then Kapukwa has the unusual strength to remove what is dangerous for his liaison with an *apapanye* but ultimately the encounter does overpower him and his life in the world of the living is destroyed.

The passion between humans and the *apapanye* has existed since the creation of humans and there are countless stories from that time that concern such relationships. The most important and commonly told[25] of these, and in a sense a template for the others, is the myth of *Yakashukuma* the Great Alligator and the two human sisters who are his lovers. The sisters go together to bathe and while sitting and talking on a branch on the bank of the river they see a huge alligator *(Yakashukuma)* appear. At first they are fearful but when they see him as he steps out of the skin of the creature as a splendidly beautiful man, they fall passionately in love. They call to him to come to make love with them both and he does, and every day they return and call to him and they do so again. In the end of this story the sisters' husband finds out about their relationship with the Alligator-*apapanye* and together with the other men of the village he kills *Yakashukuma,* but the sisters take their lover's dismembered body and bury it and from his body grows the first pequi *(akãi)* tree, the cultivated plant central to Mehinaku existence.[26] Another of the many stories that depict the desire between *apapanye* and humans is that of the Maned Fox-*apapanye* named *Awayulu* who takes a human baby left in the fields by her mother because she cries too much. The girl-child grows up to become Awayulu's wife, and the woman lives together with her husband in the world of the *apapanye.*

It is crucial to clarify that desire is not only the impetus of motion but is also the flow of motion itself; no difference is made between the two by the Mehinaku.[27] Harking back to the last chapter, it was explained how the stuff of the soul is desire and now we see that the flows of the worlds discussed earlier are streams of this soul-substance, sometimes along with other substances of that soul's world. Also, desire is not only the dynamic of motion between worlds, it is also the source of the general motions of Mehinaku experience that were described at the start of this chapter. The flow of activities and between activities, of dancing, language, and of different substances are a flow of desires being steadily satisfied according to a kind of 'pleasure principle'. The Mehinaku say that communicating with language, dancing and eating all give *'alegria',* the Portuguese word for joy, and in Mehinaku they express this with the word *awirinkyapai,* which means 'pleasurable' or 'delicious'. Those activities that are not directly enjoyable such as strenuous physical labour and painful body therapies such as scraping and vomiting, are done with a view of the eventual pleasure they will yield, such as good food, physical beauty and sexual intercourse. Furthermore, temporary limits on direct pleasure such as in the practice of various abstinences, hard work and pain, are understood to temper the flow of desire and its satisfaction to a moderate steady form that is the ideal.[28] Hence the general motions of Mehinaku experience are of desires being met moderately and ongoingly.

In summary, it is desire that makes a being move from his or her own reality into another and it is also desire that gives motion to the various activities of Mehinaku life. These are two different kinds of hunger: the encroachment into another world is an excessive, passionate yearning whereas the flow of yearning within the normal workings of the world is ideally steadily moderate.

IV. The Boundaries for the Flow of Desire:
Concentric Circles and Paths

The motions of desire that have been described do not however flow unbounded. They move within the limits of the various worlds that were
described in chapter 2, the boundaries between and within these different realities. The borders and shapes of the worlds only began to exist in
the time that humans were first created. Before the creation of the first
women by *Kwamutë*, wild consuming passions flowed unbounded in the
undifferentiated darkness.[29] The *yerepëhë* and the *apapanye* were the only
beings who lived then and the small gentle *yerepëhë* were easy prey for the
fierce *apapanye*. We will see in the aforementioned story below that the
first restrictions on desire and its satisfaction came only because of the
first human women, the *umënéshë*. These women *Kwamutë* made as wives
for the Jaguar-*apapanye (Yanumaka)*, in exchange for the fierce *apapanye*
agreeing not to eat him or the other little *yerepëhë*-people.[30] Once the
umënéshë-women were living in the village of *apapanye* with their new
spouse, the *apapanye* returned from their first hunt and their quarry was
yerepëhë-people. When the human women saw this they began to cry and
their tears made the lines that still crease the palms of human beings.
The sisters wept and said 'Our father gave us to you so you would stop
eating the Little People' and the Jaguar listened and in the afternoon explained to all in the village that they were no longer to hunt the *yerepëhë*.
In the skin of hands previously smooth and unmarked, the sorrow of the
women made the first marks of compassion, the first lines drawn, as it
were, against the boundless ardour of the *apapanye*.

The Sun *(Kamë)* and the Moon *(Keshë)* were born to the Jaguar and one
of these *umënéshë*-women, and it was the Sun who brought about the most
important of the formations that delimit the world as it is known now.
This occurred when he made sunlight by rubbing the head of the Great
Vulture (the light came from the bird's four shining eyes) that caused the
yerepëhë who could not abide the light, to make the *yeya* masks of the
world in which they hid. As we discussed in the last chapter, the *yeya* are
the structural blueprints from which the world is constituted as *ënai* copies, and it is within and between these living structures that desire flows.
Soon after the first sunshine and the formation of the *yeya*, other cosmic
bodies took their proper places. This occurred when the Sun, the Moon
and certain of the *apapanye* settled in villages in the sky, the Sun and the
Moon perceptible to the living human eye as the familiar round heavenly
bodies and *apapanye* such as the Jaguar (*Yanumaka*) and his friend the

Black Bee (*Alama*), visible now as the shining stars (*kalunté*). Again here it was *Kamë* the Sun who was responsible for the establishment of boundaries, the place and shape of the parts of the worlds. *Kamë* deemed the fierce Jaguar and Black Bee and some other *apapanye* too dangerous to live amongst human beings and so sent them up to live in the sky. Likewise *Kamë* compelled the ferocious *Anapi* Snake to stay in the sky where he is observable as the Rainbow.

The first boundaries that were formed when the worlds were created continue to give bounds to the flow of desire. Moreover within these borderlines of the shape of the worlds, the passions of beings are further contained within still smaller limits and these are in the form of circles. This is most evident in the layout of the village and beyond with different zones of life existing one within another in a series of concentric circles (Figure 2).[31] The *apapanye*, still as wildly passionate as in the time of creation, live in

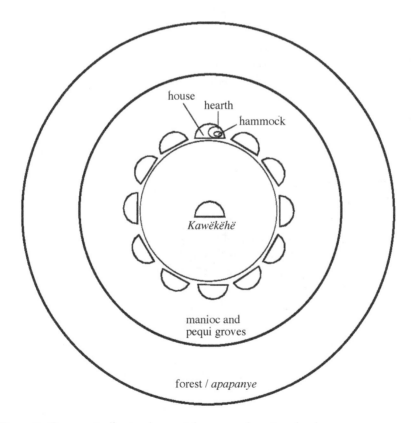

Figure 2. Concentrically circular spatial zones at the micro-level.

the forest, the outer-most round of the earth. This forest region of bound-less desires encircles the 'roças', the orchards of the Mehinaku, which is also an area of desire though of a more muted kind. Within its borders the forces of desire are restrained by the social articulations of lovers' intrigue and marital values.[32] This is the region where people most commonly meet to have sexual intercourse, husbands and wives or lovers meeting in secluded groves. The area of the orchard in its turn surrounds the round of the village with its houses spaced evenly to form a circle. The ring-shape of the village forms a zone of inward-looking domestic safety, whereas the orchards and the forest that extend outward from it are experienced as dangerous in comparison. Yet, for the extended-family members within the round of the single house, the socio-political sphere of the rest of the village is felt to be of relative peril. In turn, within the comparative ref-uge of the house, the circle of nuclear-family members around a hearth (of which there are up to four or five in a house) forms the sanctuary of utmost security. The very safest of all is the hammock and within it the ultimate bounded 'unit' which is the individual's human body, the integ-rity of which is the last bastion against the potentially destructive desires of the world.[33] At the very centre of the village however, in 'the house of the sacred flutes' (kawëkëhë), is another area of uncontrollable passion, as not only are the sacred flutes apapanye, they are their chiefs. Thus, as in the outermost circle of the forest, the epicentre of the Mehinaku village swirls with the wild desires of the apapanye.

This configuration of concentric circular zones of space of different or-ders of desire is experienced in an equivalent layout at a macro-level (Fig-ure 3). Here at the macroscopic level, Morena or Mushuna, discussed pre-viously in the chapter as the dangerous intersection place of the different realities, is the epicentre. It is surrounded by the area of the Xingu, in a way corresponding to how the safety of the village encircles the perilous House of the Flutes. The protection afforded by the village community from the strains of the socio-political climate of the Xingu region is equivalent to the security of the house from the rest of the village goings-on. And just as the orchards and forest surround the village with wild hungering forces, at the macro-level the land of 'Wild Indians' (Washayu) and White people surround the relative sanctuary of the Xingu territory.

The boundaries of circles within circles occurs over and over again in the Mehinaku experience of landscape. I was told that before contact with White people and the illnesses that ensued, the members of the Xinguano communities were far more numerous, and that the greater populations of each were housed just as they are at present with the House of Flutes at the

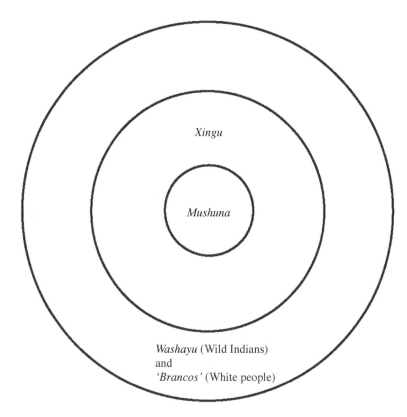

Figure 3. Concentrically circular spatial zones at the macro-level.

centre but surrounded with not just one circle but many concentric circles of houses. The movement of the stars which bring the change of seasons occur in a cycle that is also understood in the round, a kind of circular 'calendar' (one young man told me it was equivalent to the White man's *'calendario'*) which was drawn for me once with a stick on the dirt floor by the chief Marikawa, a circle with a number of points on the perimeter indicating certain stars that refer also to the season they herald.

The sense of circular boundaries is traced by various of the Mehinaku dances such as the aforementioned *Takwára* and another, the *Kapushai* (others include the *Kukuhë*, the *Eweshë* and *the Watana*). Both circle the village as the group of dancers move to dance inside each house of the village-round in turn, the *Takwára* also circling inside each of the houses entered. The *Kapushai* involves two male singers improvising words to a certain melody that is supposed to evoke (and make fun of) how news *circulates* between houses of the village, and villages of the Xingu, particularly via gossiping women.

Each of the different ringed zones is experienced with the sense of being in a circular 'whole'. The suffix *'naku'* denotes one's being present within a certain round, with the specific whole that it is, indicated by the relevant prefix, for example *pai-naku* means 'within the whole of the house'. Experientially being within a certain *'-naku'* puts ego in a certain relation to the spheres outside it. This relation is of 'inside to outside' and this 'outside' is referred to by the suffix *'taku'*; therefore when one talks of the forest while within the house, the forest is referred to as *ata-taku,* whereas when one is within the realm of the forest, this experience is referred to as *ata-naku.* The particular nature of this experiential relation of inside to outside is one of opposition, so that from within the house, the other houses are potentially hostile but the experience of being in the village as a whole in relation to the other villages in the Xingu is again one of safety versus potential danger. Therefore the experience of boundaried landscape depends on one's perspectival position at a given moment, which sphere or *naku* one feels oneself to be within, automatically implying an opposing relation of inside to outside.[34]

These oppositional areas radiate concentrically, 'onion-like', with each consecutive ringed zone more dangerous than the one before (going outward), the house more dangerous than the hearth, the village more so than the house, the orchards more than the village and the forest more perilous than the orchards. The very centre however, as mentioned earlier is as wild and hazardous as the periphery and the dangers of these two zones, it should be noted, are not fixed. At different times the peril of each encroaches outwards or inwards as the case may be, into the circular bordered regions between. This occurs every day with the shifting movement of the sun, or rather the lack of it. For darkness harbours the *apapanye,* so as it begins to fall, the *apapanye* are understood to first enter the orchards, then the centre space of the village, then the inside of the houses. People move as each domain of relative security dissolves into the dark danger of the periphery. First, the women – who in the late afternoon usually relax at the back of the houses attending to the making of the sweet evening-drink of *nukaya,* twirling cotton and painting, plucking and denitting each other's heads – move inside hurriedly as the sun drops below a certain point. Some move to sit at the front of the house (others may stay inside if they wish) where they continue their gossip by the front door, facing into the village circle. Just before the sun drops below the horizon, the women quickly move inside where people may visit each others' hammocks but as the night deepens all move to their hammocks by their nuclear hearths. Although they heed the shift of the nature of domains, men, less threatened by the *apapanye* (having a different relationship with them),[35] have more freedom in their movement with the darkening of the day.

At certain times the danger of the centre also radiates outward into the domains that surround it. This occurs when the *Kawëka* flutes or other cloaks of the *Apapanye* (costumes made from the *shepeku* palm) are brought by the men out of the House of the Flutes, into the village circle and sometimes into the orchards and forest. The *apapanye* are then understood to be dangerously present in the village circle and beyond and again the women, who are more endangered by them, move into the safety of the interior of the houses. Particularly, when the men are returning with the *Kawëka* from a trip to the forest there is the danger[36] of the women being caught out of the houses returning from bathing and fetching water and other such activities, though there is usually due warning of when this return will be happening. And in general, although the nature of domains changes through the day and with particular events, they do so with predictable rhythms and limits that the Mehinaku anticipate, thus keeping within safe borders.

Another way that the flows of desire within landscape are defined by boundaries is with various kinds of paths both within and between the circular domains. There are certain paths that are known by all to mark the border of the territories of orchards owned by particular people, the produce of these orchards being only for the disposal of those people. In this way peoples' desire for produce from the different orchards is given particular limits, although much theft of fruit and manioc and gossip about it goes on. The other labyrinthine paths, the *apui,* crisscross the orchards and continue more sparsely into the forest, humanising the landscape where they pass, forming a type of boundaried conduit of safety for people walking or bicycling[37] through the spaces. This is especially important in the forest where to be without a human-made path is to be at the mercy of the *apapanye.* For this reason all females and young boys who are more threatened by the *apapanye* do not stray beyond paths in the forest, while men are able to pass though very carefully (breaking twigs and otherwise marking trees). The *apapanye* themselves have their own paths normally not observable to human beings but which become visible as one enters their reality.[38] Rivers are also understood as a kind of path; as we have seen[39] it is by following a river-path that one can traverse the outermost boundary, that between the heaven and the earth, as one flows in death from the river below up the sky-river *Irapuéné,* the Milky Way.

V. The Ever Present Threat of the Collapse of Form:
Dangerous Desire Let Loose

In the last section it was described how for the Mehinaku desires flow within certain borders and shapes of the worlds. These first came to exist when the original human beings were created, the forms of the *yeya* and their copies, the stars, the arc of the sun and the rainbow. These exist within further limits of concentric circular bordered zones of different orders of desire, from the calm of the hearth to the wilds of the outermost round of forest. These shifting and relatively opposed circular regions are interlaced with various kinds of paths, forming yet finer boundaries for the motions of the worlds' yearnings. The existence of all these boundaries, however, is under constant threat. The excessive passions that move beings to encroach *across* the borders into other worlds (as described in the third section) – of *apapanye* in their love for human beings, of sorcerers to harm others, of humans in love with the dead – compromise the margins as they push though them. These intrusions threaten the integrity of the borders and may eventuate in utter dissolution of these boundaries of the worlds, and the letting loose of wanton powers.[40]

The notion of desire becoming utterly unbounded is commonly given form by the Mehinaku in the image of the serpent. It has been discussed how normally the passions are restrained within limits, and in terms of the notion of the 'serpent of desire', this is portrayed in stories where the snake is brought under control by humans who cut it up into many pieces. In one long tale, a great miyoka snake, *Kapëshalapikyuma,* came to the village of the *Perkaintyé,* humans of extraordinary powers and beauty. The serpent demanded that the *Perkaintyé* people give him one of their young men to eat. Nothing worked against the snake, not even their very powerful arrows so the chief had no choice but to choose and sacrifice one man to the beast. This happened day after day until only the most beautiful of the young men were left[41] and the chief decided the community must leave their village to escape from the insatiable snake. An arrow was shot up into the sky, its arc forming a ladder that all but the sister of the young *Perkaintyé* men ascended. Her name was Ayaweru and she waited there at the base of the ladder, guarding it, waiting for the snake to come. The creature arrived and seeing only the ladder, started to climb it, his enormous body going up and up. Then just as his tail began to rise up too, Ayaweru took up a knife and sliced it off and the body descended that length. She hacked again, and it descended further. The serpent screamed at the unknown source of its pain, and Ayaweru struck and struck until she reached the head that she cut off too. Thus is the serpent, the embodiment of voracious, limitless appetites, finally given limit, cut down at the boundary of earth and sky, another boundary it would disregard in its desire for human flesh. A similar myth is that told of the creation of the *yanakwimpi*[42] beads, the white shell segments which the Mehinaku use to make men's belts. The rounded segments are understood to originate from the dismembered pieces of the Rainbow, the snake *Anapi,* who descended from the sky and caused havoc on earth until it too was hacked apart.

When desire is not kept within limits it is understood to flow out of control, become 'wild', *shapushapai,* threatening to collapse the further boundaries it encounters. This is the image of the serpent on the loose and on a rampage of destruction. As mentioned earlier, in sexual relationships it is often said that if a man or woman desires another, a *sucuri* snake will come to that person in the shape of the desired one. When the person has sexual intercourse with the impersonator of his or her loved one, the act destroys the boundary between the worlds of the *apapanye* and human beings, and will usually cause the victim's human body to die as the soul is subsumed into another world. Similarly the Mehinaku tell the story of a dead daughter's soul appearing in the orchards as a snake who kills her living mother so that she will join her daughter in the village of the dead in the sky. Once again, exceeding a normal amount of love/need, in this case familial love, appears in the form of a murderous snake who distorts the usual limits of things, flouting the border that exists between the living and the dead.

Excessive desire as wild, destructive serpent also occurs in the context of adultery. In one tale the overstepping of the social boundary of marriage leads to the cuckolded husband transforming his wife's lover, the over-desirous usurper, into a snake. He achieves this by slyly inserting *sucuri* snake eggs in the fish he gives to his wife, and which he knows she will share with her lover at their rendezvous. Upon eating the eggs that are hidden in the fish, the lover does indeed turn into a *sucuri* snake.

The ultimate dissolution of social boundaries, the commission of incest, is again portrayed in terms of a dangerous serpent unleashed on the community. It is the evocative story of the young unmarried chief *Arakuni.* One afternoon Arakuni calls the men of the village to paint their bodies with genipap dye to be ready to dance in the night. That night, after they are decorated, he decides they will dance the next morning instead, and while the paint on his body is still wet, he passes his beautiful sister Ukumalu and desiring her joins her in her hammock where they have sexual intercourse. The genipap pattern on *Arakuni's* skin imprints itself on Ukumalu's body while they lie together and she discovers these the next morning when she goes to bathe. Neither brother nor sister has realised this transference has occurred until this point, as the juice of the unripe genipap is initially colourless, only gradually turning to black. Ukumalu tries to scrub the patterns away but she knows it is in vain, that the genipap will be indelible for many days.

As soon as their mother sees the marks on Ukumalu's body she knows exactly what has occurred, as the designs on her daughter's skin are those worn only by the chief and thus must have come from her son. Seeing *Arakuni* confirms this and their mother becomes enraged. *Arakuni* goes out into the forest with his brother to cut firewood and when he returns his mother has burnt his belts and other personal belongings and gossip has spread about what happened. *Arakuni* is sad and ashamed and the next day he goes to work where the small bamboo named *wikyatë* grows, and is gone from early in the morning till late in the afternoon, and goes again the next day and for many days after. His friend begins to wonder what *Arakuni* is doing every day in the forest and asks him about it over and over but *Arakuni* does not tell him. One day though *Arakuni* gives in and agrees to take his friend to show him what he has been busy doing. He warns his friend not to be afraid when he sees the thing he has been constructing but his friend is very frightened when he sees the great hollow snake-beast made of *wikyatë*. 'I am making this because I am ashamed of what I have done, I am going to put this cape on and live as an *apapanye* in the water' (Plate 12).

Arakuni's friend begs him not to do this but nothing can dissuade him and the next day he goes out into the forest and puts on the snake-shell, descending to the ground from a very high tree with a loud crash. All the village inhabitants hear the noise and when they discover what has occurred they are terrified of the dangerous beast that has been brought into being. They complain to *Arakuni's* mother of her harshness towards her son and two men go out to meet him at the river, bringing him food, asking him to return but he ignores them and continues down the river singing a sad, melodic song.

The consequence of the breaking of the social boundary precluding incest is, like the other similar breaches that have been described, the creation of a serpent that threatens the safety of the community. Voracious *apapanye,* the pining dead, adulterous and incestuous lovers, the surfeit of desire beyond ideal bounds renders all of these beings terrible serpents. In the same vein, the Mehinaku will explain how wild their non-Xinguano Indian neighbours are by exclaiming with (often delighted) horror that the *Washayu* eat snakes. As explained in the last chapter, the qualities of what one eats are understood to imbue the consumer and this is how the eating of snakes is given as a reason for the aggression of tribes such as the Suyá and Kayapo, who the Mehinaku say came in the past on violent raids into their own and other Xinguano villages.[43]

Other perilous snakes of capricious passions already exist as cosmological phenomena that may simply descend at any time for no reason but their own sudden wanton volition, such as the Rainbow snake *Anapi* previously mentioned. The rainbow that suddenly appears in the sky is not a delight to the Mehinaku but a threatening menace. I realised this on a walk with Mahí, when I excitedly pointed out a bright curve arching between clouds in the distance. '*Muito perigroso* Carla!' she exclaimed, 'very dangerous', and she continued explaining a little of the hazardous nature of the rainbow. The rainbow, she told me, is in fact a snake that is harmless as long as it remains in the sky but is a creature that is terribly destructive when it descends.

All *apapanye* are understood to be intrinsically *shapushapai,* or wild, and capable of destroying boundaries in their desire. However, the particular ferociousness of *Ateshua,* the fierce chief of the *apapanye,* and *Enutsikya,* the brutal *apapanye* of lightning, is emphasized by their association with images of the serpent. *Ateshua,* who brings chaos to the earth when he descends as a great-disc, is known to have two *miyoka* snakes draped from each of his shoulders as depicted in the palm effigies the Mehinaku make of him. The slash of white violence from *Enutsikya* is also sometimes likened to a snake, with its destructive power to break up and violate bounded forms of Mehinaku life, tearing apart orchards and houses, and causing people to hide.

Although I have discussed how the dissolution of borders and the eruption of forces of desire are commonly understood in the form of savage serpents unleashed, this is not to say that there are not other notions concerning the precariousness of boundaries. Blood and darkness are also associated with the dissolution of the borders of things and the release of tumultuous passion. Very literally, for the Mehinaku, to bleed is to break open the boundary of the body formed by the skin, releasing blood that in itself is understood to be intrinsically '*brabo*' or 'wild', and which can attract the wildness of the *apapanye.* The regular scraping of the skin with the thorned instruments called *imya,* is therefore a dangerous time of vulnerability to surrounding wild forces, and in the same 'vein', I found to my surprise (considering the uncomplaining toughness of the Mehinaku in other matters), that even a small scratch on the skin is examined with great interest and worried about. The belief in the intrinsic *shapushapai*-wildness of blood is the reason why the aggressions (the violent transgression of social boundaries) of the *Washayu,* are not only attributed to their eating of snakes but also their consuming of blood *(ëshai)* or 'animals with blood'[44]. As previously mentioned in chapter 2, at the time of creation the demarcation between the *Washayu* and the Alto-Xinguano peoples was established when the former accepted the bowl of blood *Kwamutë* offered to them, while the latter refused.

Blood, with its dangerous intimations of dangerous desires unleashed with the destruction of the skins of things, informs attitudes towards the cosmological phenomenon of the solar eclipse. An eclipse is understood to be the event of the sun *Kamë* literally menstruating (it is the term actually used for it: 'the sun menstruates' – *'kamë yumekepei'*). The darkness of the eclipse is associated with blood that falls invisibly making black marks on all it touches. Leaves of certain trees were picked to show me their spots derived from *Kamë's* menstrual blood and the beauty spots on my own back I was told were because at some time I must have exposed that skin to the rays of an eclipsed sun. The release of blood/darkness is part of the terror of the eclipse as the ultimate dissolution of all the borders between the worlds and those that are within them. *Apapanye,* darkness, blood and the forest are understood to take over, this return to darkness a return to the primordial state of chaos before *Kamë* made sunshine and in its light created the boundaries of all things. The dissolution of the differentiation made at that time of creation means that even the shapes of animals are unstable in the event of an eclipse, the Mehinaku claiming sightings of animals caught between transformations, especially from land animals into fish.

The forms that constitute the worlds for the Mehinaku, that contain the flows of yearning, are then themselves always at risk from these yearnings. The most extreme such collapse of boundaries occurs during a solar eclipse. Other events are caused by releasing the destructive serpents of desire which can mean at its most drastic, the closing of the circle of the world of earth and sky, as the rainbow *Anapi* descends on the community. Yet even on the individual level, the release of the hungering snake, the seductive *sucuri* masquerading as a lover in the orchard, is a menace threatening to destroy human life.

VI. Holding up the Form of the Worlds:
Maintaining Good Relationships (the '*Uwekehë* Complex')
and Integrity of Person (the Issue of *Yerekyuki*)

So far in our exploration of the Mehinaku lived world, it has been described how human consciousness makes manifest the human world, and
apapanye consciousness the world of the *apapanye* (fifth section, chapter 2), as well as how desires ideally flow within the boundaries of these
worlds (fourth section, chapter 3). We have seen also, however, how excess
desires may destroy these borders, or in other words, in the abstract terms
above, if consciousness manifests form, a change in quality of consciousness (i.e. an increase in the amount of desire) manifests different, flawed
form or destroys form altogether. To maintain the structures of life therefore, against the inevitable onslaught of immoderate hungers entails an
effort to assuage these yearnings to less destructive levels, bringing them
within normal bounds, as well as positively asserting these bounds defen-
sively. Since the harmful surfeits of desire may arise in both *apapanye* and
humans, the Mehinaku must both pacify excesses and promote right-con-
sciousness-form in both cases: in their relationship with the *apapanye* and
in themselves.[45]

One way then that the Mehinaku uphold the boundaries of the flow of
desire is in their associations with the *apapanye*. As has been discussed at
length, the tempestuous *apapanye* have a propensity for breaking through
into the world of humans and reeking destruction. No matter what incites
the passions and consequent trespasses of the *apapanye,* the Mehinaku
deal with the predicament in the same way, by calming and feeding the
apapanye and accomplishing this within a specific kind of structural relationship. Whether it be desire for an individual human, an eclipse, or
that they are drawn purposefully near by a human being, the Mehinaku
placate the *apapanye,* bringing them within safe bounds in different per-
mutations of an approach I will call the *uwekehë* complex.

The nature of the *uwekehë* complex is best understood in the way that
it works in the treatment of human illness caused by the desire of *apapanye*. It has previously been described how the *apapanye* in their love for a
human being may take a person's soul back to live with them in their own
world and in so doing cause the flesh-body left behind to ail and eventually die. Also, I have written that the *apapanye* will take a human soul for
killing too many of its animals and plants. All illnesses are understood to
occur in these ways[46] or at the hand of the sorcerers *(ipyamawékéhë)*. If

the shaman *(yatama)* diagnoses[47] the cause of illness as soul-theft by an *apapanye* and succeeds in bringing back the person's soul from the world of the *apapanye,* it then falls to the patient (with the help of her or his family) to curb the out-of-control passions of the *apapanye,* and keep the creature from doing it again to themselves or someone else. The way the patient does this is by becoming the *uwekehë,* or in Portuguese the '*dono*' of the *apapanye* concerned.

The word '*dono*' translated from the Portuguese means 'owner' but when asked to explain further the Mehinaku describe the relationship between the human *uwekehë* and the *apapanye* as being like that between parent and child, whereby the *uwekehë* '*cria*', 'brings up and cares for' the *apapanye.* This caring for the *apapanye* by the *uwekehë* is entailed by a very particular kind of relationship including an intricate variety of practices and this is what I have called the *uwekehë* complex. The relationship involves the calming of the *apapanye* by feeding and housing it, and the protection given in turn by the *apapanye* to its human *uwekehë* in gratitude. To feed the *apapanye,* the *uwekehë* must first bring the *apapanye* near and she or he does this by making the music (with the help of other villagers) of the *apapanye* concerned, which is understood to lure the *apapanye* invisibly into the presence of the music-makers/dancers. It is for this reason that the *uwekehë* is explained to be the 'owner of the music' ('*o dono da musica*'), as well as the 'owner of the *apapanye*'. The *apapanye* is believed to be 'housed' when the Mehinaku dancers dress as the *apapanye* and it is especially by the wearing of the *apapanye*'s mask that the numinous entity is said to be given '*uma casa*' ('a house'). This notion is evident in an explanation given by a young man Makau-Laka that summarises the nature of the *uwekehë* complex: 'If an *apapanye* likes you, he will give you his mask and then he will make you sick and you will have to look after him'. In this statement is evident the desire of the *apapanye* that causes the illness and also the duty of its human victim to bring the *apapanye* into the human world (with the mask) and care for it thus becoming its owner. In return, the *apapanye* will give their protection to their *uwekehë,* and again this is understood to be a reciprocally familial (child-parent) kind of caring. The protection afforded is mostly against other *apapanye,* especially in their own domain of the forest. For example, I was told by her son that my foster-mother Takulalu, as *uwekehë* of the *apapanye* Shapacuyawa, would be accompanied by that *apapanye* when she was out in the orchards and most importantly when on far away trips extracting salt. The *apapanye* would watch over her and '*não deixa eles*' 'not let them', that is other *apapanye* such as snakes, bite or harm her in any way.

For the *apapanye* then their relationship with the human being concerned is emotional in nature – first desiring then protective. However, for the Mehinaku person, becoming an *uwekehë* is usually a more calculated act,[48] a deliberate attempt to placate the destructive passions of the spirit-admirer, by the absorbing of the wild *apapanye* into the bounds of a relationship of care which is mutually beneficial. And this relationship is not only favourable and advantageous to the *apapanye* and its human owner. The *uwekehë-apapanye* relationship helps to maintain the forms of the worlds in general, so that the efforts of the *uwekehë* are in fact on behalf of the well-being of the entire Mehinaku community. This is because, the *apapanye*, once incited, is prone to attack other people and as the victim's illness forms a breach in the community's consensus reality,[49] other people are more vulnerable to such an assault and so the human world in general must be protected. The sense of the vulnerability of the group as a whole to the upset caused by a single *apapanye* is well portrayed by the aforementioned myth of *Arakuni*. Transformed into a huge snake as a consequence of his commission of incest, his anger towards his mother who rejected him because of his deed is not only seen as perilous to her but as endangering everyone. All members of the community set out then to appease *Arakuni* by making him food and following him to offer it, these actions depicting the beginnings of the practices of the *uwekehë* complex.

Therefore the work of the *uwekehë* also concerns all other members of the group and so when music and food is made for an *apapanye*, others apart from the *uwekehë*,[50] and sometimes the entire society participates, getting painted, dancing/music-making and fishing for the feasting afterward.[51] The cooperation of the group in the *uwekehë* complex is evident in singular events of the appeasement of a specific *apapanye* but sometimes, if many people are getting sick at the same time, a 'mass event' is held where all of the *apapanye* are danced for and fed (Plates 13, 14, 15).

These events are rare (only one occurred during my time with the Mehinaku) and do not have a particular name, rather it is simply said that the *apapanye* will appear *(puhukéhéné)*. The preparation for such a happening is long and elaborate, six weeks for the one I witnessed in July of 2001. Below, I will write of what happened in those weeks in some detail because I think that, in the spectacle of the communal event, the way the *uwekehë* complex works becomes particularly obvious.

To start with, the men went out to the distant places where they know the best buriti palm is to be found and these they brought back and gave to the women. The women carefully tore apart the palm fronds that were then dried and hence made ready for their weaving by the men into the

Plate 13. The music and dancing of the *apapanye.*

Plate 14. The *apapanye* receive their food.

Plate 15. Distribution of food to the community.

masks of the *apapanye* in the men's house. Various musics of different *apapanye* began to be played and food offered in small preliminary events for the *apapanye;* most noticeably the *kawëka* flutes were played every single night during that time.

Four days before it began, the able men of the village left for a trip that lasted three days during which all the fish for the event were caught. The last day before the event the women were not able to leave the house except to bathe and bring water, once just before dawn and then in the late morning. This is because they are prohibited to watch[52] the activities of the men and the *apapanye* that were to take place out in the open in the village centre later in the day, first the painting of the *apapanye*-effigies and then *kapushai* music/dance,[53] followed by the *kawëka* which would be played from the early evening till the early hours of the morning. Then at just one or two in the morning each household was woken by singers who entered after banging on the closed doors, singing complaints that the inhabitants should already be awake, followed by more very loud *kapushai* singing. By this time everyone had fully gotten up and out of their hammocks, with all the women of my house gathering in the cooking hut to help prepare the food for the *apapanye-Shapakuyawa,* on behalf of Takulalu as the *uwekehë*. This was supervised by Marikawa, who as Takulalu's husband is automatically also the *uwekehë* of the *apapanye*.[54] Six rounds of *ulépé* bread (slightly different to the everyday version) were made and on each was placed a large smoked fish into which liberal amounts of a salt-chili mixture (which the *apapanye* adore) were rubbed. When we were finished, a little before dawn, we women went off to bathe while it was still dark in order to return before the appearance of the *apapanye*.

When we arrived back at dawn the event was about to begin and ten year-old Kohôlupe and eighteen year-old Kwakani were already painted and *'enfeitado'* ('done up') as the epitomes of female beauty, ready to take the food offerings to the *apapanye*. The women of each house gathered by their front doors facing the men's house at the centre. From inside of it there could already be heard a great racket, in which could be made out the sounds of the individual *apapanye*, such as the hooting of the *Pahër* (Howler Monkey), the laughing, crazy babble of *Shapakuyawa*, the nasal-wailing of the *Uwéshë* (Giant Otter) and the high-pitched whistle of their chief *Ateshua* and all of it overlaid by the whooping calls of the men around them and some *Kawëka* fluting. Then the dancers in their spectacular *apapanye* masks filed out of the entrance one behind the other, with the rocking, marching motion typical of all the men's dances, each continuing to make its own particular call. They continued to dance like this in front of the men's house then formed a small arc and separated (*Ateshua* as their chief going first) to each dance over to the door of their own *uwekehë*-'owner', where specially-prepared food was presented by young decorated women of that household. Each brought this food back to the centre, until many vessels were collected before the men's house. All the men, also painted and ornamented for the occasion, also gathered there and gifts were brought for the various *uwekehë*, mostly bundles of the very long hardwood arrows the Mehinaku use. And then the event was simply over: after only about fifteen minutes, six weeks of build-up was abruptly culminated. The women retired inside, their men brought back food from the centre and then everyone sat, ate and gossiped much as usual.

In the event of the celebration of many *apapanye* together, it becomes especially evident the way the Mehinaku relate to the potentially ruinous forces of their environment as personified by the *apapanye*, as they bring them close and seek to make them happy within the safe confines of the *uwekehë-apapanye* relationship. The structures of life are defended in the same way in the event of an eclipse, the occurrence of which is the ultimate threat to these structures (as was discussed in the last section). As boundaries dissolve, all the *apapanye* are understood to be released into the midst of the village, and music/dancing of the *apapanye* is made as in the healing events described above.

As well as doing this however, a number of different practices are also performed during an eclipse in which we see the other main way the Mehinaku manage the desires destructive to the forms of their world. That is, apart from the appeasement and containment of annihilative forces, there is also the building up and assertion of boundaries in spite of these forces. So how does this occur? To defend themselves against the *apapanye* understood to be traversing all usual confines and roiling invisibly with even more wild desire than usual, the Mehinaku attempt to minimise exposure to these forces. The borders of the human world are guarded, the two small doors of the house – at the front and at the back – are shut. People avoid venturing out of the man-made world: no one bathes, men do not go fishing or hunting,[55] nor women to the manioc orchards. When night falls, which is the most dangerous time, the back of the house is protected by one of the stronger men who sits by a fire outside there from dusk into the hours of darkness, acting as a kind of sentinel against the *apapanye* and the *ipyamawékéhë* (sorcerers).

For the most part, however, during the eclipse attention is given to caring for the self, the preservation and defence of its boundaries. All members of the community are meant to scrape their skin with the *imya* so as to let the old blood pass out, now perhaps 'contaminated' by the *apapanye* writhing invisibly all around. Substances are also rubbed onto the skin to protect it, such as the red *yuku*, shielding the body from the invisible substance of the sun's menstruation. The day after the eclipse the *yatama*-shamans gather in a group and move from house to house working, on whoever wishes it, to remove whatever dangerous residues might exist in the body from the day before. Many *yatama* work together on an individual, either consecutively or at once. The cleansing of each member of each household is particular to the event of the eclipse when all members of the community are threatened at once.

As discussed earlier, the senses of body, soul and mind are not separated for the Mehinaku. The *yakulai* soul-body inhabits the *umënupiri* flesh-body, both of these being kinds of substantial consciousness and with the former having a more determinative effect on the state of the latter.[56] Another way then the Mehinaku bolster themselves from the perils of the eclipse is by a kind of deliberate fortification of self by asserting right *yaku-lai*-consciousness that promotes strong *umënupiri*-body. This is achieved in a number of ways but most generally by the deliberate cultivation of a joyous outlook *(ketepemunaki)*, held in spite of the invisible maelstrom of dangers. This intentional keeping of a cheerful attitude in spite of and even as an antidote to danger, was summed up by the following comment to me by the chief Marikawa: 'Everyone, all the villages are very sad because of the sun. For this, we stay really happy.' During this time people joke around and laugh about fearful statements made by themselves or others, so for example Marikawa's son, Maiawai laughed after telling me about the spine thin legs of the *apapanye Yewekwikyuma* which can stab a person like arrows. I laughed and then I realised we laughed together but for different reasons: I with the thrill as for a childish horror story but he because he believed and laughed to ward off its danger.

Apart from this general keeping up of a mood, during an eclipse certain bodily activities are understood to bolster this willfully positive form-consciousness such as the aforesaid scraping of the skin with the *imya* which is understood not only to cleanse the blood but also to bring strength and courage, as the heart is felt to begin beating powerfully during and after such treatment. Similarly, the whipping of thighs, buttocks and lower back with straps is meant to *'da força'*, give power or force to the person. This beating is only administered to young men, in the morning of the eclipse in the centre of the village, and the day I was there was carried out by the chief Marikawa. Likewise, it is only the young men who are sent out alone into the forest, which is terrifying during the eclipse, for the purpose of gaining *'força'*, 'getting up courage'.

The act of music-making/dancing not only contains the *apapanye* in a certain kind of relationship during the event of an eclipse, it is also understood to give *ketepemunaki,* joy. This sense of music/dance points to the aforementioned general corrective the Mehinaku see for threats to the integrity of the boundaries of things, that is, a joyful affirmation of these boundaries, not only in themselves but also of the *apapanye* as the forces of the worlds. During an eclipse, the *apapanye,* just like human beings are understood to be 'sad' and 'weak'. In the event of an eclipse, the tempestuous Sun's (*Kamë's*)[57] menstruating that dissolves the borders, puts everyone, *apapanye* as well as people, in a state of anxious insecurity that must be dealt with.

During the extreme conditions of the eclipse, the self and world preservation strategies of the Mehinaku are particularly evident. However, as we saw in the previous section, although not as great as with an eclipse, the same threats to the structures of life are ever-present in daily life and the approach to dealing with these is more or less the same although in a milder and ad hoc way. Thus in day to day life, the Mehinaku also perform such practices as the cleansing of the blood and strengthening of courage by skin-scraping, going out into the forest alone in spite of one's fears, music and dancing, and the general keeping up of a mood of joyful strength.

The upholding of both the boundaries of the self and the relationships with the *apapanye,* are performed mostly in view of the threats of the *apapanye* outside the person, who without barriers against them, may take the person's soul with them to their world where the victim's soul will become an *apapanye* too. However, the danger of *apapanye* 'wildness' does not always come from outside, it can also come from inside people themselves. In stories that have been mentioned earlier, human beings become *apapanye*-beings from an allowing of an expansion of their own wildness. This is what occurs in the tale of *Yamurikuma* when the men while camping out fishing, decide not to return to the women of the village but to keep all the fish for themselves and so begin to grow fur and sharp teeth as beasts in the forest. Likewise, *Arakuni* flees his village down the river transformed into a huge snake by the unleashing of his incestuous desire for his sister. Neither will the Waurá women who chose to become jaguars ever return to a human community. Therefore the keeping up of boundaries is not only a defensive action against exterior destructive forces but also an interior action of the checking of one's own destructive forces that are capable of irrevocably expanding out of control by their own impetus.

There is one more self-care practice to do with an important Mehinaku notion not yet discussed. I think that it is in this concept that one most clearly sees the way in which desire and its control are central to the Mehinaku understanding of the world, and I am surprised not to have found mention of something like it in the literature, considering how often it is used to explain all manner of things. It works with what causes the destructive rush, the inflammation of the desire in the first place. This is the lack, the hunger that is not satisfied and *therefore* becomes that desire we have been discussing which is excessive and dangerous. The Mehinaku call this notion by the word *yerekyuki,* which refers to the 'bad' *('mal')* that will happen to you in the case of a craving not being gratified. If an excess of desire within can either expand to transform the person into an *apapanye* or can attract *apapanye* to you, who then kidnap you and so transform you from without, it is the latter of these possibilities to which *yerekyuki* mostly pertains. The way Cuelho, the chief Marikawa's son, explained it to me is as follows: 'If early in the morning, there is no *uwitzikyuwi* (maniocwater) prepared and you go out hungry hunting or fishing, a snake will bite you, some *apapanye* will take your soul, so before we go out walking we people like to eat manioc bread, fish, salt and chili, *uwitzikyuwi.'* So it is the hunger for food then which is the cause of *yerekyuki* and interestingly, according to Cuelho, the hunger is understood to be that of the soul which is wanting to eat and which therefore becomes vulnerable to attack. This occurs because, as I wrote earlier, a human's excess of desire moves her or him into the reality of the *apapanye,* the person suddenly becoming especially noticeable to the *apapanye* who are attracted to the extreme need, as like to like. This can occur to anyone, not only working men but even to a baby crying for candy. Cuelho's niece, a baby girl called Nana was diagnosed with *yerekyuki* which apparently occurred when she was frustrated sucking on a sweet (brought from a town) still in its wrapper while she watched another child enjoying her unwrapped sweet. Afterwards, she became pained in her mouth and could not suckle. Not only illness but accidents are also attributed to *yerekuki* which are just another way the *apapanye* seek to bring the human back to their world (by destroying the human body in its world). Thus Marikawa describes how he lost the sight of his right eye by saying that the tree branch fell and gashed his brow because, 'I had the wish to eat but I forgot. It is for this that I got hurt, *niwyerikyuwiku* (*yerekyuki* happened to me).'

The destruction of boundaries that occurs in *yerekyuki* can be prevented then only by filling the 'lack' which is its cause, this lack being a hunger for food. Thus for the Mehinaku, the act of eating/feeding is not simply to sustain the body and for enjoyment, it is a practice of bodily defence against the unwelcome attentions of the *apapanye* spirits. This means that every effort is made to eat when one is hungry, and if there is no food, one does not do anything risky while one waits for some. It is for this reason that family living in different houses will bring fish to other houses, especially when none in the latter house has made a good catch. If one is watching another person eating and envies them the food, because of *yerekyuki* they must ask the person for some immediately and likewise a child who complains of hunger, or points to another's food is always given some straightaway. If one is hungrily waiting for something being cooked to be ready and then is called away, one cannot leave until after one has eaten (whoever is waiting will understand the reason for the tardiness). Once while I was sitting with members of my household in the cooking hut waiting for fish to cook, I was called away to do an interview. A few minutes into the interview a girl from my house appeared beside me, calling me back to eat and simply but gently not taking no for an answer. I could not understand the urgency of her request, as I was not yet familiar with the concept of *yerekyuki*. She had been sent by her mother and my foster-mother Takulalu to bring me back to eat the fish that was now cooked. One cares only for the *yerekyuki* of oneself and one's closest kin, those within the nuclear family. When I understood that she had been taking care of my *yerekyuki* I was moved beyond any other gesture made to me during my time with the Mehinaku.

VII. The Dynamic of Daring: to Create, Maintain and Improve Form, One Must Risk Form

In this chapter, that is part of our general survey of Mehinaku experience, we have seen how Mehinaku life in many different dynamic aspects is experienced as a continuous flow and that the nature of these streams of life is desire. These move within the structures of the worlds, but in excess this flux can overcome the boundaries that contain them and so the Mehinaku are always working to uphold the forms that define life for them. However the paradox is that in order to maintain and elaborate form against the forces of desire (the *apapanye* without and the wildness within), one must risk it to those very forces. To even simply preserve a closed form at all, the form must be periodically opened up, and further, to improve form requires risking even more opening to the powers that be. This is because the flows of desire are not, as we saw earlier, only destructive but constitute all the dynamism of life, including all the reservoirs of its possibilities. Therefore both to simply be part of life and also to go further and make the most of it, requires an opening to draw from life's flow, followed by closure in order to contain it with integrity.[58] This is what I will call the 'dynamic of daring',[59] the 'risky opening' that works as the other completely opposite dynamic of Mehinaku life to what has been discussed thus far. While we have looked at the flowing along of life and also the Mehinaku conservatism about setting and keeping boundaries for this flow, in daring there is the utterly contrary action of violating boundaries, even if it is for the sake of ultimately strengthening them. An important part of this principle is that the opening is a very quick punctuation to the ongoing continuity of life, where the danger of opening occurs quickly in order to expand and create and then closes again into safe, closed integrity.

Simply to maintain the substantial body, the integrity of the body must be opened and jeopardised in order to be worked on further and built up. As we saw in chapter 2, the human body (the flesh-body *umënupiri*) is not assumed to grow of its own accord; growth must be made to happen by human effort. Nor is the body assumed simply to continue to exist once fully grown. The existence of the body is understood to be ongoing only by dint of the work that continues to be done to it and this work involves an exposure to the motions of life. This is because, as we saw at the start of this chapter, the Mehinaku believe that all things, including humans, must flow along with the continuous movements of the worlds that they are in fact inextricable from. Therefore, to even continue to exist, one must stay part of this flow or simply wither into nothingness. The moving forces of life are actively sustaining, so in exposing oneself to them, force can infuse the body and thus transformed, the body can close over again. Even the basic act of eating involves this sense of dangerous but necessary opening, absorbing of the outside and then containing it within the self. Things that are eaten are foreign objects that may have been bewitched by sorcerers. Even if they haven't been tampered with, the consumption of manioc and fish, involves the taking in of these *apapanye*-copies that carry some of the *apapanyes'* perilous potencies. The consumption of food, though very enjoyable, is thus an anxious affair with eating being a quick and private[60] act, as bodily form is risked for a short time to connect with and absorb from the flow of life all around, before being sealed back into wholeness.[61]

This process of calculated risk for the sake of bodily form is most obvious in such practices as *imya* skin scraping, where the skin as the external covering of the body is opened all over in fine cuts. The flow of blood in the body is now perilously open to the flow of life all around. The root tinctures brewed are applied to those openings, drawing the *apapanye* related to that root into contact with the person so the powers of that being may be instilled in that person's body. As discussed in chapter 2, this procedure is undertaken by all members of the Mehinaku community in order to preserve bodily form. The root utilised for this kind of maintenance is that of a purple flowering shrub called *tërtu* that grows prolifically; however, as we shall see other rare substances are put to use in this practice for more dramatic results.

In techniques employed not simply to maintain the flesh-body but that seek to further improve it, the hazardous, quick opening of the daring principle is especially evident, as the peril braved is greater for the sake of a greater result. Such customs were discussed in chapter 2, in procedures submitted to mostly by young women and men in order to attain certain ideals of beauty and youthful powers. In skin scraping for example, the fat of the anaconda snake may be used in the potion applied to the cuts, and the Anaconda-*apapanye* thus brought near may grant the young man the ultimate strength for wrestling but is also so dangerous that the relationship with it can prove fatal. In the same way, the practice of imbibing huge amounts of root tinctures that are then vomited up, opens the body to a potentially dangerous flow of liquid; this liquid is related to a certain *apapanye* who may bestow its particular boons on the person but on the other hand can cause her or him illness.

The relationships between *apapanye* and humans that are produced by such practices are somewhat different to the *uwekehë* complex discussed in the previous section. The human who undertakes the procedure does not become the parent/owner of the *apapanye* but more the other way around so that the *apapanye* looks after the human, imbuing the person with particular qualities. The beneficial presence of the *apapanye* is understood to surround the person at all times in an aura-like invisible field, however this proximity becomes perilous if the human does anything that offends the *apapanye*. This is not a difficult thing to do as each *apapanye* has its own very idiosyncratic dislikes – some cannot abide salt and chili, others the smell of fresh fish and sex. To affront an *apapanye* who is living close in this way, can make you ill or even kill you.

The dynamic of daring therefore is at work in the relationships concerned with maintenance and improvement of the flesh-body. And yet this dynamic is not only about bodily care, it is an essential way that relationships in general function for the Mehinaku. Associations with the *apapanye* occur not only for the body but in all the different ways the Mehinaku relate to their environment, the *apapanye* being as they are the various forces of the landscape. Furthermore, this dynamic is crucial to different aspects of interpersonal relationships – such as in gender relations, as shall be seen in chapter 5 – and certain social dynamics where even simple interactions with other Mehinaku individuals are in fact anxious matters, far from what they usually seem to outsiders, concealed as they are by much laughter and banter. At the most abstract, the daring dynamic is a certain sense that the Mehinaku have about life, where although the gentle approach of flowing along with things is mostly the ideal, an occasional risky and courageous breaking through of the normal boundaries is also admired.

Before proceeding to an examination of the various ways this dynamic functions, I would like to explain the most basic sense of it. I first encountered it a few days after my arrival and never more succinctly. I was sitting with the chief Marikawa just within the doorway of his house, looking out from the shade at the spectacular sight of the *Kayapa* dance being performed in front of the men's house. A very intricate dance, with special costumes of leaves hanging from the arms, palm skirts and feather headdresses, Marikawa told me that this was the music/dance of a fish-

apapanye called *Kayapa.* He drew a figure slowly and very clearly on the soft dirt floor with a twig:

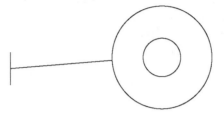

Figure 4. Marikawa's diagram depicting the 'dynamic of daring'.

He drew the diagram and explained that this was the way that humans first learned the music. The *apapanye* danced in the centre of a round lake (he pointed at the inner circle of the drawing) teeming with giant piranha and other dangerous creatures and at the edge of the lake men watched and listened hidden from view (the shorter line, the longer being their line of vision). In this way, another man called Yanapa told me, the men were able to 'rob' *('roubar')*, to 'catch' *('pegar')* the music from the *apapanye*, remembering it and then teaching it to the others in their village. And it is in this figure/story that one sees the dynamic of this 'catching' *('pegar')*-daring most clearly: the potency of the centre (in this case that of the *apapanye*) is surrounded by a field of danger (the lake filled with vicious beasts) and the humans risk coming into contact with this field (watching instead of running away, represented by the line touching the outer circle) in order to 'catch' or gain the knowledge of the centre; the humans then retreat to the safety (of the village) with the gains they have 'caught', *'pegou'.* This word, *'pegar',* is the same word as that used for 'catching' a fish and it is this sense of daring that the dynamic has in general: 'to get hold' of with all of the connotations 'catching a fish' has for the Mehinaku: that is willfulness, good memory, intelligence and quick, brave craftiness.

And it is through these qualities that the Mehinaku social order is understood to have come to exist, through the daring taking of the sacred flutes by the men from the women. The *kawëka,* the sacred flutes understood to be the *'amunão',* the 'chiefs' of all the *apapanye*, were once kept by the women. This state of affairs is described in the story of *Yakashukuma* and his human sister lovers. In the myth, which has been described previously, the women are in love with and having sexual intercourse with the *apapanye-Yakashukuma.* The women are thus joined with the *apapanye* in a kind of flow of unbounded passion. The case is similar when later in the story *Yakashukuma* is killed and the women eat the fruit of a tree that has grown up from his body, and play the *kawëka* flutes, thus bringing close to themselves the *kawëka-apapanye*. Both when the women make love to *Yakashukuma* and when they play the *kawëka,* they are engaged with the *apapanye* in a flux of forces from which the men are excluded, first the husband who hidden in bushes is forced to watch his wives having sex with the *apapanye* and later the men who are made to stay in the houses while the women dance. Again here the daring configuration is at work and according to the same basic principle as depicted above in the diagram of the *kayapa:* the desirous liaisons between women and *apapanye* form a field of dangerous potency at which the men look on hidden from view, and the men again daringly 'catch'/'rob' *('pegar')* the power from the centre and make it their own. In the myth, the men rush into the centre of the village whirling large bull-roarers *(matapu)* to frighten the women and succeed in taking possession of the flutes. Thus from what could be seen as a 'state of nature' of sorts, of a women ↔ *apapanye* continuum, the men through their action of daring created Mehinaku social structure as it is now known. Furthermore, as we shall see in chapter 5, the Mehinaku continue to live with this tension of daring, of something having been robbed and kept; for the true owners of the flutes are the women ('*a dona de verdade de* kawëka *é mulher*') and there is always the threat of them taking the flutes back.

In another version of the *Yakashukuma* story, it was *Kamë,* the Sun, who took the flutes from the women on the men's behalf while the men remained in the houses in fear of the women. And it is the Sun who for the Mehinaku is the supreme personification of the dynamic of daring. In various myths of creation it is the Sun's impetuous breaking of boundaries and 'grabbing' what is needed, which is the crucial part of the way he creates things. For example, it is owing to such an action that the waters of the landscape exist as they do today. Once all water in existence was owned by a small bird, *Yanakuma,* and his wife, held in ten huge pots in which lived many dangerous water creatures, great piranha, and snakes among others. One day the Sun and the Moon encountered on their path a tiny *bobinha* bird whimpering in thirst. The Sun assured the bird he would find water and taking a cigar, the Sun exhaled smoke which formed a straight line (like the line of the *kayapa* diagram) that they followed all the way to the house of the other bird, *Yanakuma,* the 'Owner of Water'. The *'Dona de Agua',* the 'Owner of Water' would give the Sun no more than a tiny ladle of the water so the Sun said to his brother the Moon, 'Let us go and rob the water from *Yanakuma;*' and so the two of them went with arrows and clubs, feathers and masks to the bird's house. With his arrows the Sun broke one after the other of the clay pots, releasing the water (and the water beasts), which flowed to form the waterways of the landscape as they are known today. Likewise, it was in a similarly risky, forceful act of 'theft' that the Sun created sunshine by setting up a huge net to trap the great two-headed Vulture. Once he finally caught the bird he took it by the neck and rubbed its heads against a whetstone thus releasing the blazing energy from its four huge shining eyes and the bright feathered crests of its heads.

Similar to the Sun and his daring actions in the myths of creation, many other characters in Mehinaku mythology are celebrated for their intrepid, impetuously risky ways. The most notable of these is *Ayanama*, a young man whose mischievous exploits form a whole series of stories. *Ayanama* is having an affair with his uncle's lovely young wife and when his uncle, a wily and bellicose older man, finds out, he sends *Ayanama* out on various missions which are actually deadly traps but which *Ayanama* always succeeds in escaping. So, on one foray *Ayanama* is sent by his uncle to gather precious *yanakwimpi* shells from a certain village which the uncle knows to be that of dangerous *apapanye*. The *apapanye* attempt to trick him by offering a bench which is actually a snake. But the snake cannot hurt him, as *Ayanama* has prepared for such an occurrence by applying *Mapuyene* tree-oil to his skin so that he is so slippery nothing can catch hold of him. The *apapanye* reward him for his cleverness by giving him lots of the shells he came for. In various similar incidents, *Ayanama* is sent out by his envious and treacherous uncle on false missions that *Ayanama* nevertheless accomplishes with his clever bravery, using tricks usually taught to him by his wise grandmother, such as crossing dangerous waters with the help of spider web bridges and wearing false skins made of tree bark to protect him from attack.

Similar in many ways to the character of *Ayanama*, the Toucan, *Yakawakuwa*, is likewise admired for his cunning robbery of the beautiful wife of the ugly owl, *Mulukuhë*. The Owl who has married the best looking girl of a village (one of the three daughters of the Great Eagle) is returning to his own village when he encounters the Toucan. They begin to talk and soon the Toucan invites the Owl to play a game with him before he continues on his way. The game involves diving into a nearby stream and seeing who can hold onto his breath underwater for the longest. They jump in once and while the woman looks on, the Toucan comes up before the Owl, congratulating the other bird for his superior ability. Once more they dive in and the Toucan does the same thing. The third time the Owl jumps into the water but the Toucan remains on the bank watching him. Quickly he takes the woman by the hand (who preferred the handsome Toucan anyway) and while the ingenuous Owl is still underwater holding his breath, the Toucan makes off through the forest with the other's bride.

The merit attributed by the Mehinaku to the daring dynamic is clearly evident in both these stories,[62] with the character who boldly takes the chance to '*pegar*', to seize what he desires – depicted as beautiful and clever – the Mehinaku attributes of the 'hero' of a tale. On the other hand, the adversary of the bold hero, whether it be the Owl or *Ayanama*'s uncle, is portrayed as ugly and pathetic and generally unsympathetic. However, one can go too far with the dynamic, one can be too cheeky and take too much. And this is what the daring Toucan does upon returning to the village of the woman he had taken. Living in the house of her father, the Eagle *Gerpushë*, he is warned by his father-in-law that he can use whichever arrows he likes except for a certain cluster. But curiosity overwhelms the Toucan and one day he takes the forbidden arrows and goes hunting. Upon shooting the first arrow, it passes through the quarry but comes out the other side, the arrow transforming into an eagle and flying on across the sky. The Eagle looks up and sees the eagle-arrow and knows his son-in-law has disobeyed what he bid him. The Toucan, knowing he has now gone too far, is forced to flee in shame from his new home. In the same sense, the Sun as personifying the excessive extreme of the dynamic of pure daring is depicted as viciously, mercilessly brutal and ugly, the opposite of his gentle and beautiful brother the Moon who never seeks to overstep boundaries but only to help others. So, in one story the big-nosed (a very ugly attribute for the Mehinaku) Sun destroys all the useful new things the Moon has made to help humans and put in a special holding-house. He also seduces the daughters of *apapanye* and lures them to himself only to turn them into stone.

The Mehinaku value the principle of daring such that they seek to live it out in ritual and daily life. In the weeks-long celebrations for the ripening of the *akāi* fruit, ritual involves men grabbing, catching and taking from women, although all this takes place in a humorous, playful fashion. In the *Alama* practice, that of the dangerous Black Bee, the men go into the forest where they paint their bodies completely black with a mixture of charcoal and *akāi* oil. They then run into the village, the women fleeing and squealing with laughter as the men chase and grab them (especially the ones they find attractive) and holding them tight, rub their blackened bodies against their victims until those captured are nearly as black as the captors. To cleverly manage to take or grab what one can and make away with it safely, is also admired in everyday actions. Cuelho, the oldest son of the chief Marikawa, told me a story of how a Waurá man had found a credit card on the street in Canarana, a town close to the indigenous territory of the Alto-Xinguanos. He told of how the man was frightened to take the credit card, laughing that he himself would have definitely taken it straight to a bank and withdrawn a substantial sum of money, in his words (the words of the daring dynamic), 'pegou o dineiro'. Similarly, for a Mehinaku man to venture into the White people's world to sell and buy things is a risky act that exactly echoes the shape of the daring principle drawn of the *Kayapa* incident, a daring but profitable foray into a region of danger but also of possibility.

VIII. The *Awëshëpai* Ideal: a Life of Anxious Joy, in Tension between Integrity and Risk

Thus far it has been argued that the Mehinaku both (i) maintain the boundaries of the worlds (section six) and (ii) occasionally risk those very boundaries in order to preserve and improve them (section seven). However, how can these two opposing dynamics be reconciled with the appearance of Mehinaku life as a peaceful continuity of happy contentment? In this section we shall see that the Mehinaku oscillate between the two dynamic modes of being to produce this pleasant exterior they call 'awëshëpai', which is in fact an achievement of a certain ideal[63] of shimmering balance. Moreover, we shall see that this is quite a different understanding of the good-natured playfulness that has been described as distinctive of Amazonian peoples.[64]

Both the conservative and risk-taking dynamic tendencies are parts of the Mehinaku *anaka*, their 'way of life'. The Mehinaku see themselves as having a way of doing things that is particular to themselves but related to the other Alto-Xinguano communities. *Anaka* was the only word they could find in their language to translate for me the Portuguese word for 'life', 'a vida', and in its meaning this Mehinaku word is close to the common Western notion of 'authentic culture'[65] in its sense of being all the different things the Mehinaku do, such as how they make their food, clothing, how they dance and so on but excluding obviously imported activities such as football, hunting with rifles etc. *Anaka*, apart from pertaining to the customary activities of Mehinaku life, also refers more generally to how these separate activities together form a certain 'way' or 'manner' that is particularly Mehinaku, similar to how a person is understood to have a certain 'way' or personality, *'um jeito'* in Portuguese. *Awëshëpai* then, is the ethos or ideal of this Mehinaku *anaka* or 'way', in such a way that it is the 'state of affairs' that the Mehinaku are always striving for in their *anaka* conduct.

In the following I will discuss then the nature of this *awëshëpai* ethos, the way the Mehinaku conceptualise, utilize and experience it, especially in regard to the opposing dynamic components that I explored above. The specific qualities of these two dynamics, that I will argue constitute *awëshëpai,* are understood to have derived concretely and directly from the twin brothers, the Sun (*Kamë*) and the Moon (*Keshë*). These two are the source of dual utterly opposite ways of being: the Sun is *kapakai* in character, mean, envious, spiteful and destructive; the Moon is *awëshitsi,* kind, thoughtful, nurturing and creative. A number of stories were told to me to portray these differences between the Sun and the Moon. One, mentioned earlier, was about a hut in the forest that the Moon had filled with useful things he had created as gifts to humans to make their lives easier. With his *'bom pensamentos',* his 'good thoughts', the Moon had constructed all kinds of ingenious things that are used today by the Mehinaku, such as hammocks, water containers and various tools. He worked away in secret until one day his brother became curious about where his brother was disappearing to and followed him. When the Moon had set to work his brother suddenly appeared, 'What are you doing here?' the Sun asked him and so the Moon showed him all the things he had made, all so beautiful and 'clean-crafted'. But the Sun was jealous: 'Don't give these things to humans, then they will have everything they need' (which is what the Moon wanted) and the Sun blew with his devastating breath, destroying it all. The person who told me this story went on to say that this was why everywhere there are nasty people, for example in the Kuikuro settlement (a nearby Xinguano community) and 'those bad people who went into the buildings with their planes'.[66] The corresponding traits in humans then, the conservative dynamic of caring and relationship, is understood to have derived directly from the gentle but weaker Moon, and the aggressive, opportunistic dynamic of daring to have come from the cruel Sun, more powerful than anything else in existence.[67]

People generally vacillate between the two modes of being, as they endeavour to be in a state of *awëshëpai.* Before examining how the twin dynamics constitute *awëshëpai,* let us first look to what exactly is the nature of this condition of being. The broad meaning of *awëshë* is 'nice' or 'good', used in conversation to say that some thing or situation is of pleasing satisfactoriness. The suffix *pai* signifies 'the present continuing active state' of the word it is suffix to, so that the word *'awëshëpai'*, in its most general sense, refers to a continuous circumstance of well-being. Things or situations are categorised in terms of whether they fit this *awëshëpai* ideal, or whether they do not and are therefore *aitsa-awëshëpai, 'not-awëshëpai'*. This quality of life has already been discussed to some extent in the first section of this chapter, in the description of the flowing, measured motions of Mehinaku experience and the way obstacles to this flow are actively absorbed. It has also been hinted at in the sixth section, in reference to the cultivation of a joyous outlook *(ketepemunaki)* as an antidote to the dangers of the worlds. *Awëshëpai* then is the combination of these, a kind of joyous flow of life that is constantly worked for. And it is this happy wholesomeness that is most apparent about the atmosphere of Mehinaku community life and which is therefore most obvious to outsiders who visit the settlement. Over and again, people who I met who had come into any contact with the Mehinaku, commented on how gentle and pleasant they were, how constantly laughing and generally contented they seemed to be.

Overing has written of how good-humoured laughter and bawdy play is distinctive of Amazonian communities. Her interpretation is that the Piaroa succeed in a kind of 'social psychology' concerning 'the creation of a feeling of well-being' (2000: 77) or 'high morale' (2000: 76) necessary for a society for whom 'good sociality, physical health, and proper sex are all prerequisites to their collective existence' (2000: 77). This may be true of the Mehinaku too and this aspect will be discussed in chapter 5, however it is evident from the above discussion that for other Amazonians this 'high morale' can be about more than the tone of social life. As Gow explains, 'the sustained plateau of kindness and companionship that Piro people call "living well"', 'is won from a cosmos that is governed by other kinds of reason, and which invades Piro people's lives with dramatic events of emotional extremity' (2000: 61). This notion of 'living well' as an 'intentional flatness of everyday life' is very similar to the state and the sense of Mehinaku *awëshëpai* with its sense of upholding their human world that is always under threat of collapse, this threat also associated with emotional extremity and concerning a cosmos ultimately beyond their control.[68]

However, at least for the Mehinaku, the meaning of this peaceful calm that I grasped in my first months at the village, though accurate, is only one sense of the notion. The laughing volubility and overall strident joyousness of Mehinaku life attests only to the first dynamic we have discussed, the conservative, 'upholding' dynamic. Unlike the Piro, who are concerned with avoiding as much as possible the 'sharp descents into very different regions' (Gow 2000: 61), the Mehinaku regularly and often gladly make certain 'descents' whilst in general trying to keep the steady flow of 'flatness'. These descents for the Mehinaku are the second dynamic that was examined earlier, the dynamic of daring, boundary-breaking risk, and we shall see that this too, though less evident, is mixed into the sense of *awëshëpai*. The question is how can it be reconciled with the smooth flow of happiness that *awëshëpai* appears to be? A clue to this is in the construction of the word *awëshëpai* itself. Apart from the common sense meaning of the word mentioned above, its exact definition reveals a more subtle aspect of its significance. When broken down even further into its parts, the word '*aw-ëshë-pai*' literally means 'the continuous action of being' *(pai)* 'of all that / that thing' *(aw-ëshë)*. Here is evident the assertion of existence, of the identity of its elements, that is also *awëshëpai*. This involves affirmation of 'the being of things' by the combining of both of the dynamics, the being inside and holding up of the form of the world and the risking of form to maintain and improve it. Therefore beneath the outward contentment of Mehinaku life is a struggle against non-being *for* being, that entails mostly the conserving techniques of the first dynamic and also the occasional furtive, daring ploys of the second as they were discussed in the previous sections. One sees then that in fact in spite of their carefree appearance, life for the Mehinaku is one of creative tension between the dynamics, of making and staying on the surface, the 'skins' of the world, and the other of dancing[69] on these edges to occasionally draw from the darkness that pulsates with possibility, beneath and all around.

This is not to say that the outward show of happiness is a false front, with the existential 'dance with darkness' kept secret beneath. There is no such distinction made by the Mehinaku between sincerity and pretence. The joy of *ketepemunaki* even when consciously cultivated can be sincerely, thoroughly experienced.[70] Moreover, the appearance is the socially accept-able expression for the 'struggle for being', which in itself is not meant to be made obvious or much discussed. *Awëshëpai* then *is* the struggle and also the benign way it manifests visibly. Once this is understood, it is possible to detect elements of each of the dynamics in the *awëshëpai* exterior. For example, there is an ambivalence in manner, in attitudes and in statements people make, that seems incongruous without an awareness of the complexity of the *awëshëpai* way of being. For example, though the conduct of Mehinaku people is characteristically peaceful and gentle, a 'sharp' shine to their gaze can also be seen, an almost 'fierce' sparkle in the eyes. This edgy,[71] sometimes even panicky look, seemingly so at odds with the same person's laughing, nonchalant behaviour, is in fact an indication of the artfulness of the 'daring dynamic', of hyperawareness of the nuances of the present moment so as to be able to take the fullest advantage of them. Part of this edginess is also attentiveness to the ever-present threats that exist to the continuation of things as they are, to which the Mehinaku then respond by subsuming their edginess in the positive and casual behaviour which serves to maintain the form of things as discussed in the sixth section. Even at times of distress – when speaking of grief at the death of someone close, of the threat of dangerous spirits, or of the nature of the *kawëka* – a Mehinaku person will keep a serene and even smiling, laughing demeanour.[72] Mostly then what is visible in *awëshëpai* behaviour is the action of the conservative dynamic: while the oscillation of both dynamics is always at work within people,[73] the daring is only at times observable as a certain nervous restlessness, or in private *pegar* actions that are inadvertently seen by others.[74]

This chapter has been an exploration of the dynamic aspects of Mehinaku lived worlds, part of our general exploration of Mehinaku experience on the way to understanding the particular event of experience that is the walk to the river. First I looked at the general nature of the motions of Mehinaku life and found them to be an ongoing and measured flow, consciously cultivated, within the structures of experience that were the subject of the previous chapter. I then looked at how there are also movements not only within but also between the structures, trespassing motions that take place across the two main configurations of realities, vertically between the worlds of earth and sky and horizontally between the village and the world of forest, dreams and spirits. At that point a question was posed in regard to what is the impetus for all these movements, the general flowing motions within the structures and also the intrusive and often forceful movements between them. It was found that desire (which in chapter 2 had been identified as the stuff of the Mehinaku soul) was the source of these dynamics, both the steady and moderate desire giving motion to the various activities of Mehinaku life, and also the extremely passionate longing that makes a being move from their own world to another.

After investigating the motions of life, I turned to the borders and shapes of the worlds within which they flow. I looked at how the first forms were made when the first human beings were created, and how within these there exist further limits of concentric circular zones, and how these are in turn differentiated by yet finer boundaries of various kinds of paths. I then described how these borders of desire are however always at risk from the desires themselves, which, when excessive, compromise borders as they push their way through them, sometimes eventuating in their complete destruction and the unleashing of terrible forces. To uphold the structures of life therefore, against this constant onslaught, the Mehinaku work to assuage these immoderate hungers to less destructive levels, bringing them within normal bounds in the practice of methods of preservation of integrity of self *(yerekyuki)* and of artful relationship with the *apapanye* (the *uwekehë* complex). However another and opposing dynamic was found to come into play that, apart from conserving form, risks must be taken to open it up and hence improve it (the 'daring' dynamic). Finally I considered how the two dynamics, the conservative 'upholding' dynamic and the dynamic of 'daring' come together in one Mehinaku life, one of creative tension, the cultivated happiness of *awëshëpai*.

Notes

1. Such as the *Takwára*, which will be discussed in more detail later in this section, as well as the *Tineshukuma*, a dance of the women. In regard to similar sense see Gell's (1999) interesting discussion of the similarities between the Umeda dance of the *ida* ritual and non-dance.
2. This flow of Mehinaku language is akin to what Feld writes of the Bosavi experience of '[S]inging like water' (1996: 132).
3. Following Taylor (1992), Sobo writes of how liquid symbolism with 'an emphasis on maintaining a continuous, unimpeded flow … is common among those who value reciprocity and emphasise the obligation kin have to share with each other.' (1993: 54).
4. See a similar sense of the cleansing action of vomiting in Gow (2001: 139).
5. The cyclical and indeed circular sense of flows of the world is evident in the 'circular calendar' of stars discussed in section IV. It is also similar to what Gow finds for the Piro people for whom 'days and months are most salient … as periods within an annual cycle, and are hence treated like cyclical star movements, rather than as part of a cumulative series of days, months, and years' (Gow 2001: 281). Gregor has written of Mehinaku spatial expressions of time (1977: 36–37), that is, they think of one in terms of the other (time in terms of space). I would argue that the Mehinaku experience cannot be subsumed into either of the Western concepts of space and time but that the sense of the landscape as substantial, cyclical flow blends the notions inextricably.
6. See a similar formulation by Sobo (1993) of Jamaican kinship ties created by a flow of mingled fluids and resources and whereby '[A]ny blockage of goods, services or familial love leads to or indicates social discord' as in the case of 'jealous hoarding' that is regarded as one of various kinds of 'social pathologies' (60).

7. The way the Mehinaku deal with aggression and conflict will be explored in chapter 5, sec. III.

8. Which will be discussed at the end of this chapter.

9. For example, washing the hair with commercial shampoo is common but judged by some as 'not Mehinaku' as I was told by my foster-mother Takulalu, who would chasten her daughter for using mine.

10. The Mehinaku are extremely tolerant of the differences of behaviour of outsiders and are similarly quite tolerant of the behaviour of other Mehinaku individuals, though there is a fair amount of indirect pressure on conformance, that goes on through gossiping and other surveillance mechanisms to be discussed in chapter 5.

11. Heckenberger and Franchetto (2000); Heckenberger (2000); Dole (2000).

12. I think that the Mehinaku feel it is possible to absorb outsiders (even White people) into their way of living at least on principle, having something to do with what Gregor has written of Mehinaku 'social identity' as being 'a matter of degree' (1977: 318). Yet this 'absorption' does not occur without certain 'racial' antagonisms in certain contexts. More on this in chapter 5, sec. III.

13. This value given to work of ongoing industriousness has associations with a kind of moral goodness, *awitsiri,* discussed in the next chapter. See Griffiths on similar Uitoto ideas for whom 'continuous work is advocated and esteemed' (2001: 249).

14. For more detail about the 'life of the dead', see chapter 2, sec. V.

15. For example in the Amazon where the Araweté are described by Viveiros de Castro as believing that in dying 'alterity takes place' and they become as their 'gods' (1992: 3–4). The Barasana understanding of death is of reincarnation, where 'the souls of the dead … go either directly to the people's waking up house in the east, or down the Underworld River and thence to the east … to be reincarnated as human babies' (S. Hugh-Jones 1979: 216).

16. See Overing (1985) for similar conceptualisation for the Piaroa for whom there is an 'existence of a number of real worlds separated from one another … which are today in constant interaction: elements from one world, … continually entering, becoming part of, and leaving another' (169).

17. These 'Star Birds' are in a category of their own; they are not *apapanye,* nor the *enai* copies of them (which were discussed in the preceding chapter). They live in villages in the sky and are antagonistic and more powerful neighbours to the villages of the Mehinaku Dead.

18. When *apapanye* are spoken about specifically, they are named as though only one of each kind exists, though in conversation and in response to my specific questioning of the matter, it is evident that in fact a number of each kind of *apapanye* exist (and often different genders thereof). However there is a subtle relation of equivalence made between the one and the many, between the archetypal *apapanye* and the different individual *apapanye* associated with certain events. This way of understanding things will be discussed in chapter 5 as part of a general exploration of what I will term 'thingness' for the Mehinaku.

19. As we have seen in the last chapter, to encounter a being from another reality can be a highly transformative experience to the extent that it can bring you into the reality of the other. How exactly this occurs in dynamic terms shall be explored in more detail later in section VI of this chapter.

20. The practices of both shamans and sorcerers will be discussed in detail in chapter 5.

21. Gregor has written at length about Mehinaku desire in his book *Anxious Pleasures* (1985). However, very differently from my own findings, he discusses it chiefly in terms of men's sexual desire for women. The way he does this will be addressed in chapter 5, sec. II.

22. This story was told in the previous section.

23. Almost exactly the same story is often told only with the characters of the young man and his dead friend substituted with a mother and her dead daughter.

24. This event was previously mentioned in chapter 2.

25. The central significance in Mehinaku life of the related myths of *Yakashukuma* and *Yamurikuma* will be explained in chapter 5 as part of a general discussion concerning Mehinaku gender issues.

26. This story and the significance of the pequi tree in Mehinaku life will be explored in detail in chapter 5.

27. The Desana have a similar conception of flow or 'currents' through the world. However these currents, *bogá*, which are conceived in terms of 'energy', are distinguished from a force that is their impetus or cause, *tulári* (Reichel-Dolmatoff 1971).

28. This ideal way of conducting and experiencing one's life according to a kind of tempering of desire to its right form is part of what the Mehinaku refer to as *'awëshëpai'*. This 'life principle' will be discussed at the end of the chapter, once other necessary aspects of it have been discussed.

29. For more details of the stories of the beginnings of the worlds see chapter 2.

30. As I have mentioned previously, *Kwamutë* is often identified as a *yerepëhë*-being.

31. These have been discussed to some extent in the last section of the previous chapter in regard to the horizontal configuration of worlds.

32. The Mehinaku experience of 'love' and marriage will be discussed in chapter 5 as part of the exploration of gender relations.

33. The crucial role played by the integrity of the boundary of the human body in upholding the form of the worlds will be discussed in section VI of this chapter.

34. The experience of 'spheres of being' (the implications of the words *naku* and *taku*) will be discussed in more detail in chapter 4 as part of the exploration of the general Mehinaku 'sense of things'.

35. This relationship will be explored in chapter 5.

36. The specific danger for a woman of seeing the *Kawëka* is in fact that the consequence is rape by every man in the village, a phenomenon that will be discussed in chapter 5.

37. Some bicycles have been brought into the Park and are used mostly used by men.

38. As mentioned previously in this chapter, in the story of the *Mawaya* tree.
39. As in the story of Yapikyeku's journey to the village of the dead, from earth to sky and back (chapter 2, sec. V).
40. See Gow for a similar sense of precariousness of existence for the Piro, who writes that 'surrounding them is a cosmos based on very different principles ever ready to impinge on their lives' (2000: 59).
41. Here is portrayed the great value placed on beauty by the Mehinaku as discussed in chapter 2, sec. I.
42. *Yanakwimpi* (a large pinky white river snail-shell) is commonly known in the Xingu as *Karamushu.*
43. See Heckenberger (2000b) on history of Xinguano contact with other Indians of the area.
44. I repeat what I have mentioned in the previous chapter, that animals 'with blood' (boar, snake, anteater etc.) are differentiated from certain kinds of birds, water tortoises and fish that the Mehinaku and other Alto-Xinguanos allow themselves to eat. A particular species of small black monkey (*pahër* in Mehinaku) is an exception to the prohibition against eating animals with blood as their perceived closeness to humanity means that their blood is not wild like land animals but more like humans. To explain this the Mehinaku tell a story about how the *pahër* originate from a human baby who was abandoned in the trees by his mother.
45. Also between themselves, which will be explored in the discussion of Mehinaku sociality in chapter 5.
46. Illness for Piro as similarly caused by 'forest and river demons' and for predation of animals by humans' (Gow 1991: 79–80).
47. The act of shamanising will be explored in detail in chapter 5, sec. I.
48. Having said that, the love of the *apapanye* can be reciprocated so that the calculating intention of entering in to the role of *uwekehë* can be mixed with some emotion from the human side. This kind of relationship usually occurs between *apapanye* and people whose relationship transmutes from *uwekehë* to that of *yatama,* shaman, whereby the *apapanye* becomes the personal spirit-helper for that shaman. Such an association is exemplified by Kaiti a shamaness, the chief Marikawa's late mother, whose love affair with *Uikyuma* the Great Snake was to continue even after her death. A little of this story and this type of relationship in general will be described in more detail in chapter 5.
49. The notions of illness as a change in state of consciousness that enters one into another reality (as in the example of the man and the butterfly lake) and that each reality is produced by many 'consciousnesses' perceiving together (consensus realities), was discussed in detail in chapter 2, sec. V.
50. Who participates in such events depends on the nature of the event, i.e. different dances require different constituents, and the motivations of volunteer dancers can be anything from friendship with the victim, a love of dancing or a wish to paint and show off one's beauty.
51. The food offered to the *apapanye* and eaten by them invisibly as the Mehinaku consume it, is given either to the music-makers only or is distributed in the centre to each male head of a nuclear family who brings it back to his house

and gives it to his wife who then divides it up for each member of the family. The food is usually a fish stew called *wakula* consisting of fresh or smoked fish and manioc flour and sometimes flavoured with chili and when in season the pungent pequi *(akāi)* fruit that is especially delicious to the *apapanye* (not to mention the Mehinaku who adore it as an incomparable delicacy).

52. The complex reasons for this and other such prohibitions are explained as part of a general discussion of gender relations in chapter 5.

53. The *kapushai* music, as has been mentioned previously, involves a pair of men entering each house of the village round to dance back and forth before the front door mocking the women (usually the way they gossip) in improvised chants to a regular meter, melody and dance step. This music will be explored in more detail in chapter 5 in the context of a wider discussion of Mehinaku gender issues.

54. Husbands and wives are understood to naturally share the role of *uwekehë,* as they share all activities, with each playing their necessary and complimentary part (again, more on this in chapter 5 in regard to notions of gender).

55. There is a story told of a man who did not believe in the particular danger of the *apapanye* during an eclipse and so went into the forest fishing in spite of the warnings against it. There a great noise heralded a terrible encounter with an *apapanye.*

56. See chapter 2, sec. V.

57. '*muito aitsawëshëpai sol!*' 'very bad sun!' I was told by a number of people that day.

58. See the comparable Barasana 'sense in which the secular world of human society is really too cold and social; it requires purposeful use of natural forces to heat it up and sustain life' (C. High-Jones 1979: 233). Also, Viveiros de Castro has written of the similar Araweté 'impulse leading outside itself, a passion for exteriority' (1992:3) but as part of a very different kind of 'cosmology'.

59. Thus when I use the word 'daring' from this point onward, I am always referring to this Mehinaku dynamic. I use this English term as there is no Mehinku word that particularly refers to it.

60. Though household members will very often eat at the same time in the cooking house or near the fire, this is not a gregarious act of joining to interact over food as it can be in other cultures. Nuclear families will huddle together as food is distributed by the women of each and once the food is in hand, the eating is a solitary and mostly silent act (though some gossiping can take place, usually afterward), with individuals usually turning or walking away, often even going to sit facing a wall or to eat while walking around.

61. See the very similar finding of C. Hugh-Jones for the Barasana: 'whether the orifices are open or closed the bad effect will come along with the good; this is prevented … by the regular alternation of opening and closing, a kind of dynamic alternation' (1979: 119).

62. The way that stories are related and 'applied' to life by the Mehinaku, will be discussed in chapter 4, sec. II.

63. The meaning of 'an ideal' as it occurs in the Mehinaku context will be explored in the next chapter.

64. The particularly social dimension of this way of being, *ketepepei,* will be explored and compared in chapter 5, sec. III.
65. This finding, that the Mehinaku do have quite an abstract indigenous conception of 'culture' is quite different to the findings of modern fieldwork in general, which is that notions of 'culture' and its 'authenticity' is peculiar to the Western perspective and imposed with misconstruing results on others, see for example Wagner (1975).
66. It was shortly after 'September 11', and the members of the community had heard varying versions of the event from people in town, television and on transistor radio.
67. The opposing qualities of the Sun and the Moon relate to the opposing qualities possible for all souls (as described in terms of the 'soul continuum' in the previous chapter), of wildness and gentleness, but represent specifically the two extreme aspects of the human soul, the Sun and the Moon being the children of one of the First Women, and being the creators of the first men.
68. For the Mehinaku, the 'upholding' dynamic involves not only the winning of a calm social life, but also the very structures of their human world, their very bodies, as we saw in section VI of this chapter.
69. I use the term 'dance' here as it is seems particularly appropriate since dancing is a crucial way that the Mehinaku create relationships with the forces beyond themselves (in the dancing for/as the *apapanye*) (chapter 4, sec. II).
70. That is to say, the joyful appearance of the upholding aspect of *awëshëpai* is not fake happiness but rather 'made happiness', the choice by people who believe that quality of consciousness manifests reality, so that to act happy one really feels happy, with all the beneficial effects of such a mode of being on the continued integrity of the form and flow of the worlds.
71. See Gregor's interpretation of this quality as specifically 'sexual anxiety', which I will refute in chapter 5, sec. II.
72. See Gow (2000: 56) for a similar joking way of reacting to the trauma of death among the Piro.
73. Interesting similarity between the Mehinaku sense of flow of desires and Jung's more abstract notion of the flow of psychic energy that is 'libido', with comparable sense of two 'life-movements' (1960: 37), 'regression' and 'progression' that are the forward and backward movements of the libido (40), contraction to conserve the boundaries of the individual and the expansion outward to embrace the all, very like the oscillating 'upholding' and 'daring' dynamics that have been discussed.
74. Such as stealing, skin-scraping, making deals with spirits.

4

Experience of Mehinaku Experience

Working towards the ultimate goal of coming to terms with what ordinary reality in particular is like for the Mehinaku, in the last two chapters I have investigated their experience of reality in general, the fundamental categories, connections and dynamics of their existence. In doing this, I have sought to avoid finding pieces from the Mehinaku worlds to fit into a preconceived theoretical model. Details of Mehinaku existence were not broken up and put to the service of an extrinsic explanation, rather it has been the other way around: Western language and its categories (which are the only explanatory media at hand) are mixed and shaped in order to construct a Mehinaku model. Now, after investigating what the Mehinaku conceptualise, I would like to go even further in the effort to avoid taking anything for granted, by asking what is their process of conceptualisation; for example, not only what are their concepts but what is a 'concept' itself for these people, *what is their notion of a notion*? Here I want to proceed past anthropological analyses that stop short of this point, either assuming the fundamental aspects of consciousness to be universal, and/or deeming the experiences of others as ultimately lacking such abstractions as concepts of concept, their 'thought ... non-conceptual, conveyed in images and symbols, rather disguising ... ultimate objects in myth and rites than expounding them logically' (Jonas 1958: 21). I will argue instead that the Mehinaku conceptualise their own 'ultimate objects', which their 'myth and rites' do not disguise, but rather express, with their own intricate logic.

Therefore in this chapter we will look not only at what experiences the Mehinaku have but how these experiences actually occur in a Mehinaku person's consciousness. Harking back to the introduction, in the discussion of my phenomenological approach, I wrote that I would discern (i) the saliences, (ii) associations between them, and (iii) how they are lived in streams of Mehinaku consciousness. Therefore in these terms, in the last two chapters we have looked at the 'content' of these aspects of Mehinaku experience. Here then we will focus on how this content is experienced as consciousness, looking at those three facets of human experience in turn. As I said above, I will start by (i) examining not only what 'things' occur to a Mehinaku person but what a 'thing' even is to a Mehinaku person. We will then explore (ii) how these 'things' are associated in consciousness in general, and in a certain 'story logic', as well as a Mehinaku 'ritual logic'. Finally, we will turn to see (iii), how these ways of making associations can come together in the Mehinaku case, in an ideal way of thinking/being that could be called by the Mehinaku term – *awitsiri*.

I. The Concept of a Concept: Mehinaku ' Thingness' and the Blending of Entities

What is a 'thing' to a Mehinaku person? What if anything gives objects, occurrences, acts, thoughts and utterances a sense of entity to the Mehinaku? In chapter 2, we saw the two main kinds of 'things' in existence: the *yeya* forms (the true forms of the *apapanye*) that are understood to have always existed and the *ënai* copies of these that are made from amorphous materials lying about. Here is evident the basic way the Mehinaku comprehend discrete 'things' in their own and other worlds, that is, that all things have distinctive identities that are archetypes from creation, or derive from these archetypes. This is the Mehinaku understanding of 'things' that in Western terms would be defined as 'objects'. However, in chapter 2 we also saw that for the Mehinaku other aspects of life also have an objective 'thing-like' identity that they do not have in the West. Not only objects outside 'in the world' but also objects inside consciousness are similarly substantial. Sense-perceptions, thoughts, emotions and social solidarity are impersonal substances with independent causal efficacy, so that senses and feelings are in fact experienced as 'forces' or 'things' that move into and between people. Other 'intangibles' in the West are also objectified by the Mehinaku as 'things' that can be owned and passed onto others, such as different 'musics' and stories that are inherited, traded for and used as a currency of prestige. In the last chapter we saw that even thoughts, concepts, ideals of behaviour and attitude, are 'things' that derive concretely from creation, for example the opposing principles of graciousness and aggressive opportunism that came directly from the Moon and Sun respectively. Thus, an idea or a concept for the Mehinaku is not an intangible production of an intangible mind, each is a concrete and specific 'thing' that is not differentiated in its substantial 'thingness' from the other things that constitute the Mehinaku worlds.

There is not then a separate 'concept of abstract concept' as in the West, which is derived from the ancient Greek notion of *'logos'*. Rather, Mehinaku 'ideas' fall into the general category of 'substantial thing'[1] we have been discussing, which in fact has its own abstract term, *yakawaka*. However, harking back to the previous chapters, it must be remembered that the substantiality of things is a subtle and complicated matter for the Mehinaku. The natures of the things of the world are subject to the different consciousnesses that perceive them and subsequently exist in a certain state of precariousness. This lends a certain creativity to the Mehinaku people's sense of their relation to the things that surround them, as the things they perceive become malleable to, exist subject to the quality of their own perception. The role of language in this creative kind of experience of the world is fundamental. It defines and hence supports the identity of things that already exist in the consensus reality concerned. Also with language, by naming things, aspects of life that are ambiguous in nature come into existence as distinct entities. This role of language in the sense of Mehinaku 'thingness'[2] is suggested by the very word for 'thing': *yaka-waka* where *'yaka'* means 'speech' or 'talk' and *'waka'* indicates what is being referred to; so that the general category of 'thing' means approximately 'that which is spoken of'.

The way that naming with language can actually create a 'thing' from amorphous 'no-thing' is one part of elaborate methods of constructing entities. When an object is made by the Mehinaku, whether it be a palm mat, a basket, an arrow or animal-bench, there is always a critical threshold, where the materials being assembled meld into the thing being made. For example in the construction of a *matapu*, a ritual object whose purpose is to 'house' the *Matapu* Spirit, the small piece of wood in the shape of a fish may only be called a *matapu* once the wooden shape has been properly painted. It is understood that only at the point that this painting is completed does the *matapu* become what it is supposed to be and function as such,[3] that is, become a vessel for the *Matapu-apapanye*. The Mehinaku speak of having to make things 'beautiful', *awitsiri*, where 'beautiful' means to them that the thing is as new, clean and perfect as the original *yeya*. Things therefore, can be made but only by imitating as far as possible the original *yeya* types, where the closer it approximates the archetype, the better and the more beautiful the thing is considered. Objects that are not made properly in this way, lack real identity as 'things', remaining amorphous matter moved together but without a result in meaning. The process of making these 'copies' is connotative for the Mehinaku of the reenactment of the archetypal process of creation, the creation of humans by *Kwamutë,* when he put together materials lying about to fabricate the first human bodies.[4]

These entities identified as *yakawaka* or 'things' – that is, both the *yeya* 'true originals' and their *ënai* constructed copies – have certain boundaries. There are two ways this boundedness of 'thing' is understood, and that is in terms of notions denoted by the suffixes: *naku* and *taku. Taku* refers to the limits of a thing and *naku* denotes all that is inside those limits. One can see the difference between these concepts in the two Mehinaku words for 'sky', *enunaku* and *enutaku.* One young man explained this difference to me by drawing a diagram of two concentric circles, the inner one representing the land *(gehë)* and the one outside it representing the sky. *Enutaku,* I was told, is the line of the outside ring, it is the 'sky place' at the limits of one's vision of the heavens, to where one can point with one's hand directly, whereas *enunaku* is that which is within the outside ring, above and around covering the earth, and to indicate the meaning of this, he waved his hand all around rather than pointing directly. The sense of *naku* meaning all that unifies a thing in identity, is evident in the very word the Mehinaku use to identify themselves, that is, *Mehi-naku,*[5] where the suffix denotes all those and all that which make up these peoples' identity as they themselves see it. In regard to the idea of *taku,* most importantly it designates what defines or rather differentiates an entity from all else, its identity from what is outside it, what it is from what it is not. For the Mehinaku, ostensibly, the defining limits of *taku* and the strong identity of the *naku* of things are firmly drawn and perceived, so that the features of the Mehinaku world seem striking in their bold outlines. This is obvious at first contact with the Mehinaku, in the plain unambiguous ways the people discuss all manner of things and in the different kinds of 'material culture' they produce, where from body painting to the designs on pots, the firm clear line is always preferred.

However, the entities that occur in Mehinaku consciousness are in fact not at all as clearly discrete from one another as it at first appears. The reason for their aesthetic of bold clarity is that the Mehinaku deliberately promote or project definition because in fact the opposite is the case. As described in the last chapters, the world is constantly shifting and fluid for the Mehinaku and so they must consciously uphold the forms that constitute their reality.

We shall now look then at the following question: if the 'things' in Mehinaku experience we have been describing are not in fact as distinctly separate as they seem, how exactly *do* they shift and even blend in consciousness? This occurs in a number of ways. The first of these is that different things are identified as one another in a way that would be contradictory to a Western perspective. This became apparent to me in a recurrent concatenation of motifs in discussions about the causes of illnesses. The same sickness would be attributed to a sorcerer *(ipyamawékéhë)* and then to one or other *apapanye* spirit interchangeably, even in the same telling of a story. For example, in the chief Marikawa's story of the illness of his mother, the great Shamaness Kaití, he began by saying that she was made sick when she went alone to relieve herself in the bushes and the Snake-*apapanye (Uíkyuma)* took her soul. In another telling of the story by Marikawa however, she storms into the men's house to declare that she knows the identity of the sorcerer who attacked her and made her sick. Confused, I tried to discern which in fact had been the cause of Kaití's illness, the *apapanye* or the human sorcerer, or had it been in some way both? No matter how I phrased my questions on this matter to Marikawa and others, no one understood my enquiries.

Again and again the same apparent contradiction would surface in discussions of people's illnesses. I found that a similar lack of differentiation between *apapanye* and *ipyamawékéhë*-sorcerers was evident in regard to a being called the *Tsi Tsi*, a dangerous creature with legs like a man, talons like an eagle and a head like a jaguar. In fear of the *Tsi Tsi*, men do not like to hunt at night and women even avoid walking in the dark. On the rare occasion that I was walking at night with women, often they would point to the sky and exclaim to me 'Tsi Tsi, *"muito perigoso!"* – very dangerous!' and other nights '*feitiçero* –sorcerer', and then once they pointed and said first one, then the other. 'Tsi Tsi, *"feitiçero, mesmo"* –the same?' I asked and they agreed. Another example is that in a certain myth recounted about a being that descends from the sky to kill all the members of a now extinct neighbouring tribe, the perpetrator is named as the *apapanye-Ateshua* and then as a sorcerer, even in the same telling of the story.

Confronted with such ambiguities, my initial tendency was to attempt to tease out some clear sense from the blurred information I was receiving. This analytical approach is common in most anthropological studies, including those of the Xingu, where what is told to the researcher is organised into misleadingly clear categories of types of animals, spirit-beings etc.[6] The error here on behalf of ethnographers has to do with assumptions that their own ways of thinking/perceiving (for example, the logic of categorization) is shared by the peoples they study. For example, common to the classifications of beings produced by the researchers of the Xingu, there is an imposition on their findings of the oppositionality inherent in the common sense Western view of the world, that 'things' or beings are either 'this *or* that'. For example Basso writes of the Kalapalo that 'the four categories of the paradigmatic set are ... "possessions", "pets", "living things", "monsters"' (Basso 1973: 17–18). When however, one does not try to understand the material in such ways, it is possible to discover whether there are in fact different kinds of logic at work.

If therefore, an ambiguity in the identification of various entities, though presenting a contradiction to a Western sense of things, does not to the Mehinaku, how does it make sense to them? There are two related aspects to this Mehinaku way of understanding 'things'. First, in the comprehension of an occurrence there is a lack of feeling it necessary to determine one way or another, the exact identity of agents or causes, which is I believe a tendency in the Western process of understanding and explaining an event. For the Mehinaku, ambiguity is not disturbing: put simply, it is bearable to them for different possibilities to coexist in consciousness. This is how a person can understand the cause of such an illness to be an *apapanye* and/or a sorcerer, without experiencing such understanding to be contradictory. Similarly, there can be an overlapping of the nature of things (such as that of *Ateshua* and sorcerers) such that entities are perceived as so alike that at times their identities are able to be transposed, once again, without their separate identities having to be absolutely defined.

Another way that the boundaries of 'things' blend or shift is in a kind of flickering of consciousness. This occurs for ordinary humans but more often for the *yatama,* the shamans. It has been mentioned earlier how one may glimpse an entity from another world. For instance, while out in the orchard one might hear the flap of birds' wings, turn and out of the corner of one's eye, glimpse the fleeting spirit-form of an *apapanye*. As described in chapter 2, this occurs because of 'over-desiring' that causes one to leave one's consensus reality so that one sees into another, in a kind of super-imposing and intersection of worlds. Two examples discussed in that chapter were of the man who saw a lake of butterflies instead of fish and the woman in the forest who is seduced by a man she then finds is an *apapanye*. The shamans on the other hand do not have to be ill to see such things. At any time but especially when they are smoking, a *yatama* may observe an object or creature that he then suddenly sees in a different form, for example, Monaim told me he may see a hummingbird *(ahira)* and then when he looks again he sees the spectacular man-form of the *Ahira-apapanye.* This is not a blending of category as discussed earlier but rather the experience of the shifting appearances of the one category. This is why the same name is given to the *apapanye* spirit, its palm mask used by the Mehinaku for dancing, and also the animal one sees scampering in the forest. In a profound way they can be perceived as the same by the Mehinaku, different faces of the same being that one can see or simply imagine as one thing then another from one moment to the next.

There is also the blending of meaning in activities. There is not simply one purpose for a particular activity, there can be many that may be experienced alternately or blend and be lived at once.[7] For example, when the Mehinaku scrape their skin with the *imya*,[8] there is a number of ways this event can be understood. The basic bodily sense of the action is that scraping the skin so that blood is let, gets the heart pumping to make new blood as the old blood flows out, giving a feeling of vitality and force. When a person scrapes or is scraped there is also a sense of doing a thing that the creators did, skin-scraping being first performed by the creator of men *Kwamutë* on his grandson *Keshë*, to colour his pet-parrot bright red. Also, parents will scrape their children as a punishment for being naughty. Skin scraping then, may involve just one of these three experiences, or all of them, with one or the other experience foregrounded, or a person may alternate continuously between them. In the same way, women's practices related to menstruation and the post-birth period,[9] are understood and lived in varied ways. Women do not partake of their usual diet of fish (eating certain types of bird and monkey instead) and must avoid contact with objects that men drink or eat from. When asked the reasons for these practices, the responses, even from the same person, are varied. There is a sense of them being a very discrete set of observances, one man translating their distinct importance as '*o lei do Xingu*', 'the law of the Xingu'. Other reasons given for the practices can be social and/or physiological: that if one carries water, cooks and eats fish during one's period, the other women will make fun of you; that if you breach normal practice by eating fish, it will make you sick and your cooking will make the men ill. Therefore there is not one sense of the purpose of these observances, rather they have various meanings that can blend in lived experience.

The intermingling of categories in consciousness is also evident in a certain logic of myth. Myths are told in such a way that if one compares details and takes ideas to their 'logical conclusion', the myths told lack coherence and appear contradictory. For example, in the myth of creation the *yerepëhë* lived in absolute darkness and sunshine was only made by *Kamë* some time after all the acts of creation by his grandfather *Kwamutë*, and of the various stories of *apapanye* such as the Jaguar, *Kamë's* father. According to 'logic' then, confusingly, stories such as the tribal gathering of

the animal-*apapanye* and the fish,[10] must have occurred in utter darkness.
But when I told people such 'logical conclusions', they always stared back
at me perplexed. I began to realize that the Mehinaku did not necessarily
always feel the need to piece together conclusions from the myths they
listened to, nor apply such 'findings' to other myths. I found more of this
difference in logic as I heard other stories. One person would say that the
origin of the sorcerers, the *ipyamawékéhë*, is the *apapanye-Ateshua,* who
brought down the 'sorcerers' things', their ensorcelling paraphernalia, in
his disk-like head when he descended to earth. Another person would
then explain that it was the evil grandmother of the Sun and the Moon,
the Great Jaguar's mother, who was the first and hence the origin of all
sorcerers. If one then goes, as I did, back to the first informant to question
the apparent inconsistency, he will say, 'Yes it was *Ateshua* and it was the
Jaguar's mother.' Falling back on Western logic, the anthropologist asks
the questions: which one happened first; if they were origins of different
aspects of the same creation, what are these and how are the two creation
events related? But asking these questions, one receives baffled silence in
response. This is because, this Western demand for consistency is mis-
placed, a different sense of meaning is at work here. There is no 'worked
out' (by experts) timeline that the facts of myth have to fit within,[11] there
is no need to ascertain an ultimate and singular answer to a question.
Once again, as discussed above, for the Mehinaku it is unproblematic for
there to be more than one answer to a question, as for them many possibilities of reality can coexist.

II. How Things Are Associated: at the Most Basic Level; in a 'Story Logic'; in a Certain Understanding of Ritual

Thus far in this chapter I have discussed the way the Mehinaku conceive
of the various aspects of their experience as entities, and how these entities can blend in consciousness. Sometimes however, things or entities can
be linked in consciousness but without actually going so far as to blend.
Thus the boundaries of each entity remain clear while they are associated.
In this section I will look then at the general nature of such relations and
then how this occurs in a certain 'story logic', and also as part of the Mehinaku understanding of ritual.

The issue of how associations are made is crucial to the purpose of this
book, of coming to terms with the way ordinary reality is experienced by
the Mehinaku. To get to that most imminent sense of living, 'the imme-

diate flux of life' (James 1947: 83), it is necessary to investigate not only what and how things are perceived but also how these things make other things 'come to mind'. The way that experience is constituted by associations made in human consciousness was explored in the introduction. The question here is how the Mehinaku specifically make these associations in their experience, for there is no reason, especially for an anthropologist, to take for granted that all humans make associations in the same way. In spite of this, it is common for anthropological writing to do so. As Overing has eloquently discussed, there has been an 'evasion by anthropologists, and by structuralists in particular, of the issues of similarity, knowledge and belief' (1985: 153), with the assumption or claim that statements such as '[T]he tapir is our grandfather' is not a belief in an actual relationship between the human and the non-human world but of an intellectual kind, part of a system of analogical classification of a universal and rational thought process (Overing 1985: 153).[12] In contrast then, I will be looking at how the associations that I myself have described thus far, such as 'sex is like eating' or 'night is associated with danger', are understood by the Mehinaku. That is, *how* is eating like sex, or what exactly does 'like' mean to the people concerned?

This problematisation of such Western notions as 'symbol' and 'representation' is concerned with what might be called the '*how* of the lived metaphor'[13] and will be explored here for the general terms of the Mehinaku case. Also, it is in these terms that at the end of this discussion, I hope to contribute somewhat to an understanding of 'the most strange identifications' that are those of 'mythic thought' (Lévi-Strauss *in* Overing 1985: 153), particularly how they work in the activities of story and ritual, a contribution to just one of what Girard, Goody and Overing have argued are the 'large number of interesting questions having to do with religion, belief and morality' that through structuralism Lévi-Strauss has purged from anthropology (Overing 1985: 175).

There are a number of ways the Mehinaku make associative relations between things. The first is that entities are associated because they are in fact different appearances of the same thing. This has to do with the fact that superimposing realities exist (as discussed in chapter 2), so that for example an *apapanye* who has a basically human-form in his own world, will normally be perceived by a human being as a slightly larger than normal and particularly beautiful-looking animal. The sighting by a human person of such an animal therefore, brings to mind the human-form of the *apapanye* who the animal may actually in fact be, as well as its outward animal appearance.

The fact that most things in the world are not the *yeya* originals which are very rare but rather are the *ënai* imitations leads one to another manner in which the Mehinaku make links between things in consciousness. The Mehinaku have a specific word for the 'like' of 'the lived metaphor', which is *épéké*, translated to me in the Portuguese as *'parece'*, and which translated literally into English means 'to appear' or 'seem like'. However exploration of the meaning of this word led to a more nuanced understanding, whereby the way that any one thing is 'like' another, in fact has the sense of its being an imitation, in the way that the *ënai* is a copy of the *yeya*-archetype. This is most obvious in the very literal kind of association, of deliberate representation. One sees this in the various things the Mehinaku make in the image of other things, for example, the painting of designs on the skin such as the *kulupé-yana* that are in the image of small fish, or a wooden stool made in the likeness of animals *(shepi)*. Always there is the sense of these representations being a copy of the original, in much the same way that most creatures, plants and other entities in the world, are believed to be copies of archetypes made of the archetypes' own substance, as 'children from their mother'.[14] When I did not at first understand this, a man called Yanapá attempted to explain it to me by saying: 'The *kulupé-yana* are not like *("como")* fish, they are exactly the same *("igualzinho")'*, that is, of the same stuff.

Representations and other kinds of 'symbolic' understandings may also involve the sense of the building-up process of creation by imitation. For example, I have said that the Mehinaku perceive their own bodies as being like fish. So the question here is *how* do the Mehinaku experience their bodies as 'fish-like'? And what does 'like' mean in this statement? We have seen above the sense that by emulating the fish who they so admire (painting their bodies with fish-designs etc.), the Mehinaku are in a way substantially linked to the original they are copying. There is also the feeling of one's body being 'made of' fish because one eats fish. For the Mehinaku this has to do with the aforementioned mythic sense they have that the body continues to be made up of materials (by eating fish, for example), just as the first humans were made by *Kwamutë*. It is here that it is most evident that the substantiality of this understanding of the world is not simply the same as a Western radical physicalism. Rather, the Mehinaku understanding of themselves as 'like fish' and other such associations made between things, are imbued with a logic that occurs in their myths but is not isolated in them, so that this rationale of a kind of ontological bricolage, pervades even the most mundane associations of experience.

'Metaphorical' understandings for the Mehinaku do not necessarily have a sense of one thing as a copy of another but there is always the substantial sense to the metaphor. Even the most vague kinds of association are perceived in a material, often bodily way. The fact that night calls to mind the *apapanye* spirits, fear and sorcerers for the Mehinaku, is not abstract conceptualization. Although it is hard to comprehend from a Western perspective, for the Mehinaku, fear has night in its very substance, and the substance of darkness inevitably contains traces of the *apapanye*. This is because, coming back to chapter 2, everything for the Mehinaku is substantial, including emotions like fear, and even acts of perception. Therefore, not only are the links of association not understood as abstract, the act itself of perceiving these connections is not mind-bound theorization, rather it takes place as substantial process, so that feeling fear of the night is an allowing of the dangerous 'stuff' of fear into one's body; and thinking about the *apapanye* effectively draws them near.

There is even a material literality about the way associations may gather around elements of experience. In chapter 3, we saw how people/things have a haze-like locus or aura of invisible substance surrounding them, this being the residue of the activities they have been involved in, smells they are thus carrying, *apapanye* they may have attracted. In many cases, associations in general are perceived as substantially clustering in this way around the thing they are associated to, for example a rifle bought from the 'White people', apart from being understood to be a copy (and thus of the substance) of an archetypal 'Rifle-*yeya*' (the first metaphorical sense we have been discussing), the associations of power and danger to the rifle are also perceived as materially perilous presences emanating from the 'rifle-object'.

From what we have seen so far then, in the way that, for example, a psychologist might understand many elements of what she encounters – the motifs of films she sees, world events and her own dreams – as causally linked and consequences at different levels of fundamental psychological processes, so too do the Mehinaku make associations in their consciousness in their own particular way, which is pervaded by a substantial sense of the world, infused with a certain mythical logic and a view of the world as multi-dimensional.

Having explored how elements are linked in Mehinaku consciousness, I will now look at how these associations very often cluster in the pattern of 'story', *ownaki*. In general for the Mehinaku, the occurrences of life do not 'just happen'. The ways that things occur are understood to have to do with entities and forces often beyond human perception, giving a kind of meaning to events, so that they are perceived and spoken about in the form of stories. Even one's whole life is circumscribed by story, the omen of which is dreamed by one's mother. When she is pregnant, she dreams that someone gives her something and the thing she is given indicates the nature of the baby and the life it will have. For example, to dream of a jaguar means the baby will be a strong person and long-lived, or to dream of the hard white shell *yanakwimpi*, tells that the child will be beautiful. Kwakani's mother, dreamed of a small parrot called *Watapu*, which means, Kwakani told me laughing,[15] that she will die when she is still a young woman. There is a sense then, of a particular understanding of destiny, the whole story of which humans are only able to glimpse in dream.[16]

To say that the Mehinaku make associations in their lives according to a certain kind of 'story logic'[17] begs the question as to what exactly is the meaning of *ownaki*, 'story', to these people. Creation stories that we would label as 'myth', as well as stories of more recent history and also everyday events, are not differentiated among, but rather are all referred to as *ownaki*. The tales we would categorise as myth, of the *apapanye* before the creation of humans, do not have the particular aura of magic that the word 'myth' conjures in the Western imagination. For example, even the words of the most important song, the *Yamurikuma*, which tells of the women who decide to live without men and hence become the 'huntress-women'-*apapanye*, consist of the most prosaic kind of dialogue: '[O]h, so now I'm good for you,' a *Yamurikuma* woman taunts sarcastically, 'You are like a fox crying but I am happy!' This understanding also lacks the common Western designation of certain narratives as religious or fictitious allegory, these often being associated with exaggeration and 'constructed-ness'. For the Mehinaku there is not our sense of fiction as I found one day when the chief Marikawa asked where the animal on the front of my book was from. It was a Harry Potter book and the animal was a griffin. I didn't know what to answer, then finally said that the creature was not from anywhere, that it did not exist. Marikawa stared back at me for some moments, then asked, 'It is from Australia?'[18] 'No', I said, struggling for a way to explain the Western meaning for fiction that suddenly seemed foolishly pointless to me. Finally Marikawa concluded 'so, it is a lie' and satisfied with his own answer walked away.

So, how then does this story logic pattern the associations of Mehinaku experience? The Mehinaku perceive, act and explain in terms of stories. The most ordinary associations made in everyday life can be imbued with story. In narratives about *Kamë*, the Sun, we have seen that he is portrayed as persistently cunning and cruel, for example seducing *apapanye* close to him on the pretext of having a wrestling match and then turning them to stone when they come near, only to take their women, the *apapanyéshë*, to have sex with. The experience of these accounts is not contained in the narratives of their telling. My foster-sister Kwakani, vain with the beauty of her young, pale skin, would exclaim – *"aitsawëshëpai Kamë, brabo!"* 'The sun is not nice, he is wild!' – to explain why she avoided the midday sun. The associations Kwakani made with the sun and its light, her experience of it on her skin, was of the angry touch of a being she had been told about in stories.

The Mehinaku not only sense in terms of story, they explain events post facto in the form of narratives. *"Nownakitsalapitsu"*, 'I am going to tell you a story': this is how a great many conversations begin in Mehinaku, the way the events of the day might be told, confusions explained, questions answered. Sitting in the cooking house, making the *ulépé* flat bread, or waiting for fish to cook on the fire, my enquiries about various matters would be responded to in this way, story after story told to me to explain everything from a word or practice I did not understand, to the social 'goings-on' in the village. I would ask a question but it would not be answered directly, a story would begin and it would seem so unrelated that I would not at first realize that it was a less direct form of answering the question. This propensity to tell stories to explain and make sense of things is most evident in events that threaten the preferred seamless flow of daily life. One such thing occurred to me when, while cooking, I upturned a full vat of boiling oats onto my bare feet. In the days that followed the disturbing event, people would gather around and talk about what had happened to me. They would come and look at the huge blisters and ask me questions: what had I dreamed the night before it happened, what had I been thinking about immediately before? Gradually with my answers and their discussion, interpretations and reinterpretations of what had occurred began to take shape. The first version of events concerned the way the cooking tripod had not been set up adequately and the final one was that it had been an invisible *apapanye* who tipped it over. In the telling and listening to these discussions I felt the coercive pull of this story-forming tendency, as I was forced to find in the elements of my experience pieces to fit the story-form that the Mehinaku felt the need to fill. And as the narrative took its shape, I was surprised to feel myself curiously satisfied by the way the tale wrapped around the bare elements of the event, containing it with a spiritual meaning that separated it from the disruptive possibility of fault and blame on my own part or theirs.

Apart from perceiving and explaining in stories, for the Mehinaku, stories are also a kind of parable, the form for the way things are to be done. This is in keeping with the basic structural-functionalist view of myth and mythical notions as 'templates' of action, for example, in Reichel-Dolmatoff's interpretation of Desana myths wherein 'the structure of the universe […] is a great code of signals and signs that determines and guides the programming of cultural conduct' (1971: 246). In the Mehinaku case, there is a particular sense as to why and how the mythical relates to present human action. Just as we have seen the *apapanye* are archetypes from which things are copied, so too are their actions as depicted in myth/story, the original or real way things are to be done, which human action must imitate. This is evident in what we have seen in chapter 2, as one works on one's body according to the building-up method of the creator *Kwamutë* and in the image from the stories of the ravishing *Shapushënéshë* (if you are a woman) or the handsome hero *Ayanama* (if you are a man). Likewise, it is because of a story, that of *Arakuni,* that one avoids incestuous feelings, having been warned in the narrative of the horrific consequences of such sentiments and although one does not eat other mammals one does consume the black monkey, *pahër,* because one knows from the story of its creation that it was once a human baby and is therefore not dirty to eat like the other hairy animals of the forest. The *Kuarup* – the funereal rite for the Mehinaku, a ceremonial gathering of various Xinguano villages – is conducted as closely as possible to their knowledge from the story of the very first *Kuarup* that *Kamë,* the Sun, carried out for his dead wife's/ mother's soul.[19]

I will now turn to look at how elucidation of the way the Mehinaku make associations in their experience, clarifies the manner in which ritual is perceived by these people and may shed some light on one aspect of the perpetual debate that has always surrounded the subject of ritual in the field of anthropology. That aspect is the question of what ritual practice means to the people participating in it. In the case of the Mehinaku, it became the question I was most obsessed with solving during my fieldwork, and I asked it over and again in different ways, trying to find a chink in the answers that were at first impenetrable to me: what does my young friend Kwakani think/feel when we hear from outside the house the sound of a person 'playing the part' of the *apapanye Shapacuyawá?* When she points and exclaims to me – '*Shapacuyawá!',* does she somehow think it is *Shapacuyawá* himself? What does the man himself experience dressed up in the woven-palm costume and making the sounds of the spirit-creature? That is, what does 'playing the part' mean? How exactly are the palm and wooden objects related to the *apapanye* they are supposed to represent? In fact, what does 'representation' mean here?

We saw earlier that in the anthropological literature, the structuralists deign to bestow their own Western 'rational thought process' (1985: 153) on the way the 'savage mind' makes representations, maintaining that they have 'comparable intellectual application and methods of observation' (Lévi-Strauss 1966: 3). The structuralists were not the first to do this. Tylor (1958[1871]) and Frazer (1890) had already attributed the quality of rationalism to the beliefs and ritualism of the so-called 'primitive man' in the nineteenth century, finding that despite these peoples' rationality the conclusions reached were in error: 'magic as a false physics' (Wittgenstein 1979[1931]: 7). In the functionalist view of ritual, with Durkheim's (1995[1912]) seminal notion of it as providing a means for social cohesion and other ideas of function discerned by structural-functionalists and other kinds of functionalists after him, ritual is deemed as having purposes that are somehow beyond its evident ones, and which the participants are usually not even aware of. In the functionalism of the dramaturgical model that Gregor uses to analyse Mehinaku life, he writes that despite the ostensible function of curing illness, the details of rituals are self-interested responses to the dilemmas of staging roles (1977: 331). His approach negates any actual truth to the supposed intent of the ritual, maintaining that the nature of Mehinaku ritual is completely constructed, to the extent that he trivializes their rituals as akin to Western 'fads': '[A] final line of evidence suggesting that spirits, as well as the attendant ceremonies, are personal discoveries is that many of them have a faddish nature like popular songs and other ephemeral creations in our own society' (Gregor 1977: 326).

There are of course still countless other approaches in anthropology to understanding ritual but the point I want to make here is that rather than looking beyond the experience of the ritual to find functions or structuralist relations, or interpreting the experience according to any other extrinsic model (psychological, symbolic etc.), in keeping with the phenomenological approach of this book I will look to comprehend the experience according to its own terms. Moreover, I will go phenomenologically further than looking at ritual in terms of which categories are at work in consciousness. The problem with only doing this is that the Western linguistic apparatus for explanation can still be left intact. Therefore, statements such as the following are still made: 'the initiate *identifies* with the jaguar by wearing its pelt', where, for example, the word 'identifies' is not problematised in terms of how this relation actually occurs for the people concerned. Above, I have attempted to investigate how such connections are made in Mehinaku experience, and will now look to how knowledge of such first principles can be built up into a certain theory of ritual.

The most crucial question in the Mehinaku case, is how does the participant of a ritual[20] understand the manipulation of a representational object, or her or his imitation of a powerful non-human, as effective on things beyond those actions? The first aspect of the ritual experience that must be comprehended is that the Mehinaku perceive all aspects of the event, the invisible actions of *apapanye* etc., with certainty of their absolute actuality. It is in this numinous quality of ceremonial situations that Western skepticism tends to come to the fore, with its propensity to divide the 'real' or the material from the 'unreal',[21] obscuring understanding of the degree of imminence with which other people experience such phenomena. Once this attitude of the Mehinaku is fathomed, we can turn to look to how it all actually works.[22]

Thus far, in this section we have seen how in varied subtle ways, associations are not abstract but substantial for the Mehinaku. In the same sense that creatures and things are *ënai*-copies created from the substance of their 'mother/father' archetypal-*yeya,* so are human-made copies or representations understood to contain substance of the *yeya* they are copies of. The sense of identification is indicated by the way the Mehinaku call the representation by the same name as they use for the *yeya*-original, with a tacit understanding of the actual difference between the two and the way they are related. In a ritual, when a representation of an entity, for example an *apapanye,* is made, either a skin-costume *(ënai)* out of palm-leaves, or a drawing of the image of the entity *(pëtala),* the *apapanye* is drawn near to this part of itself. It is drawn close to the copy, or rather its own substance in the copy, as part of a kind of 'law of nature' in which like is drawn involuntarily to like. How does this occur? Once the ritual representation of an *apapanye* is completely made, it must make its appearance, animated by a Mehinaku person inside it who dances the *apapanye*'s movements, makes his sounds and music and talks with her or his personality, with some of them cursing and taunting the women and others whining like babies. The event of the appearance *(hekwatatuwá)* is crucial. It is not enough to simply construct the representation. The music *(nakai),* the dancing *(turukai)* and the noises and chatter *(herakai)* of the *apapanye* are just as necessarily parts of the 'stuff' that constitute the *apapanye*-copy as the woven palm costume (see Plate 16). In coming together in the *hekwatatuwá,* the complete likeness attracts the 'real' *apapanye* close and the Mehinaku understand the *apapanye* to abide inside or nearby the copy, describing the copy as a kind of *'casa'*, or 'house', for the *apapanye* (see Plate 13). The better made/performed the various aspects of the imitation-*apapanye*, the more surely the *apapanye* will come and stay happily and invisibly in the presence of the community for the proceedings. If a likeness is badly painted, or the words of a song sung incorrectly, the *apapanye* might reject its summons or in its disgust, even punish the singer with illness.

Thus once the *apapanye* has entered the midst of the village, the participants with their paint, opening their throats with the *apapanyes'* songs, believe the entities to be close, making their noises and dancing in their very midst, though imperceptible to the human senses.[23] The point of the ritual is to satiate the desires of the *apapanye,* who because dissatisfied, have turned their destructive desire on human beings. To do this, once the *apapanye* have been 'housed' as has been described, and join the Mehinaku in their joyous dancing and music-making, they need to be fed. This is achieved with food especially prepared the way the *apapanye* like it (with extra chili, salt and the usual flat bread made to a special thickness) that is given to the participants when the main ritual finishes (see Plates 14 and 15). The *apapanye* are understood to partake of this meal, consuming what humans perceive as the invisible substance of the smell *(iníya)* of the food. Having been summoned in a satisfying manner, danced, made their music and eaten their fill, the *apapanye* are joyous and contented and are thus less likely to inflict harm with their usual wanton craving on humans, with whom, at least for some time, they have established harmonious relationship.

Therefore the basis of rituals for the *apapanye* is the association between the representations made by the Mehinaku and the original *apapanye.* The link, which we have seen is substantial, is deliberately forged by the Mehinaku, a yoking of the spirit-entity close to its own matter that has been made as a lure by imitation. Similarly, Basso found that when the Kalapalo sing 'song spells', their human versions 'are weakened replicas of the originals that were first invented and used by the *itseke* (the Kalapalo word for the *apapanye*)' (1985: 70) .[24] However, she does not say how these song spells actually work, writing simply that they are 'an act of magic' (Basso 1985: 253), 'naturally creative through sound' (Basso 1985: 71). Maybury-Lewis similarly writes that for the Xavante, singing summons the strong and fierce spirits (1967: 287) but also does not tell how this occurs and Gregor (1977: 38) writes in the same way of painted objects drawing the *apapanye* close.

The details of how the process of 'copy luring original' takes place is in terms of the substantial presences in the 'clouds of association' that were discussed earlier. The interaction of different key elements in the ritual includes an interaction of the constituents of the clouds that surround each of them. For example, a young participant just emerged from seclusion, is associated with beauty and purity. For the Mehinaku these are not abstract qualities but rather a lack of unpleasant substances (purity) and the presence of pleasant substances (beauty). Most of these are insensible to humans but some are perceptible to the *apapanye* and they react strongly to them because of the nature of their own substance-associations, either adversely or positively depending on the compatibility of these substances. Similarly, the happiness associated with dancing and music-making is felt to exude from the participants invisibly but materially, and also from the *apapanye,* in this case enclosing not one part but the whole proceedings of the ritual in a palpable aura of joy that conjoins all within, a kind of medium in which the necessary interactions can take place.

Therefore the vague notion of 'mythical thinking' is here given content. The supposition in the field of anthropology, that it is a mode of perceiving that involves a 'leap of faith' or belief and a consequent lack of causal logic, is in this case shown to be inaccurate. The reason these assumptions are made is because the anthropologist does not see a link between the elements of the symbol, so takes for granted that belief in ritual action must be a leap of faith between them. Now however we have seen that for the Mehinaku there are in fact very material connections between the associations that are made and furthermore, very concrete understandings of how these work and can be worked; it was only that the anthropologist does not recognise they are there at all. In summary, there are forces in the world that the Mehinaku are aware of and we are not (the question of whether they 'actually' exist or not is not relevant here, is not in keeping with the aim of understanding their reality), and it is with the knowledge of these they make sense and act in ritual.

Ritual for the Mehinaku then, does not involve a belief in a kind of magic but rather is a way of interacting with things in a very palpable way. One aspect of this interaction that I have not yet discussed is a certain openness of attitude in the participant or observer to proceedings, a sense for them of various things going on, some of which are not in immediate awareness or able to be completely grasped, and an allowing of that. This is an example of the mode of consciousness discussed earlier in the chapter that I called 'blending of entities'. It does not contradict the proposition of logic in ritual. The Mehinaku have a definite sense of how it all works but at the same time, they are not necessarily adamant about mapping it out, in other words, there is a lack of attachment to the idea that there must be an answer found to everything perceived. This is an especially appropriate mode of thought for ritual, where the focus of the practice is on the *apapanye,* who as we have seen previously, are by nature prone to a shifting of boundary and identity.

I said that I would give here a Mehinaku theory of ritual based on how we have learned these people make associations. So far I have only looked at public rituals for the *apapanye* but the reason I have done this is that these can be seen as a 'basic unit' of ritual in which others can be understood. This is because almost all ritual for the Mehinaku has also to do with the manipulation of relationships with the *apapanye* as the embodiment of all the forces of the worlds. Other rituals, more private ones (as well as those of sorcerers and shamans which will be discussed in the next chapter), have the same basic logic and practical steps: the *apapanye* must be brought near by the creating of a substantial link and then made happy for the sake of a beneficial relationship. Let us take for example, the use of 'sacred roots' *(atatapa)* for the building-up of one's body. The substance of the root is either rubbed into opened skin or drunk in tinctures of huge volume and vomited up. This physical taking in of the root emanates a smell from the body that draws close the *apapanye* who is the 'owner of the root' *(atatapa uwekehë).* Like the making of the representation discussed earlier, the *apapanye* is lured in by the substance it recognises as its own, materially linked as they are as copy and archetype. As long as the ritualist still exudes this smell, the *apapanye* will remain around her or him, and as long as the *apapanye* is happy with the ritualist, it may bestow its special favours. For example, I was told that if the spirit of the root *puyalu* is drawn close by the consuming of the root substance by a ritualist, the *apapanye* will *'fica em volta, se cuida',* that is, 'will stay in the surrounds, taking care' of the person. The *apapanye* will appear as a woman to the ritualist in dreams, talking to her and gradually the spirit will make the body of the girl or woman bulge with lovely plumpness. If however the ritualist has sex or eats certain foods the *apapanye* dislikes, the odour of these things will so irritate the spirit – who smells it being so near – that it will leave the proximity of the ritualist and at worst punish her with illness.

It is evident here how clearly and manifestly the Mehinaku understand ritual, without mystical haziness, the forces at work known though invisible. The *apapanye* spirit is pulled in by a physical link, where it stays in the vicinity of the ritualist. The ritualist does not somehow 'become' the *apapanye* in some kind of mystical union,[25] the *apapanye* is understood to be simply 'looking on' as it stays invisibly close. What is more, the presence of the *apapanye* is so distinctly understood that it was once drawn for me in a diagram as a shaded region completely surrounding the figure of the person. This aura contains the material associations of the ritualist, which if offensive to the associations contained in the *apapanye*'s own aura, will repel the spirit-entity; the overlapping and thus interaction of the constituents of two substantial 'clouds' more chemical reaction than mystical possession. And finally the effect of the relationship thus formed is material – either of physical building up of the ritualist by the spirit, or physical harm.

III. *'Awitsiri'*: the Principle of 'Care/Grace'; Living with the Right Consciousness in a World Made Manifest by Consciousness

Having looked at the basic aspects of the nature of consciousness for the Mehinaku, the way entities occur to them and also how they are related, I will now turn to examine how these people themselves are aware of this experience. The Mehinaku in fact reflect on their own consciousness and strive towards a certain kind of it. In the last chapter certain attributes that the Mehinaku deliberately seek to cultivate in their ways of perceiving were discussed, in particular the dual aspects of the *awëshëpai* ethos, the conservative absorbing flow and the occasional exploits of the daring impulse. I will not repeat the discussion of the dynamic balance of *awëshëpai* with the qualities of tension and balance it engenders for Mehinaku experience. *Awëshëpai* we have seen, is a conception that concerns behaviour more than consciousness itself, while there is another notion that pertains directly to Mehinaku consciousness of their consciousness, one that overarches *awëshëpai*, a way of perceiving and acting I will call *awitsiri*.[26]

The word *awitsiri* was translated to me in the Portuguese as *'lindo'*, 'beautiful'. A pretty young girl painted for dancing or a finely made hammock were referred to with this word and at first I understood it to refer only to the objects themselves as an adjective, the way they would in English, and it was some time before I realized what was fully meant by the word. *Awitsiri* does not simply refer to the thing. Because of the way that consciousness is understood to manifest reality for the Mehinaku (as discussed at length in chapter 2), *awitsiri*, whilst referring to the object, also always implies the consciousness that must have manifested it. One day her aunt exclaimed about eight-year-old Ërpunaya, how beautiful was the block of manioc flour the little girl had produced all on her own. I was surprised that Mahí had used the word *awitsiri* and with such enthusiasm as it seemed an excessive compliment for such a mundane, everyday thing as flour. Later I came to realise that Mahí was referring not only to the flour itself but more importantly to the beautiful state of consciousness of little Ërpunaya that allowed her to produce such flour.

There is here the sense that the Mehinaku may determine the quality of their reality by the way they choose and are able to perceive, that is by the quality of their consciousness. This includes a kind of Mehinaku morality, whereby a beautiful appearance indicates that the person is living with the ideal character and conversely that ugliness is proof of an insalubrious disposition. This explains why in most myths the hero of the story is established at the very start by the thorough extolling of her or his beauty. One series of myths is about the *Perkaintyé*, a people now extinct who exemplify this beauty. Superior in every way, they were a kind of 'super-people' who could do everything other humans could do but far better, one of the expressions of their preeminence being their supreme beauty. Because of their beauty other peoples wanted them to join their villages and would sometimes even try to kidnap them. As described earlier a giant *miyoka* snake once came to the village of the *Perkaintyé,* and demanded a young man to eat. There was nothing to be done, no amount of arrows, nothing could stop this creature, so the chief chose one of the less good-looking of the men and he was offered and eaten. The snake came back day after day, and each time took another of the young men. When there were none of these less handsome men left, the chief decided they would all have to flee from the snake and an arrow was shot upwards becoming a ladder into the world of the sky to where they escaped.[27]

In stories of the *Perkaintyé* we see a moral logic of the natural priority of beauty, that is, beauty is primacy for the Mehinaku and for them, it is produced by a beautiful 'state of mind'. So two questions follow: what constitutes the Mehinaku aesthetic, that is the appearance of beauty one is judged on and why is it so important, and second, what do the Mehinaku believe is the kind of consciousness that produces such beauty? We have seen previously that 'things' (people, animals, plants, objects) are either copies of substantial archetypes or the archetypes themselves, with the originals as beautiful and perfect and the imitations beautiful in so much as they resemble the loveliness of the original. There is a striving then to construct copies as perfectly as possible, and the degree of the perfection of resemblance exactly equals how beautiful *(awitsiri)* they are, so that their newness and wholeness is crucial because as things age, the wear and tear will render them less like the original. The seeking to make the world in this way is not a purely superficial pursuit, because as we saw in chapter 3, the forms of the worlds are always under threat of dissolution and so the 'holding-up' of the integrity of these entities is of literally vital importance. In addition, the lovelier the forms amidst which one lives, the more pleasurable life is.[28]

Thus, what is the *awitsiri* kind of consciousness that yields and preserves *awitsiri* forms of the worlds? A crucial aspect of it is what I will call 'care'.[29] This is the 'state of mind'[30] that nurtures all things towards which its attention is turned. This careful way of thinking/doing is evident in the manner in which people generally strive to conduct themselves. Some individuals are seen to be particularly successful at achieving this active state, such as little Ërpunaya, and after a while it was apparent even to me, the calm and painstaking way certain people attended to even the smallest task.

An important part of this 'care' is the quality of attention given. Once, a young man, Maiawai, sought to teach me the importance of this way of doing things when in a hurry I was frustratedly pulling at a zip that seemed completely stuck. He stopped me and motioned for me to watch as he sat and with slow, calm deliberation attended to the task. He knew I was time-pressed and still he instructed me, *'devagar, Carla, siempre devagar'*, '...slowly Carla, always slowly'. The careful nurturing concentration is a form of the principle of child-rearing *(paparitsa)* applied to all matters in the world. It is the very opposite of the destructive effects of uncontrolled and thus rampant desire, since in *awitsiri*-consciousness, one's desires, loves, are restrained into the ultimate caring form. For example, the desire to open the zip is not allowed to go out of control as it was near to doing in me, and probably would have resulted in breaking the zip. Careful loving, attentiveness to the task on the other hand, preserves the form of the thing (Maiawai closing the bag, all parts of it still intact). Similarly, in the making of a ceramic pot, for example, nurturing attention creates the most beautiful object, whereas impatient desire will result in a flawed product. The importance of this intensive kind of 'paying attention', in fact has the tone of a 'spiritual' injunction, wherein *Kamë*, the Sun, chastises a lack of concentration by giving the negligent person an injury. I found this out one day when a man called Arako chided me for my scratched hands, cut from grating manioc, asking me whether I had been thinking about something else while I was working and laughingly scolded me that *Kamë* had punished me for this with those injuries.

One of the nurturing aspects of this 'caring' consciousness is a certain 'lightness'. In Mehinaku child-rearing, children are cared for in a comparatively less controlling manner than in the West:[31] they are allowed to go and do what they want from the time they are old enough to wander off, only casually telling their mother or other caretakers where they are going; they work from a young age but only if they choose to; and literally, when they are young they are only held with the lightest touch and as they get older, from the time they can walk properly, they are hardly touched at all. There is an expansion of this delicate conduct into the quality of consciousness. There is a sense that, as in the treatment of children, to be too attached, to grip too strongly may be damaging, that this might be the case not only for the selves of children, but also that overly strong attachment in consciousness may also be destructive to the integrity of any entity one relates to, as well as the relations between entities.

Another aspect of the *awitsiri* consciousness is that the careful attention involved intertwines one utterly with all aspects of the world(s) around. To at every moment devote complete attention to the things and creatures one encounters is to be joined in strong relationship to all those entities. White people, the Mehinaku say, do not live in an *awitsiri* way. They are not caring or attentive to the forces they share their world with, they are exploitative in their unrestrained desire, thus neglecting or utterly destroying relationships with other kinds of entities. For example, I was told that White people upstream kill too many fish-copies *(kupatë-ënai),* thus angering the archetypal fish, *kupatë-washë,* who has become so angry it now creates fewer copies, which is why there are so many fewer fish in the waters of the area these days. Although the Mehinaku constantly strive to maintain an integrity of selfhood (as we saw in the last chapter), they are able to conserve this integrity while also cultivating another kind of integration that takes place between themselves and the things that surround them. In chapter 3, the flowing dynamic characteristic of Mehinaku life was discussed, and the way it works here in the case of their intertwinement with their surroundings is that this flow means that one does not remain attached to what one perceived a moment earlier. Rather, there is an integration of self and place that shifts with the flow of consciousness. The lightness we have seen to be an aspect of this flowing integration means that, one does not attach to just one thing in consciousness, there is an expansion in this flow and more things can be experienced at once, even if only glimpsed. Also, the lightness allows the sharp, clear attention of the Mehinaku to move in this integrated flow, quickly and with utmost effectiveness.

It shall be seen in the next chapter how the consciousness of various elements, even of other realities, combined with an ability to react with extreme alacrity, benefits shamans especially, but here it will be said that even in the ordinary reality of ordinary Mehinaku individuals, there is the possibility of this flowing integration with all things that in many ways resembles the notion of 'ecstasy' usually reserved for ritual experience, and part of this, a hyper-awareness that may allow an expert negotiating of reality (or realities). This bright and light, careful, skilled, integrated 'flow-ingness' of consciousness and the ecstatic pleasure it can bring, has as its manifestation an outward appearance of gracefulness,[32] and is especially evident in certain individuals. In one old man in particular, Matawarë, before even I knew that in his time he was the best wrestler, the best archer and even still the best fishermen of the community, I was struck by some-thing about the way he moved, spoke, or did anything at all, and which, early on, I could not put my finger on. It was the concentrated *awitsiri* quality of him exteriorized as a certain gracefulness that he characterized, but with which all Mehinaku seek to live.

Having sketched out in the previous chapters the general contours of what Mehinaku experience is like, in this chapter I have looked to how the Mehinaku experience these experiences, that is, how they actually occur in their consciousness. I examined how 'things' are perceived as such by the Mehinaku and also the way that associations are made between such entities. As part of this discussion, I wrote of how these relations have a substantial sense and tend to be made with a certain 'story logic', and also how an understanding of the way these relations are made can be used to come to terms with Mehinaku ritual. Finally, it was seen how the Mehi-naku are self-conscious of their own experience and cultivate a particular quality of this consciousness that they call *awitsiri*. In the next chapter we turn to explore one last aspect of this outline of Mehinaku experience, before we come at last to use this picture in order to envisage a living in-stance of this experience, a girl's walk to the river.

Notes

1. Which is in fact very close to the ancient Greek word for 'idea', 'ίδεα' meaning 'real image' or 'visible form' (Tylor 1958: 82).
2. Interesting I believe for Western theories of the role of language in the construc-tion of reality, for example in the fields of linguistics, development psychology and philosophy.
3. Gregor writes similarly but only of ceremonial objects (1977: 38), not of things in general as I will below.

4. For the story of the creation of humans, see chapter 2.

5. It should be noted that I was told by a number of people including the 'chief' Marikawa and his wife, that the correct way to pronounce the name of their *"povo"*, their 'people', is in fact *Imihinaku* and not Mehinaku (or Mehinaco) as it has been spelt ubiquitously in the literature of the Alto Xingu. This comment was always made in pride and with an indignation that I believe was mostly about aesthetics (the prefix to the word is purely nominal and so doesn't change the meaning). I use the common word here and elsewhere so as to avoid confusion in relation to the relevant literature, only pointing it out because I was directly asked to do as much.

6. For example, Basso (1973), Fénelon Costa (1978: 1988); Gregor (1977: 1985).

7. This, I would say is also commonly the case for Western experience of activity.

8. This activity is repeatedly described in chapter 2.

9. Discussion of these practices is to be found in section II of chapter 5, as part of an exploration of Mehinaku gender issues.

10. See chapter 2, sec. I.

11. For further discussions of the issues of myth and history in Amazonia see Gow (2001) and the collection of essays in an edited volume called *Rethinking History and Myth Indigenous South American Perspectives on the Past,* edited by Jonathan D. Hill (1988).

12. Overing (1985) made this argument as part of an analysis of the nature of the relational properties of kinship categories.

13. See Jackson (1996) for a detailed explanation of the concept of the 'lived metaphor'.

14. For detail, see chapter 2, sec. IV.

15. See chapter 3, sec. VIII in regard to laughing in the face of danger.

16. See Gow (2000) on the relation between future and dreams to the Piro.

17. For excellent, detailed analyses of story/myth/narrative in the Amazon, see Basso (1995) and Gow (2001).

18. They heard about Australia often as the place where my family and I come from.

19. See chapter 2, sec. I.

20. There is not a special Mehinaku word for 'ritual' but it is used here to refer to those Mehinaku ceremonial actions or procedures that the word generally denotes in the anthropological literature.

21. See Corbin who has discussed 'Western man's "agnostic reflex"' (1972: 97) as a cultural orientation with a long history having its roots in early Western metaphysics.

22. See Basso (1985) who also discusses Kalapalo ritual as 'actually transformative'.

23. Except shamans', as we shall see, who as we have mentioned earlier and will explore fully in the next chapter, can perceive the reality of the *apapanye* and inform the community as to what the *apapanye* are doing during rituals, that is, whether they are happy, celebrating etc. or showing dissatisfaction.

24. Bracketed explanation is my own.

25. See for example Eliade (1964).

26. Gow writes of a similarly deliberate way of being for the Piro that he translates as 'thinking beautifully' (2000: 61), which is qualitatively very like the sense of *awitsiri* in its concern with beauty, albeit defined quite differently. The Piro notion of 'living well' (2000: 56) has more to do with behaviour and was compared to the similar Mehinaku concept of *awëshëpai* in the last chapter and will also be compared to the Mehinaku social ideal in the next chapter, sec. III, as will Overing's discussion of *huruhuru*, the deliberate cultivation of 'good-will', also relevant here but more related to sociality in particular. Guss (1989) writes of a very similar intentional cultivation of consciousness to that of the Mehinaku's, as shall be seen in this section in a note below.

27. Some of this story was told before, in section IV, chapter 3.

28. The importance for the Xinguanos of beautiful beings and things and the pleasure one gets from living in their midst is also mentioned in Gregor (1977) and Basso (1973: 1985).

29. Correspondingly, Guss found that Yekuana purposefully cultivate a similar kind of consciousness during activities and like the Mehinaku, see this as a way of constructing and maintaining their reality: '*towanajoni,* "the one with wisdom", approaches life accordingly. For him each task is a work of meditation, a way of being present or conscious in all that one does … [T]he ability to reconstitute the whole with every artefact, every gesture, every ritual' (1989: 170).

30. I use this turn of phrase with the common-sense meaning as it renders this Mehinaku sense of experience as a continuous quality of consciousness, but do not want to imply a mind-body separation for the Mehinaku, which as we have seen would be incorrect.

31. There will be more discussion on this subject in the next chapter as part of the analysis of Mehinaku sociality.

32. Compare to Bateson's (2000) conception of 'grace' as similarly recognisable cross-culturally (see text below of same paragraph) and also to do with kinds of 'integration'.

5

Experience of the Mehinaku Social World

We have been exploring Mehinaku lived experience so that at the end of this book we are ready to come to terms with a particular experience, one of ordinary reality, a walk to the river. Here in the final stage of this exploration we will focus on their experience of their social world. We will look at some social phenomena that have already been touched upon in the previous chapters, and it will be seen how what has been found out thus far about Mehinaku life in general helps to explain its main social aspects. I will consider the shamans *(yatama)* and sorcerers *(ipyamawékéhë)*, who stand out and apart from the rest of Mehinaku society, forming two specialized kinds of human being against which the rest of the community understand themselves as ordinary. I will then turn to explore the complex and contentious issue of gender for the Mehinaku, presenting quite a different view of the subject than has been thus far discussed in the literature of the Alto-Xingu, and of the Mehinaku in particular. Finally, I will discuss the general sociality of Mehinaku life, including the behavioural ideals, the reality of social life and the forces and institutions, political and otherwise, that help shape it.

I. In the House of the Jaguar:
Shamans and Sorcerers in Mehinaku Experience

Shamans and sorcerers play prominent parts in social life among the Mehinaku. I will explore this by looking at each of them separately and also by seeing how they are related. It shall be seen how notions explored in previous chapters, especially that of *awëshëpai,* of *awitsiri,* of ritual, of the differences between *apapanye* and humans and of the existence of multiple realities related to these different kinds of consciousness, will help to elucidate these two kinds of unusual persona.[1] First I will turn to the figure of the *yatama*,[2] the Mehinaku shaman. I will use the term 'shaman' to refer to the *yatama*, as it is a cross-cultural category that informs the reader of many of the general attributes of the Mehinaku counterpart. We shall see that the *yatama* does more or less share the crucial characteristic of the shaman as defined by Eliade, that sets her or him apart from 'other members of the collectivity', that is, the 'capacity for ecstatic experience' with the 'magico-religious universe that is thenceforth accessible to him' (1964: 107). It will also become evident that many of the other main traits outlined by Eliade are also evident in the *yatama*, such as the initiatory sickness, the obtaining of shamanic powers, some aspects of costume, symbol, myth and rite and especially the role of psychopomp, retriever of lost souls (1964). There has been much criticism of Eliade's synthesising interpretation of shamanism, as well as of other general theories of shamanism before and after (Atkinson 1992: 308).[3] I agree with assertions that the categorisation of shamanism, especially in the case of Eliade, crystallises out a context-free model (Humphrey 1994) that can homogenise and 'devitalize' ethnographic data (Geertz 1966: 39). A danger of such conceptualisations is in using them as 'ready made patterns, for which [the ethnographer] … has only to select the facts' (Shirokogoroff 1935: 57), so that what the reader learns of the people studied is only how the society concerned fits the external model being applied. As I have stated from the outset of this book, this kind of analysis runs directly counter to my aims as part of a phenomenological anthropology, where extrinsic assumptions are avoided as far as possible in an attempt to describe the subtle and profound particularities of experience that exist. Therefore, as has been done with other key terms thus far, the word 'shaman' will be used only out of the necessity for translation, as a starting point, but will then be problematised as a 'picture' is built up from 'Mehinaku first principles' and the original concept is turned and reshaped, this way and that, until it comes as close as possible to the unique sense of *yatama* that the people have themselves.

I would like to begin my discussion of the *yatama*-shamans by looking at how they are perceived by the rest of the community. The *yatama* are such outstanding figures in the social field that one is bound to come across one or talk of one shortly after arriving in the village. To White people, they are referred to as *'pajé'*, the Portuguese term for 'shaman', in a way that implies that everyone, even White people would know what a *'pajé'* is.

The crucial characteristic of the *yatama* is that they are those individuals who have established a particular kind of relationship with the *apapanye*, which affords them special powers including the ability to move between the human and *apapanye* realities and to cure illness in various ways with the help of the *apapanye*. The position of *yatama* is one of prestige, partly because of their 'richness' owing to the payments that as we shall see are made to them, together with a certain respect and awe for what the *yatama* experience and accomplish in shamanising.[4] This special status of the *yatama* is easily understood when one remembers that they are the only recourse when serious illness occurs or any other event that is held to be outside of the realm of normal human understanding. The role of the *yatama* was established at the time of creations, '*o Sol criou os* yatama', 'the Sun created the *yatama*'. The Sun, *Kamë*, also created all the different illnesses that exist. The story goes that *Kamë* gave himself an illness and it was three *apapanye* that managed to remove the sickness, becoming the archetypal shamans with whose help all human shamans are able to heal with their hands and mouths. These are *Yulá* and two bird-*apapanye*, *Tsekyatëshu* and the very small bird *Itsuku*. In the initiation process of the shaman, these *apapanye* are understood to each place an invisible stone, one in each of the shaman's hands and one in the throat, in this way remaining present[5] in the shaman's body, enabling him or her to heal with the hands and mouth. The start of the process of becoming a *yatama* is very much in accord with Eliade's shamanic model, with the individual suffering an illness caused by soul loss. Monaím, the eminent *yatama* of the Mehinaku village, fell ill when he was twenty- or so years-old and none of the local shamans could help him. A great *yatama* from the neighbouring Yawalapiti community was called and he found that the *apapanye-Ahira*, the Hummingbird, had taken Monaím's soul so as to make of him a great shaman. After this, Monaím underwent a rigorous and years long instruction/transformation into a *yatama* with the Yawalapiti shaman. This development[6] involves long periods of seclusion, abstinence from sexual relations and the consumption of certain foods, and the imbibing of certain roots, *akukutë* in particular, known as 'the root of the shaman'. The novice-*yatama* learns to smoke the tobacco of the shamans' cigars and is instructed (in return for massive payment)[7] in the various aspects of the *yatama*'s knowledge, such as the intricate healing songs.

However, as I have mentioned, the crucial part of becoming and being a *yatama* is one's relationship with the *apapanye* spirits, especially with the particular *apapanye* who chose the individual. The defining characteristic of being a *yatama* is one's ability to enter the reality of the *apapanye*, to conduct oneself there according to a healing or otherwise helpful purpose and to be able to return to human reality unharmed. To do this one must know how to relate to the *apapanye* and one also needs the direct help of one or more specific *apapanye.* Therefore, to learn how to do this, during the initiatory period the apprentice-*yatama* is often in contact with the *apapanye,* seeing and communicating with it in dreams and when she or he smokes. There can be a number of 'helper' *apapanye* for one *yatama,* but there is always one special one, usually the *apapanye* who chose/called the *yatama* in the first place (causing the initiatory illness), accompanying the *yatama* invisibly everywhere she or he goes. It is by this special *apapanye* that the *yatama* is identified in the community, so that in the Mehinaku village there is for example the Hummingbird *(Ahira)* Shaman, and the Black Monkey *(Pahër)* Shaman, to name just two of the seven or so *yatama* of the community. Once the initiate is a 'fully-fledged' *yatama,* it is with the special *apapanye*'s assistance that he or she is able to perform the most important of shamanising tasks, the fetching back of a human soul stolen by other *apapanye* (loss of soul being the main cause of all illness). The 'helper-spirit' also assists the *yatama* to do other things such as search for missing items and as we shall see, detecting and dealing with signs of sorcery. The way the *yatama* might appear to an outsider is either dramatically bizarre (as in the grunting, seemingly possessed state of trance the *yatama* enters when intoxicated by cigars and in communication with the *apapanye*) or as normal (if a little aloof) as any other member of the community. However, to ordinary Mehinaku people, the *yatama* are not normal at all, since, although they cannot see them, they imagine surrounding these figures at all times the entities that accompany the *yatama,* so that each *yatama* is envisaged as walking in a haze of the roiling forces of *apapanye.*

I will now turn from exploring the ordinary Mehinaku person's view of the *yatama,* to the experience of shamanising for the *yatama* her or himself. I spoke to all of the shamans of the village but the most detailed, revelatory information came from the most renowned *yatama* of the community, and perhaps of all the Alto-Xingu, Monaím (see Plate 16). One of the first things he told me was in fact about the experience of becoming a shaman not for himself, but for his mother Kaití.[8] She who, according to the Mehinaku, was the greatest of *yatama* in the Upper Xingu, had her first contact with the *apapanye* as a young woman. She had been out in the orchard alone when the Spirit of the Great Snake, *Uíkyuma,* came to her and led her into the forest. Accounts of the initiatory illness of shamans usually tell of the loss of soul and the accompanying illness of the physical

Plate 16. The shaman (*yatama*) Monaím.

body. In Monaím's description of this event, one also gets a sense of what the experience of soul loss is like for the neophyte shaman. He explains: 'Your body becomes like wind, disappears and you fly with the spirit up into the tops of the trees.' That is, the sensation of the flesh-body, the *umënupiri,* is left behind as the consciousness of the *yakulai*-soul flies up and outwards, to the tops of trees that is the location of many of the houses of the *apapanye* in their parallel reality. The young Kaití disappeared into the forest for three days, during which time 'she dreams and dreams of the *apapanye*'. We have seen in chapter 2 that dreaming involves the movement of the soul *(yewekui)* into another reality, in which one may encounter the *apapanye*. And this is where she stays for these days, being cared for by the *apapanye* in its house and meeting others who live in its village.

The experienced *yatama* can spontaneously enter the world of the *apapanye,* as during their first experience, but can also do so again and again at will by smoking their special cigars of wild tobacco. Unlike the first time, the soul of the *yatama* does not need to travel away from the body. He or she learns to maintain an integrated self, the flesh-body moving wherever the soul *(yakulai)* perspective moves and in this way the shaman appears in both realities at once. The *yatama* learns to manipulate the parts of her or his self in this way by the use of tobacco. The smoke is understood to warm the body to the hotly desirous state of consciousness of the *apapanye* (who smoke all the time instead of eating), thus bringing them into the same perspectival world.[9] Once the *yatama* will be able to see and communicate with the *apapanye,* she or he calls to the companion-*apapanye* with song[10] to get the advice and help needed. Therefore, it is not that the *yatama* become possessed[11] when they are intoxicated by the smoke, rather, they are simply talking with the *apapanye* whom they can see but others cannot. In the most serious case of the illness by soul loss, the *yatama* in his or her smoke-trance runs into the forest which is where the villages of the *apapanye* are located, and is led by his or her spirit-companion to where the soul of the patient is being kept. It is usually held in the house of one or other *apapanye,* and the *yatama,* with the help of his *apapanye*-friend, will try to negotiate or even steal the human soul and brings it back to the patient. While in the *apapanye*-reality, the *yatama* can also locate the arrows sent and bundles made and buried by sorcerers, which may also be an alternative cause of illness (as we shall see below). In addition they can simply find lost objects with the aid of their omniscient *apapanye*-companion.[12]

The experiences of the *yatama* described above involve the Mehinaku ethos of *awëshëpai* and the overarching principle of *awitsiri,* except that these qualities are even more necessary and enhanced in the *yatama,* their possibilities more fully exploited. *Awëshëpai,* with its concern for the integrity of self and the aspects of one's world are of exaggerated importance for the *yatama.* She or he actively battles for the continuity of the human world, most significantly the human soul, against the pulls of the *apapanye,* and whilst doing this must resist extraordinary strain on the wholeness of their own selves. The risks that must be taken to achieve these things, require even more than those usually necessary for the 'daring principle' of *awëshëpai,* submerging themselves not for moments but profoundly and for lengths of time in the worlds beyond the skins of their own world, so that the *yatama* may even begin to find that during a normal day, her or his perspective may shift inadvertently between realities. Also, the *yatama* exaggerate their ability to live in an *awitsiri* way, as the lightness of this principle of 'integrated flow with all things' allows an expansion of consciousness that gives greater awareness of aspects of the different realities, and also bestows a heightened alacrity to this richer consciousness, whereby the perspective is able to move far more effectively and in ways not possible for ordinary people.

There is another group of people that stand apart in Mehinaku society and they are the *ipyamawékéhë*, best translated as 'the sorcerers'. Although the category of 'sorcerer' is not as controversial as that of 'shamanism', for the same reasons as in my discussion of the latter category, I should state that I do not use the term definitively but rather as a necessary starting point for conveying a Mehinaku idea, that shares only some qualities of the universalising English word. The notion of the sorcerer as possessing 'magical' powers usually used for malevolent ends is generally relevant to the Mehinaku concept, but here magic is not about achieving impossible feats but rather extraordinary feats that as we shall see are possible and comprehensible according to the Mehinaku understanding of their worlds.

The extraordinariness of the *ipyamawékéhë* derives, like that of the *yatama,* from the *apapanye.* However, whereas the *yatama* maintain their human identity while establishing relationships with the *apapanye*, the *ipyamawékéhë* in a sense identify with the *apapanye* while relating with and masquerading as humans. In fact, as was mentioned in the last chapter, there is a blending of categories between those of the *apapanye* and the *ipyamawékéhë,* such that they can sometimes even be mutually identifiable. The *yatama* master the techniques of their calling but the *ipyamawékéhë* inherit their identity, born into certain families who have a continuous line back to the time of creation. Stories tell of how the 'things' *(yakawaka)* of the *ipyamawékéhë* were bestowed upon their male hereditary lines by either the Sun *(Kamë)* or the *apapanye-Ateshua.* This was mentioned in chapter 2 where it was described how, in a hole in the ground that is called 'House of the Jaguar', an *ipyamawékéhë* keeps these things, most importantly his 'skins' of animals (mostly of different jaguars), which he puts on to wander unrecognised and do his business.

This ability to change *'capas'* or skins, a definitive characteristic of the *apapanye,* is therefore also possessed by the *ipyamawékéhë.* There are numerous other attributes that also associate sorcerers with *apapanye* beings or show that they are simply these beings in disguise. For example, it is said that like the *apapanye*, the *ipyamawékéhë* are always hot,[13] heated with the wild passions of the *apapanye* perspectival reality, unlike the *yatama* who must smoke to temporarily attain this perspective. The consequent awareness of two realities at once means also that, like the *apapanye,* the *ipyamawékéhë* are understood to be more or less omniscient. As we shall see in section III, the effect of this is that the *ipyamawékéhë* exert a kind of surveillance power over the community, even punishing those who have erred by Mehinaku standards, for example those who have stolen something, or women who have looked on the *kawëka* flutes.[14]

Their motivation for doing this is not moral. The impetus for all actions of the *ipyamawékéhë* is malevolence. The *ipyamawékéhë* will harm people for reasons such as if they are sexual rejected by a young girl (this is very common) and often for no discernible reason at all. The *ipyamawékéhë* hurt others in two main ways, either by tiny invisible arrows *(kaukí)* that they shoot at people from hiding places in the brush or by making the *ipyama* bundles. The deadly *kaukí* must be removed from the patient's body by the *yatama* who, with the help of their *apapanye*-companion, can sense and remove them, with their hands or by sucking. These bundles are made with a scrap of anything related to the victim: a hair, nail, a fish bone spat out, a strand of their *uluri* belt. The bundle is buried in the ground and the tightness of the way it is bound affects the body of the victim, so that she or he feels like some part of the body, most commonly the head, is being squeezed. The result of the illness is inevitably death, unless a *yatama* finds the bundle in time, defusing its power by throwing it in the river. The fear every person (even the *yatama*) has of such sorcery is extreme and I found that it preoccupies the Mehinaku a great deal. However, an outsider would never know, perhaps never find out about the *ipyamawékéhë* at all, as they are hardly spoken of so as not to draw their cruel attention to oneself. The details of which individuals of the community are *ipyamawékéhë* and what they do, are only whispered amongst people that one trusts, in fact I never even heard mention of them for the whole first phase of my fieldwork. However, if enough attacks occur, and a large consensus grows as to the identity of the perpetrator, it may be agreed that he be discreetly killed. This occurs extremely rarely (perhaps once every twenty or so years), with the trauma of such a violent act (which we have seen previously, is so abhorrent to the Mehinaku), affecting the community for a long time afterwards.

II. Paths through the *Akãi* Groves:
Some Ideas about Mehinaku Experiences of Gender

In this section the aspect of Mehinaku sociality that will be examined is that of relations between men and women. This is a rather contentious matter in studies of the Xingu, with the seeming disparity between the violence associated with the sacred flutes and the peacefulness that is supposedly characteristic of the people of the area, as well as issues of anxiety that Gregor (1985) has claimed mark Mehinaku interactions between the sexes. Although the findings I will present are quite different to the literature on the subject of gender in the Xingu and the Amazon in general, I will engage with others' work only in notes, in keeping with my approach throughout of avoiding lengthy discussions that deviate from my prime purpose of phenomenological description. First there will be an explanation of the extent to which I found the different sexes are understood to be substantially different, defining the nature of interactions between them. We will then see how the two most important mythical stories for the Mehinaku may be used as a starting point to elucidate the way the Mehinaku themselves experience the interaction between the sexes, that is, not the way it has been written about, as a dynamic across a gender divide that is fraught with misogynistic aggression and anxieties, but rather a differentiation that allows an intricate and creative tension and interplay of a world sustaining nature.

Unlike in the West where the two genders of humanity, though possessing different specific features, are understood to be of the same 'species' and thus of the same kind of flesh and blood, for the Mehinaku, women *(tinéshu)* and men *(énéshu)* are believed to be radically different in their very material make-up, so that the sexes, though sharing the same consensus reality,[15] are understood to be two utterly different kinds of being.[16] As discussed in chapter 2, men and women were created at different times, for different reasons, by different entities. The first women were made by *Kwamutë* in the image of his own daughters, the *Apapanyéshë*, and were called the *Uméneshë* for the reason that the main part of their bodies was made from the *umé* tree, with the rest of their bodies made up from various other materials. The first men on the other hand, were made much later by the Sun and the Moon, their bodies made from arrows. Although the bodies of women and men are constituted by some of the same substances, such as the manioc and fish they both eat, apart from these, as described previously,[17] the bodies of men and women today, as in the time of their creation, are of fundamentally different materials and continue to be constructed with the use of various found substances, these being highly gender-specific.

Therefore the interactions between men and women are understood as the coming into contact of different substances with varying effects.[18] The transfer of matter involved in sexual relations can be beneficial in the creation of offspring, however the same act also involves a depleting of one's own substances and contact with foreign (those of the other sex) ones that threaten the integrity of one's bodily constitution. For example, by embracing a woman, the milk scent *(iníya)* ever present on her chest enters the man and will weaken him if he does not wash it off in time with neutralising water. Alternatively, semen from sexual intercourse is understood to inhibit the growth of a young woman in seclusion. We saw in chapter 2, that these interactions may even occur at a distance, with for instance the smell of a menstruating woman's blood thought to affect the growth of a secluded youth. Consequently, 'romance' is tempered with a necessary pragmatic concern with the exchange of substances and self-preservation. Even excessive emotions of love and passion, as we have seen, are dangerous to one's bodily integrity.[19] On the other hand, men and women carefully living together, in their production of fish and manioc respectively, as well as the other gender-specific products,[20] are perceived as a necessary complementarity for material daily life. The subsequent necessity of marriage for all Mehinaku adults was thus explained to me by chief Marikawa in terms of absolute physical need: *'Quando nao tem mulher, soffre,'* 'without a wife, one suffers.'

The substantial differences and exchanges between men and women are part of an intricate interaction of vital societal dimensions. A way to begin to comprehend the crucial aspects of the relationship is to explore the two most important Mehinaku myths,[21] that of *Yamurikuma* and *Yakashukuma,* and also the phenomenon of the sacred flutes, the *Kawëka,* whose origin is depicted in the latter story. Both these narratives have been mentioned in earlier chapters but I will repeat them here in more detail because of the importance in which the Mehinaku hold them, and for the sake of their revelatory quality for the explanation to come.

In the story of *Yamurikuma,* all the men have gone on a fishing trip together and they are gone so long, one young boy is sent to find out if there is anything wrong. When he arrives at the fishing camp, his father hears him coming and quickly hides the full basket of fish he holds between the trees and pulls out the hair that has already begun to grow all over his body. For the men have decided to stay and become beasts, *apapanye,* not to return to the village, and to eat all the fish they catch themselves instead of sharing it with their families. The boy sees his father and though the man tries to act normally, the boy can see the remains of fur on his father's body and catches sight of the rest of the men covered with fur and acting like animals. The boy runs away and finds the fish his father has hidden and taking the basket returns home to tell his mother what has occurred. She cooks the fish, makes manioc bread and brings it to the centre of the village. She calls all the other women to join her there and discuss what has occurred. They decide they will learn to live without the men and they dress themselves up to celebrate, also putting on the men's adornments that have been left behind, their belts, arm bands and feathered headdresses.

Then the women dance and dance without stopping for five days and the men far off hear them and return, watching them from a little way off. The mother of the boy sings *kamata pirari*, a song of humorous scorn for her husband: 'You left and I am happy, now it is you who is crying like a fox,' *'neketepemënapai, awayulu nurituani.'* The song goes on, taunting in this way. The men look at how beautiful the women are, all painted and adorned, dancing and singing and want them back, want to return to their life in the village, and go to offer the women their great baskets of fish. But the women will have none of it and with the help of an anteater, dig a tunnel through which they escape from the men to set up another village without them. Again and again the men eventually find them and each time the women escape deeper and deeper into the forest. And somewhere out there they are understood to still live, a village of women, now immortal, the *Yamurikuma*, hunting and fishing for themselves and making manioc and everything else they need.

The other story tells of *Yakashukuma*, the Alligator *apapanye* and the two sisters who fall in love with him when they see him stepping out of his animal-skin as a beautiful young man by the bank of a river. They call to him: *'Yakashukumaaaaa, awainkaritsawaka'*, '*Yakashukuma*, come and have sex with us,' every teller of this story emphasising this refrain, calling it out in the same melodic, drawn-out way. Each sister has their turn with him and then they go home in great happiness. Every day they return to the same spot, painted and decorated with beads and *uluri*, bringing food spicy with chili they know *apapanye* like and then he eats and each have sex with him. This continues until their husband finds out and the men secretly plan to murder the *apapanye*. They hide in the brush and watch, the husband included, as the women have sex with *Yakashukuma*. When the *apapanye* is lying exhausted from his exertions, the men attack and kill him, hacking him apart. Later, the women secretly return to their lover's remains and bury them. A moon or so after they return to the burial site to find that a small tree is growing there which they realise has come from the body of *Yakashukuma*. They return time and again and the tree grows, eventually issuing fruit, the first *'pequi,'* or *akāi* as it is called in Mehinaku, the most cherished foodstuff of the Xinguanos. Like in the previous story of *Yamurikuma*, the women take the fruit and leave to set up another settlement, the other women of their village coming with them. There they live happily without the men, eating *akāi* and playing large flutes called the *kawëka*. The men come looking for them and when they see what the women are doing, they desire the fruit and decide to steal the flutes from the women. This they succeed in doing by storming the village and swinging the bullroarers *(matapu)* so that the frightened women drop the flutes and run to close themselves in the houses.

These two narratives condense in many ways the dynamic between women, men and the forces of the world, that is, the *apapanye*. There are two main aspects of this dynamic, or stages, as it were. The first stage is one of blissful harmony of women with their environment (that is the *apapanye*). This occurs in the *Yamurikuma* with women finding themselves happy to live in the world, which provides for them without any need of men. In the story of *Yakashukuma*, this joining with the powers of the environment, again to the exclusion of the men, takes place as, literally, an ecstatic (sexual) union. In the second stage, the men must seize, with all the mischievous forcefulness of the dynamic of daring,[22] the fruit of beneficial life between humans and *apapanye*, the transformed bodies of the *apapanye* – the *akāi* and the *kawëka*. They must take these things and make them their own, keep the *apapanye* from the women and keep the women in the houses, if they are to be part of it at all and not left out in the cold, unneeded, half-human-half beast, far from the village hearths the women enjoy by themselves. This is how the men establish what becomes the ongoing world structure for human beings. Therefore, maintaining this configuration – which we saw in chapter 3 is always a concern – is about keeping the flutes stolen, preserving the separateness and thus necessary tension that sustains Mehinaku society as we know it. This is the essential significance of the *kawëka* flutes to the Mehinaku which, far from signifying a socially enshrined brutal subjugation of women as generally inferior, are things of beauty to the Mehinaku, associated as they are with a sweetly illicit, passionate love affair. And the fact that the *kawëka* are now possessed by the men is not an indication of their superior power[23] but instead a state of affairs, rather poignant with the tragedy that an ecstatically unified world must be ruptured to create and sustain the normal Mehinaku world.

And it is important to note that Mehinaku men themselves perceive the *kawëka* in this way, that they keep them unfairly from the women and they themselves will say to you that women are their 'true owners' *(uwekehë-washë)*. The men maintain their hold on the flutes with one main threat. The consequence of seeing the *kawëka* for a woman is rape by every man of the village.[24] It is by intimidating the women in this way that the men see themselves as enforcing their hold over the sacred instruments, even though it is carried out so rarely that no one was sure when it last happened (perhaps twenty or so years ago was an estimate told to me). Still, the women are very careful to avoid any sighting of the *kawëka*, locking themselves inside the houses when they are played and will not even go close to the walls. Men feel differently about this state of affairs, some pitying the victims of the sanction, others happily smug about it. To reiterate, men do not see themselves as simply superior and dominant over women, rather they have at some point managed to take hold, mischievously, of what is not rightly theirs. In fact, what is clear in both the *Yakashukuma* and the *Yamurikuma* is that the women are in fact the 'true-humans', sharing and caring for one another and powerfully so, while the men are not as strong and are swayed by greed, desire and violence, tending toward wildness such that they may even become *apapanye*.[25] In both narratives, the women do not need men and finally leave to set up a village without them, and in both stories the men find they cannot live without women. In *Yakashukuma* the men have to actually force themselves into women's lives, with the *Yamurikuma* story serving as a warning that if they do not, then the women will continue human life without them. In short, the essential plots of the two most important Mehinaku myths portray how, though women are human, men need to strive to be human and cannot be without women.[26]

These aspects of the relationship between men and women are evident in both ritual and everyday life. The particular articulation of separation between the sexes is played out in every kind of ritual, with men and women performing distinctly different roles. As we saw in the previous chapter, in ritual the *apapanye* are brought into the presence of the Mehinaku by use of imitations of them. In music and dancing the relationship between humans and the *apapanye* is acted out in a way that brings it as close as possible to an ideal harmony, with the women acting as the human part of the interaction. As established in the mythical narratives, the men must insert themselves in the midst of the interplay that then occurs between the *apapanye* and the women, which they would otherwise be excluded from, by acting as the representatives of the *apapanye*. In the different music-making/dancing that occurs for each of the various *apapanye*, the men usually perform the part of the *apapanye*, while the women dance as the human characters of a story (such as in the *uwéshë* dance, see Plate 17),[27] or act as the human audience to the antics of a menagerie of *apapanye* who 'appear', '*hekwatatuwa*', to the human women.

In everyday life, the physically, substantially differentiated sexes, to a large extent also live distinctly separated lives. The strongest relations between different gendered individuals are those between family members, which are of extreme closeness and love, but are always understood to be associations between essentially different beings who are supposed to lead

Plate 17. Women and men dance opposite each other in the *uwéshë* dance.

almost completely discrete lives. The division of labour is very clear, with women producing the manioc products, cooking and fetching water, and men fishing and hunting, tending the manioc gardens and building houses etc. Generally one also sees the way that males and females are not only different in substance and activity but also in general behaviour. The position of women as proudly, alluringly self-sufficient is not only a mythical theme, but in fact is very much the way Mehinaku women are.[28] As mentioned earlier, they will spend hours painting and adorning themselves for no specific reason, after which they haughtily, often teasingly flaunt their beauty to the men and each other. The men are also proud and do much the same thing, although as in the myths, there is often a noticeable insecurity about whether their attempts at being desirable will be successful. This tension is commonly articulated in affection,[29] or even attachment and a flirting joking framework with a particular repertoire of bawdy motifs that is so rich it deserves a study of its own. The humour then is one kind of expression of the tension between the genders, as there is another very different kind as we have seen, in the aggressive impulses that have their extreme articulation in the threat of rape by men and the pride and the acerbic anger of women: there are these and many other possibilities. It becomes evident how the dynamic, first occurring in mythical time – of the taking of the flutes and thus the sustaining of world order – is not only played out in ritual, but takes place in everyday situations in the variously toned expressions of the individual personalities of the male and female members of the community. From the sexual encounters that take place in the *akãi* groves, to the centre of the village, there is still resonating that which first occurred in those groves – the call of the flutes.

III. The Owl and the Toucan:
General Tendencies of Mehinaku Sociality

In the course of this book thus far, general aspects of Mehinaku social life have been touched on, however in this section I will focus on this subject. In the following we will see how certain principles of individual experience that we have already discussed work in interpersonal interactions and we will also look at some phenomena that are almost entirely of a social nature.

I would like to begin with the most basic question of how a Mehinaku person 'feels' other people, that sense of others that one has which is usually taken for granted, the primordial sense of interaction that is not necessarily conceptualised. There is an intense closeness of social life for the Mehinaku. In the houses, extended families of ten to fifteen or so people live in a space without walls, moving quite[30] freely between the hammocks, so that there is very little spatial privacy at all. Retreating to my hammock, I found that people might suddenly appear above its rim and that this behaviour was not reserved for me. In fact in the village one is almost always with others, usually even going to the river or to defecate with others, and as a woman one almost always works in the orchards with others, though there is some solitude for the hunter or fisherman who may choose to go out alone. This sense of almost never being alone, the familiar warmth and love of closest family[31] always nearby, is for the Mehinaku felt to be a sort of natural state of affairs.

To be alone on the other hand, is dangerous, a laying of oneself bare to attack by *apapanye*, who also recognise solitude as unnatural and try in their own way (deadly for the human, resulting as it does in soul-loss) to comfort the lonely person. When I once wanted to stay behind in the house when the family were to leave for a fishing trip for some days, they were afraid for me, saying that by my being alone, the *apapanye* would be drawn to me there. Even for a man, to go into the towns outside the Xingu reserve is an unashamedly fearsome and lonely affair. This constant proximity of others does not cause friction because of the flowing dynamic that as we saw in chapter 3 characterises Mehinaku life, absorbing small frictions and also greater conflicts. Certain social customs enshrine this principle, such as the way newly married people avoid direct talk with their in-laws for at least the first few years of marriage. There is also an individuality, a strong discreteness of character that means that even though the Mehinaku crave close company, there is a natural space given to others in respect for these personal boundaries that curtails extreme invasions of others' senses of self. Also, the constancy of the concentric boundaries of the spaces of the landscape, as discussed in chapter 2, lends a clarity that delimits social fields, preventing confusions.

Apart from the basic expectation that others will maintain the standards of 'humanness' described in chapter 2 (non-violence, sharing, no incest, stealing etc.), the Mehinaku also conceptualise an ideal kind of sociality.[32] This standard, or principle of behaviour to which people aspire, is called 'ketepepei'. It is characterised especially by the generosity[33] of a person, and always men and women would explain this quality in the following way to me: as a person who welcomes you and will immediately offer you the *uwitsikyuwi* drink or even food when you come into her or his house. Also a *ketepepei* person has a joyful and gentle comportment as opposed to a harsh and aggressive one. These virtues, the closest thing to what might be called a Mehinaku 'morality', are reminiscent of some of the attributes also quasi-moral in character that were discussed in chapter 3 in regard to the concept of *awëshëpai*, and in chapter 4 in regard to the idea of *awitsiri*. The crucial differences between these conceptions being that whereas *ketepepei* describes behaviour, *awëshëpai* concerns a state of affairs of person and situation, while *awitsiri* pertains to a quality of conscious being, with all of these as mutually conducive.

The sense of joy in the notion of *ketepepei* also includes an element of playful originality. Within the ideal limits set by the standards of the *apapanye* as archetypes, that as we have seen both men and women seek to incarnate, the Mehinaku prize and desire to stand out for individual, original qualities. In seclusion, it is up to individuals how they develop their bodies, what qualities they especially want to enhance (strength, beauty, knowledge of stories), the young person her or himself deciding at what point to leave their isolation. As adults, people are admired and discussed in terms of their special attributes, as great wrestlers, beauties, industrious workers and funny-men. To be *ketepepei* can imply these kinds of particularity of character that are enjoyed and commented on by others, especially inventive humour,[34] people in each other's *ketepepei*-company bantering back and forth amidst much laughter.

There is a mythical story that has distinctly allegorical[35] qualities, the two main characters embodying the two extreme departures from being a *ketepepei* person. This tale of the 'ugly bird' *Mulukuhë,* a kind of night-owl and the beautiful Toucan, *Yakawakuwa,* was already recounted in chapter 3 to portray the way that the dynamic of daring works, so here I will only highlight the pertinent points in the story. What happens to the Owl, tricked out of his lovely new wife by the cunning Toucan, warns of the dangers of being gullibly dull-witted and ugly. One part of the narrative tells how, once he is back home, out of shame *Mulukuhë* hides the fact of the absence of his wife from his family, concealing himself behind a barrier at one end of the house, pretending he is the wife, making womanish voices and producing women's products – hammocks and manioc that he hands across the partition. When he is found out, he is so repulsive to his family that he is exiled forever. The Toucan on the other hand, goes too far in his brazen confidence and takes a dangerous arrow he has been forbidden to take by his new father-in-law, the Eagle *(Gerpushë),* but is found out and must also leave forever. In each of the personalities there is a warning of the kind of social behaviour intolerable to the Mehinaku: the timid, fearfulness of *Mulukuhë,* cutting himself off from the group, and in his repulsively secretive behaviour conducting practices not appropriate to his sex; *Yakawakuwa,* on the other hand, is admirably upbeat and daring in disposition, but goes too far in his boldness, contravening respect for other individuals, their wishes and possessions. In both cases great deviance from the desirable social conduct is punished with exile from the group, with such consequences, as for the characters of the story – and as in the cautionary tale of incest discussed in chapter 3 – still operating as an implied threat for deviance from social norms, negating the need for any formal castigation.

However, although the ideal of *ketepepei* is generally lived out, the reality of Mehinaku life is also undercut by some of the opposite kind of intention and behaviour. Beneath the appearance of jolly camaraderie, greed, envy, anger and fear may grip the members of the Mehinaku community. Generosity is the first quality extolled as *ketepepei* but Mehinaku people can be loathe to share food.[36] Likewise, until I eventually got used to it, I was shocked by the things some people would whisper to me about others they seemed very close to, and had even just been very friendly *(ketepepei)* with. In fact, complimentary things are rarely said about someone not part of one's nuclear family. Apart from some people talking badly of and laughing at the ugliness, weaknesses and age of others, there were also sorcery, and more rarely bashing, rape, and murder allegations. At one point I realised that a man from every single house had been accused of sorcery to me.

Similarly, although social relations between Xinguano groups is of markedly jovial pacificity, it is also often constituted by an underlying, strong,

xenophobic antagonism.[37] I use the word 'peoples', because it conveys the
sense the Mehinaku have of the different groups. When the Mehinaku
want to speak of the other communities in the area, they do not have a
word for them all as a totality, instead they name every individual group.
The differences between them are understood to be of an essential kind, of
history,[38] physical and social characteristics, which are felt and expressed
in antipathetic general statements like: 'The Yawalapiti are full of sorcerers,' 'The Kalapalo are violent' and 'The Aweti and their language are ugly.'
There is a common belief that the Mehinaku should marry within and not
with the other peoples. In the event that the latter occurs, and a man or
woman from another group marries and comes to live in the Mehinaku
village, people have no compunction, in fact it is vaguely traditional, to
torment the newcomer with cruel taunts and exclusion, even discussions
of murdering him or her, and they expect the same treatment by other
groups in the reverse situation. Former lovers of the individual marrying
an outsider, are especially cruel, one woman telling me that she had slung
mud at a Waurá girl when she had found her bathing alone. The 'foreign-
ers' will never be absorbed completely into being a 'Mehinaku', but will be
distinguished as outsiders for the rest of their lives.

Therefore, there is a striving towards *ketepepei,* and the general impression of social life portrays this: gentle talk and behaviour, much laughter,
food changing hands and a respect for other people's individual choice.
And there is much genuine graciousness, generosity, and respect for the
desires of individuals. However, beneath the apparent social atmosphere,[39]
there is also fear, anger and hatred felt and expressed in less obvious ways.
In the discussion of *awëshëpai* in chapter 3, it was explained how fear and
resentments are struggled against for the sake of conserving a flowing,
harmonious 'state of reality (or realities)' and here we see how this struggle
occurs socially. As in the more general maintaining of an *awëshëpai* state
of things, to be *ketepepei* is to live on a knife-edge, in the latter case, to
be constantly attempting to act out a specifically social ideal while feeling
and being aware that often something very different is going on. *Ketepepei* is a struggle to uphold social humanness under the constant threat of
becoming bestial, as the story of the *Yamurikuma* so vividly warns of. The
notion of sincerity is not really an issue then for the Mehinaku. As in the
discussion about *awëshëpai,* one even pretends the ideal if necessary so
as to come closer to it, as part of what amounts to a battle to maintain
the Mehinaku way of life from anti-social vagaries of its own people and
even oneself, a battle which, to Mehinaku people's credit, is almost always
won.

Apart from some very general ideals about how to perceive, be and behave in the world – that is *awitsiri, awëshëpai* and *ketepepei* respectively – the Mehinaku do not possess an abstract 'moral code' as such. We have seen thus far how these general principles deter and contain the 'darknesses' of life, not in a systematic way but by individuals in their individual ways,[40] these interacting and balancing into what is an acceptable social atmosphere. Also, this occurs without recourse to any centralised controlling body that might judge and administer punishments. There are however some saliences and institutions of sorts in the Mehinaku social world that, overarched by the three ideals, conserve its shape.

The basic articulation of social relations – apart from the principles that have been discussed and the basic likes and dislikes between individuals – is given form by a kinship and affinal system[41] that is loosely defined and highly negotiable,[42] related to constant trading, ceremonial interaction and intermarriage extending throughout the villages of the Upper Xingu.[43] Overarching this locally is the closest phenomenon to a kind of government for the Mehinaku, the existence of *amunão*, which might be translated into English as 'chiefs', although it shall be seen that the usual connotations of the latter term, of a 'Big Man' with much power and prestige, are somewhat misleading in the Mehinaku case. There are a number of chiefs for the Mehinaku, all of them called by the same name, *amunão*. There is usually one main chief[44] for the men and one for the women, each overseeing the goings-on in the village. These roles are generally inherited and then there are six or seven chiefs who are the leaders *('liderança')* of different aspects of life. The *amunão* do not hold any special privileges of wealth or respect and they do not ultimately control or command others in their group, but rather loosely instigate action,[45] supervising, but without any overriding authority in making decisions. They are expected to set an example in the way they live.

Apart from these very vague responsibilities and expectations, the nature of leadership is almost completely determined by the personalities of the individuals. And no matter how personally powerful the *amunão*, they never have direct control of the rest of the community. This means that the way things eventually *come to happen* is that people react to a situation, come to decisions, as individuals acting alone, and informally influence others by their actions and suggestions, so that a group consensus is reached in a flowing, piecemeal fashion, without it being really possible to tell exactly how it occurred. Social pressure plays a part in this dynamic, as it also does in preventing what Mehinaku perceive as antisocial behaviour. We have seen that it is this oblique influence, of mostly

silent disapproval, that is the 'discipline' exerted on children, and later it
also operates together with surveillance and gossip, rather than any formal
law enforcement apparatus, to prevent people from perpetrating adverse
actions, with various degrees of exclusion and exile as the ultimate of implied consequences. And it is not only other people who are watching but
sorcerers and the *apapanye*. They see far more than ordinary human beings, with sorcerers in particular punishing 'wrongdoing', such as stealing
and violence, with their deadly curses.[46]

Apart from the tensions of surveillance acting preventatively on unde-
sirable social actions, the instigations of the *amunão* and the general ideals
of behaviour already discussed, the interactions of the Mehinaku community are shaped by institutions of exchange related to the kinship and
affinal networks mentioned earlier. The literal, substantial sense in which
the Mehinaku experience the 'give and take' of life has been discussed in
chapters 2 and 3, the flow of foods such as *uwitsakyuwi, nukayá* and *akãipé*
binding together household members and the different groups of the Alto
Xingu (see Plate 18). There are also the *Chuluki* (the ceremonial exchange
of objects in each house), peacefully gregarious social relations, as well as
inter-communal rituals,[47] wherein the Xinguano communities come to-

Plate 18. Sharing food between houses.

gether and ceremonial as well as less formal interchanges take place. However, these openings to exchange are brief; the perils of such Mehinaku sociality, as in so many other aspects of Mehinaku life[48] requires a closing of oneself afterwards, that is, before the inevitable, necessary opening once again.

As the concluding part of a broad survey of Mehinaku experience, I have here discussed shamans and sorcerers, gender relations, as well as general aspects of the Mehinaku social world. Now I will finally look to see how all the various aspects of Mehinaku life that have been described in the preceding chapters can actually make up a particular experience, one of ordinary reality, my friend's walk to the river.

Notes

1. Giving a somewhat unusual understanding of shamans and sorcerers of the Xingu, of the Amazon and in general. See especially Gregor's (1977) interpretation of Mehinaku shamanism as 'performance'. Also for example, Basso (1985); Carneiro (1977) for Xingu; Reichel-Dolmatoff (1971, 1975); S. Hugh-Jones (1996) for other Amazonian areas; and in general Thomas (ed. 1996, see ref. for S. Hugh-Jones) and Eliade (1964).
2. The word *yatama* refers to both the singular and plural.
3. The morass of literature on 'shamanism' includes the pseudo-scientific 'objective' analyses of early scholars such as Tylor, Frazer and Marett (Hultkrantz 1978: 27), then the interpretations of the theorists such as historians of religion like Eliade. There are also the more recent multidisciplinary studies which render 'shamanic' phenomena in neurophysiological terminology, as well as anthropologists who seek to contextualise shamanism using models such as Foucaultian discourse theory.
4. The amount of wonder and deference a *yatama* inspires varies greatly between individual shamans, who are often suspected of actually being sorcerers posing as shamans and therefore more feared and despised than anything else. Alternatively they may be believed to be charlatan *yatama*, without any real ability and mocked behind their backs.
5. The talismanic stones have the basic nature of the 'copy-things' discussed in chapter 4 (in general and in regard to ritual) that, being of the substance of the *apapanye* are able to draw them near so that they might act with their ability to heal. It is not the *yatama* himself therefore who is understood to actually effect the healing (somehow magically with 'stones of power' as it at first seemed to me) but the *apapanye* through the shaman.
6. The process of becoming a *yatama* and the various aspects of being one is a vast subject of its own for which I have collected much information but which,

except for the short exposition here, must be reserved for another work as space does not allow it here.

7. Like most payments among the Alto-Xinguanos, this payment can be of varied kind, for example, everything from ceramics, to labour on building a house, to necklets and harvests of pequi oil.

8. The story of the great shamaness Kaití is one so rich and unusual (the only case of a female *yatama* I have heard of in the Alto Xingu, not to mention the greatest of her time), it deserves a work of its own which I am planning.

9. See chapter 2, sec. V, on how state of consciousness manifests reality for the perceiver.

10. The *apapanye* is drawn close by the sound of its own particular music by the process described in the previous chapter, sec. III.

11. A common practice of shamanism (Eliade 1964).

12. The various methods of the *yatama* are too numerous and too intricate to discuss in detail here, such as their healing songs and the aforesaid power to heal with the stones in the throat and hands, invisible to the ordinary human eye.

13. Their aversion to the cold means that they only pretend to bathe, as the water would cool them down. Also, they secretly eat the bloody meats that we saw in chapter 3 the Mehinaku avoid because of their qualities of inflaming desire.

14. A discussion of women and the *Kawëka* is to be found in the next section.

15. See chapter 2, sec. V.

16. This is dissimilar to others' findings such as Gregor's (1979, 1985), who sees gender as problematically amorphous for the Mehinaku, requiring definition of sexual differences by such 'devices' as the cult of the flutes, that will be discussed later in this section.

17. See chapter 2, sec. I.

18. See also Viveiros de Castro (1977) and Gregor (1985).

19. See chapter 3.

20. Women make hammocks, while men make houses and stools, men prepare the orchards and women harvest them etc.

21. The Mehinaku will tell you themselves that these are the most important stories. Also evident is the importance of the *akãi* ('pequi' in Portuguese) season and the evoking of the myth of the fruit's origin (*Yakashukuma*) during this time, and the music/dancing of the *Yamurikuma* which also takes place during this period, that is so hallowed that even one mistake in performing its song will cause the singer to die ten days hence.

22. As discussed in chapter 3, sec. VII.

23. Gregor (1979, 1985) has maintained a view of Amazonian society, not uncommon (Bamberger (1974); Goldman (1979)), where the interactions between men and women are fundamentally antagonistic and hierarchical whereby men use various devices, especially the 'men's house and the sacred flute' ('the throne and sceptre of male power' (1979: 257)), to enforce their control over women. I agree with McCallum, who has criticised Gregor for his 'problematic theorization of myth and ritual' (1994: 91), arguing that Gregor's functionalist and psychological notions, with their Western assumptions of the way representation

works and the idea of male sexuality as an essential locus of power, leads him to inaccurate conclusions (which for me always jarred with the obvious pride, strength and sexuality of the Xinguano women and the generally joyous relations between males and females) and does not allow for understanding the subtle interplay that I propose above.

24. I agree with McCallum following Basso (1985), that the understanding of the rape by the Xinguanos themselves (and not with Western constructs about human sexuality, power, representation etc.) is about the flutes as 'powerful beings' (Basso 1985), the rape 'considered a compulsive effect of the performance observed, rather than a punishment by men of women who have violated a rule … the combination of the sexual feelings of male flute players and the sexuality of the flutes themselves' (McCallum 1994: 99). I found this to be in keeping with the Mehinaku understanding of ritual discussed in the last chapter, where making the music of the *kawëka*-flutes is *actually* understood to draw the *kawëka-apapanye* near, the human dancers emulating as much as possible the wildly desirous *apapanye* they are representing..

25. In terms of the 'soul continuum' discussed in chapter 2, sec. IV, women are securely at the human end of it, whilst men can find themselves anywhere on the continuum and must therefore work to maintain their humanity and reduce their *apapanye* spirit qualities. Perhaps this has something to do with the fact woman were first made by the *Kwamutë* in the image of his gentle daughters, while men descend from both a human woman and the Jaguar-*apapanye*. Also, the trace of *apapanye* understood to be in men is maybe why they can be sorcerers (they can shift to the *apapanye* end of the 'continuum') but women never can be.

26. The opposite to other findings of Amazonianists who have found women to be 'marginal to the centre of society, "somewhat natural"' (Seeger 1981: 107) or 'leity' (Goldman 1979), in keeping with ideas ubiquitous in the anthropological literature and firmly established by Lévi-Strauss (1964), of men as sacred/cultural and women as natural, 'raw', 'earth-like'.

27. An exception is in the *Yamurikuma* music, as in this story (depicted above) the women do ultimately become *apapanye*.

28. This is a very different picture to how lowland Amazonian women have been described in the literature, Gregor (1985) describing women as quiet, lacking in libido and at the mercy of the sexually frustrated, boisterous men. Similarly Bamberger (1974) describes the women of lowland South America as 'forever the subjects of male terrorism, hidden in their huts fearing to look out' (1974: 274–5). Seeger writes that the Suyá women are considered property, which is for that matter insalubrious, 'bad property … our rotten-smelling property' (1981: 107).

29. Very different to the picture portrayed of interactions between men and women as frightened and agonized by Gregor in his book *Anxious Pleasures* (1985).

30. There is some sense of definition to the space where nuclear families form clusters of hammocks, or young unmarried men sleep alone, so that although one may pass through these spaces, one would not linger unless in some way invited.

31. Which comes with a profound empathy. I was deeply moved when I experienced this myself in the accident described in chapter 4, when the boiling oats fell on my feet and as I screamed I heard another screaming with me. It was Takulalu, my foster-mother, as she ran over to me, frantically shouting (which was completely out of character) as though she herself had been burned, holding my feet as I held my feet in those first few agonising moments.

32. See Basso (1985) on almost identical *ifutisu,* Gregor's (1990) discussion of *ketepepei,* Gow (2000, 2001) on the Piro notion of *gwashata,* 'living well', and Overing (2000) on Piaroa sense of *huruhuru.*

33. The attribute of generosity is also referred to as *awushitsi,* and this word can also denote a 'good person' in general. However, *ketepepi* is more of an umbrella concept for general comportment.

34. This witty ingenuity is evident in the improvised words of ceremonial songs as well as in regular conversation.

35. In chapter 4, sec. II, it was explained how myth may form a kind of template for action for the Mehinaku, the principles of which form the closest thing to what we might call a 'moral code'.

36. Usually with those who are not part of the family. Generosity occurs in the context of pre-existing relationships, there not being a universal, altruistic notion of it. See Basso on the same (1973: 7).

37. See Gregor (1990, 1999, 2000).

38. Recent detailed archaeological evidence confirms this (Heckenberger 2000).

39. This is similar to the sense of kindness and compassion described in other ethnographies of Amazonian peoples, in which these qualities also require effort by the people, such as the Piro sociality of *gwashata* 'to live well, to live quietly' (Gow 2000: 56) and *huruhuru,* the Piaroa social aesthetic of good words, laughter and thus communal good-will (Overing 2001: 57). The empathy amongst the far more individualistic Mehinaku does seem to be somewhat different from the 'narcissistic attachment' of the Piro to their kinspeople as 'multiple other selves' (Gow 2000: 56). The Mehinaku reserve this kind of attachment only for close family.

40. Xinguano social life as 'person-centred', social organization centred on the 'construction of personhood' and not the construction of "corporate groups" or "society"' (McCallum 1994: 105).

41. For some detail on the network of kinship, of which the most significant behavioural and terminological distinction is that which is made between 'parallel' and 'cross' relatives, see Gregor (1977). The consequent social forms are, for example, the particular kinds of conduct that characterise affinal relationships (ibid.: 279–80). See also Basso (1973: 74) in regard to similarities for the Kalapalo.

42. Gregor writes: 'villagers do not regard themselves as members of rigidly defined social units' (1977: 318), going on to say that social identity is a matter of degree that depends on a multiplicity of factors, including networks of involvements.

43. See McCallum (1994: 93). This together with social values such as *ketepepei* has been the reason given for the peacefulness of the groups of this region (Gregor 1990, 1999, 2000).

44. There are in fact two of these chiefs at the moment, the role being shared by the brothers Marikawa and Monaím, their deceased father and mother having been the chiefs before them, Marikawa's daughter holding the position of *amunão* of the women.

45. For both regular, everyday activities – such as bathing very early in the morning (when it is still dark, this is no longer done), wrestling in the afternoon, making arrows for collective hunts – and also activities for unusual events such as the larger healing events.

46. This is the opposite of what has been written before about social deterrents and sorcerers for the Mehinaku. Gregor claims that people avoid doing the unacceptable for fear of being labelled a sorcerer. However, I was told that the sorcerers are fearless and that even Monaím, the most powerful of the shamans would not speak of who was a sorcerer, though he knows who they are, for fear of his own life. It is true that if it is unanimously decided that someone is a sorcerer and a present danger to the community, it may be agreed that he be murdered. However, this occurs extremely rarely and the sorcerers are not understood to be intimidated by this or anything else for that matter.

47. For detailed accounts of these events, see Gregor (1994), Basso (1973), Menezes Bastos (2000).

48. See especially chapter 3, the opening and closing involved in the *awëshëpai* ideal.

6

Some Conclusions

In the preceding chapters we have learned of what and how the Mehinaku experience in their lives so that in the next and final chapter we will
have the terms with which to describe the way Wanakuwalu might have
experienced her walk along a path to the river. Before we finally arrive
at this walk let us review here what we have understood so far and what
significance this knowledge may have ethnographically and theoretically.
After this, I will discuss some ideas to do with the writing of the phenomenological description of the walk.

In chapter 2 we saw the main configurations in Mehinaku experience:
the marked substantiality of these, but then how this apparently solid
materiality is in fact shifting 'skins' of things, and the nature of these differentiated into various realities determined by perspectives of distinctive
soul-groups. We saw that what distinguishes these soul-perspectives and
thus the particular worlds they engender is desire. In chapter 3 we looked
at the motions of the formations described in the previous chapter, and
how these are in fact the flows of soul-desire-substance. However these
formations are also under threat from the very soul-desires that produce
them, as desires tend to excesses that are destructive to the boundaries of
the worlds. Thus the Mehinaku work to uphold these boundaries whilst
also occasionally taking risks to augment them according to an oscillatory
ideal way of being called *awëshëpai*. After having investigated *what* the
Mehinaku experience, we turned to consider *how* exactly they perceive
these things. This was a focussing in on the Mehinaku articulation of the
general aspects of human consciousness described in the introduction. We
looked at the Mehinaku sense of a concept, how these are associated and
then how these come together in a flow of consciousness that the Mehi-

naku strive to attain. Finally, the specifically social aspects of the Mehinaku lived world were examined.

In the course of making an overview of the Mehinaku sense of life, diverse issues of ethnographic and theoretical import were brought up. In chapter 2, the contentious anthropological topic of animism (especially discussions of it in the Amazonian context) was engaged with, with a particular view of it given that is suggested by the Mehinaku case. The related notions of cosmology and the nature of reality for Amazonian peoples were also comparatively discussed in this chapter. Particularly unusual here is the Mehinaku conceptualisation of the relationship between consciousness and reality, with desire and its restraint as the critical factors to the substantiality and configurations of worlds. These notions are also significant in concepts introduced in chapter 3, as are more typical anthropological themes – such as 'models of flow' and human/non-human relations – as well as some unusual aspects of the Mehinaku way of being (integrity, the ideal of *awëshëpai* etc.) that have implications for the much discussed theme of Amazonian ontology. Chapter 4, with its close focus on the workings of consciousness, is suggestive in regard to the extent to which problematisation of categories can take place in anthropology. The Mehinaku concept of a concept, and the way these concepts are associated, sheds a particular light on the theoretical topics of ritual and storytelling and also on the way people reflect on and cultivate their own consciousness. The discussions of gender and general sociality, with their somewhat uncommon findings in chapter 5, will be of comparative ethnographic interest for those studying both the Upper Xingu and the Amazon overall.

Looking at the findings of all of the chapters together, they are also of some theoretical significance simply as an example of what one gets from employing a phenomenological approach to making a general outline of people's experiences. The body of this text portrays how, when one is not using approaches that involve fitting things into preconceived ideas but rather attempting to see how they 'just are', the picture produced is not of a complete whole or system. Rather what emerges are some intricately interconnecting aspects and others piecemeal; that is, the 'coherent meaningfulness' discussed in the introduction is discernable but its qualities are in fact somewhat rambling, in keeping with the actuality of the life it represents. Also, perhaps due to the phenomenological method, certain atypical ideas were allowed to emerge in the course of the body of the text that should be of interest to other disciplines. As Michael Taussig suggests in *The Devil and Commodity Fetishism* (1983), so-called 'anthropological objects of study' in fact give critical insight into the anthropologists' own culture. For example, the Mehinaku experiences of the multiplicity and perspectival nature of reality might be of interest to philosophers and also to scientists who study quantum physics, whose postulates are not dissimilar to these. The Mehinaku notion of *yeya*, so similar to the ancient Greek conception of Plato's archetypes, might also be relevant to comparative philosophers. In addition, the way the Mehinaku cultivate a certain flowing quality of consciousness *(awitsiri)*, could be instructive to Jungian psychologists (for whom the notion of 'psychic flow' is crucial), as examples of people who in many ways actually live what psychotherapists advocate.

Therefore some specific ethnographic and theoretical points emerge from the general study of the Mehinaku experience that are of some consequence for Amazonianists, anthropologists in general, and possibly even philosophers and psychologists. However, as I said at the start of the book, these points have been discussed only briefly, or restricted to notes, as they are only incidental to the central aim of this project. The previous chapters are only really meant as instrumental to the endeavour of finding out about ordinary reality for Mehinaku people and this is still to be seen in the description of Wanakuwalu's walk to come, that is, how what we have seen to be the content of the Mehinaku lived world actually works in that event of experience. Hence we will finally come to the fulfilment of the three main aims delineated at the outset of this book: first, how facets of more distinct and studied activities (dancing, working, shamanism) in fact figure in an in-between experience such as 'just walking along'; and second, how representations made by anthropologists, of 'cosmology', 'sociality', 'personhood' etc., in fact enter into life. In the previous chapters I have discussed various Mehinaku practices and formulated abstract descriptions to communicate certain aspects of Mehinaku experience. The way we will see how these come into play in the walk is that as it is described there will be references back to the body of the text to portray where the generalised notions enter into the specific incidence. These cross-references will show how in a stream of consciousness, moments of the discussed conceptions feature, are absent and mix with prosaic moments. Obviously it is not possible to see how every one of the ideas discussed earlier comes into life, as they could not all figure in a half-hour walk to the river but it will be seen how certain of them and most of the principle ones do.

In the conceptual framework, most concretely in the anecdotes given in the preceding chapters, some sense of Mehinaku experience will have built up for the reader in a piecemeal and indirect way. Only in the description itself will the third and principal intention of this book be directly realised, that is, it will finally be seen what ordinary reality might actually be like for a Mehinaku person. As has been explained from the start, getting a sense of what life is like for people studied has been central to the anthropological project since Malinowksi's enjoining the investigation of the 'outlook on life ... the reality which he breathes' (1999 [1922]: 517). I have suggested that looking at interstitial reality in particular is to look at what life is like for people in the most basic sense, and to come to terms with that part of experience that in fact makes up most of life. I believe the value of such a venture is also in its appeal to a general audience, or those with only a nascent interest in anthropology, because gaining insight into the way others (especially those ostensibly most different) see the world is I believe a fundamental part of human curiosity. Stephen Hugh-Jones told me that after his mother had read his book, *The Palm and the Pleiades* (1979), a structural analysis of Barasana cosmology and initiation, she asked him: 'But what are they like?' I myself have found that reading the conceptual frameworks constructed by ethnographers has often provoked in me a similar sense of wanting to know what it all really comes to, what it all 'feels like' to the people described. This book and specifically the following description addresses this simple but very difficult question to answer and does so with a knowledge of the unavoidable limitations (delineated in the introduction) of such an ambition, holding that the effort – the little one can hope to share of the experience of others – is worth the attempt. Also the whole-to-part method of doing it – of tracing a framework and then using that framework to write a description of an incidence of consciousness, with cross-references between the two parts – might be found useful by other ethnographers investigating the same or other kinds of experience in various ethnographic contexts.

This brings us to the actual writing of the phenomenological description of Wanakuwalu's walk (see Plates 19, 20, 21, 22, 23). In the introduction, I discussed and justified how methodologically speaking I might come to know something of Mehinaku experience, including Wanakuwalu's experience of the walk and also, that the writing about the walk would be constituted by my portrayal of this experience according to this general knowledge. The problematics of using written language to do this is especially crucial here, as it attempts to communicate not only drawn out concepts, as in the previous chapters but is employed to literally convey one flow of consciousness (Wanakuwalu's) to another (the reader's).

This issue concerns what Bachelard calls the 'transsubjectivity of the image' (1969: xix). It begs the question: '[H]ow can an image, at times very unusual, ... How – with no preparation – can this singular, short-lived event constituted by the appearance of an unusual poetic image, react on other minds and in other hearts, despite all the barriers of common sense?' (Bachelard 1969: xix). This is what language must do if it is to transmit not only a concept but may also have to express an inchoate sense of things that is not yet familiar. The possibility of this 'communicability of an unusual image' (Bachelard 1969: xvii) has the implication that there are certain generalities in human consciousness that allow some intersection of understanding despite the profound cultural particularity of experience. Thus if in approaching another culture, we discern 'lived metaphors', instead of imposing models, as Jackson proposes (1996: 9), then perhaps we can employ words to evoke in the consciousness of the reader, connections that occur in the consciousnesses of others, and perhaps a real 'sense' of that experience. These metaphors would be able to work in this manner because of the way poetic words can evoke what are even beyond themselves, 'forces' that 'are manifested … that do not pass through circuits of knowledge' (Bachelard 1969: xxi).

To accomplish this kind of 'poetic' anthropological writing requires careful thinking about how to enter into words in order to do this. We can not simply use the 'fetishised' (Jackson 1996) words of intellectualist models that lose their power to evoke life, that are tired, 'fossilised' (Bachelard 1969: 221). Words must be employed with sensitivity to their potency, to their ability to convey what is beyond themselves. This poetic use of language, Bachelard writes, 'puts language in a state of emergence, in which life becomes manifest through its vivacity'(1969: xxvii). In this way words are 'brought up out of habit of expression to actuality of expression' (1969: 221–222) and thus can evoke 'life', the indeterminate actuality of another's experience: 'Stories become moods, and are moods unfurled' (Okri 1996: 47). This writing therefore, is not concerned with exactitudes of linguistic translation and so on but rather, what is crucial here is that the writing succeeds in 'induc[ing] in the reader a state of suspended reading' (Bachelard 1969: 14), in which she or he can imagine this other experience. Such imagination is not mere fantasising, it is the result of communication in the most profound sense, a coming closer to real understanding. The words have conducted what transcends them and attained what the Nigerian author and poet Ben Okri calls, '[T]he transparency of excellent stories: words dissolve words and only things stand in their place' (1996: 30). This then, more than anything else, is what I aspire to in the forthcoming description: that with it the reader will be able to walk some way in another's footsteps.

Plate 19. Path from the houses to the river through an *akãi* orchard.

7

Her Walk

This book started with a walk to the river, the narrator and reader unfamiliar with the Mehinaku and their world. Following this, the rest of the book has been an attempt to come to terms with this lived world, so as to return to that walk here* and see what can now be understood of Wanakuwalu's experience of these moments of ordinary reality.

> Small plants that encroach on the dirt path are coolly wet on her feet, as Wanakuwalu begins her way down the path towards the river. She thinks of all the manioc they dug up this morning, that they are leaving behind them and that they should make this trip to the river quickly, to get back to what needs to be done.[1] 'Carla will be slow but it is always better not to be impatient!'[2] Near to the white woman now, she smells[3] that Carla's scent[4] is still a little strange but now closer to her own: soft and clean, without the sharp tinge of wildness from the cities.[5] She has been drinking our *uwitsakyuwi*

* Some notes on the presentation of the description: I have used capitals for the names of *apapanye* translated into English and their personal pronouns, e.g. for Yanumaka. 'the Jaguar, His voice'. Key Mehinaku conceptual words discussed in the previous text are italicised and repeated before or after in English. In general, for the reasons explained above, the writing style is an attempt to strike a balance to keeping true to the Mehinaku point of view whilst also making the description not only comprehensible but effectively evocative even to a reader who has not yet read the whole body of the book. Therefore though I have made it clear that the following text describes Wanakuwalu's point of view and thus for the most part simply 'relates' her consciousness, still, I sometimes write 'she thinks' or 'she feels' or I indicate discrete thoughts using inverted commas, this being only for stylistic purposes, using this and other forms of Western narrative convention, to make the text as optimally effective as possible (according to the tensions of translation discussed above: that is, only being able to use what the reader already has to convey to the reader something else).

Plate 20. Across the floodplain.

Plate 21. Into the forest by the river.

manioc-water, Wanakuwalu thinks and glances back at her companion with affection.[6] 'I wonder if people saw us walk together and so see how close we are?'[7] Through the *akái* trees at the back of her house, in the green-yellow sun-stuff[8] slanting through the leaves, she first hears (a buzzing whir) and then sees the swift figure of tiny *Ahira*, the Hummingbird.[9] The bird flew right by my ear, I must walk on, quick and content,[10] she thinks, as she knows she walks through His house though she cannot see it.[11] She envisions[12] Him in his human-form, bright with desire. It will be okay though, she thinks, because only a few days ago *Ahira-apapanye*[13] was fed and made joyful and so He is unlikely to be desirous to steal souls right now. The *Aláma-Nututai* star-pair have just appeared[14] and so she knows that *Ahira* and the other spirit-owners of the orchard trees, through whose village they are now walking, will be nurturing the trees, helping them make flowers and fruit.[15] Anyway, there is little danger from *Ahira*: Wanakuwalu does not feel hungry, she drank the sweet, cold *nukaya* before leaving for the manioc orchard this morning and so there is no chance of *yerekyuki*.[16]

They continue on through the *akái* and *ketula* groves. 'I wonder who else will be bathing and fetching water at this time?'[17] She glances to one side, at a tiny path that leads to another and so on, further and further into the orchards. This is the way she takes to go the place where she and her lover meet. Wanakuwalu often thinks of this when she reaches this point on the main path to the river, wondering when she will next make her way between the trees to the tiny clearing,[18] where she knows gentle happiness[19] waits, having gathered[20] there over the many meetings, waiting to envelop them in pleasure.

Out of the trees now and onto the floodplain. It is *awitsiri*, beautiful, she thinks, as she almost always does when she crosses the cleared area that has been made with the long care of the Mehinaku community. Within the whole, the *naku*[21] of this grassy plain, she also feels quite safe. It is more or less a human place this clearing, but still the danger of the dark[22] forest surrounds, onwards and outwards, with its centre, *Mushuna*,[23] and then the forest encircled by White peoples' places. Only in the village-round is it really safe; But then in its very centre, swirling darkness too,[24] the *Kawëka*, the Flutes, *our* Flutes.[25] 'Is that...?' Yes, she recognises him immediately, though he is far off, by the jaunty cock of his head.[26] It is Kamëluvé riding his bicycle out from the river tree line, taking the path to the back of his house. The Flutes[27] are not meant to be returning until the Sun enters his house[28] but still, with the sudden sight of a man[29] on such a day,[30] a hole[31] made by fear opens up in her being. 'Be strong,[32] there is no danger till later and at least it is not night[33] and things are in their place.'[34] Her gaze falls[35] on the forest to one side and she remembers her dream of the night before, how her soul had been wandering there.[36] The memories, certain actions in the midst of some green misty spaces, fill her, and the event in those hazy regions, perhaps ominous,[37] which had thus almost prevented her from leaving her hammock that morning. She had told her husband about it upon waking but he had said there was no threat to her: the canoe was not a bad omen, he had also dreamed of it, that it was his and he had used it to take her away from the danger of a sorcerer.[38]

And indeed this morning *Yanumaka* had come to the manioc orchard, a jaguar, and was perhaps[39] the *ipyamawékéhë*, the sorcerer from the dream, using the skin of the animal.[40] And as her husband had said,[41] she had not been harmed. The jaguar had barked at the women and she had felt his angry voice enter[42] her, blood-red.[43] Even now she feels it hot[44] in her belly and head. The coolness of the water will help wash it away.[45] Perhaps she will need to scrape her skin with the *imya,* to make her blood flow till it is completely clean.[46] She thinks all this with a shudder of her body.[47] She should not think of the jaguar now, as the thinking will attract him to her.[48] She would not be so afraid[49] if she were still the *uwekehë*[50] of the *Shapacuyawa apapanye.* While she was making His mask[51] and feeding[52] Him, she knew that He would always be following her invisibly and would protect[53] her from the desire, the threat, of other *apapanye* spirits. Like when she saw *Uíkyuma*[54] – first in His snake-clothing[55] then in the form of her lover – she had not fallen ill as she had expected. However she is no longer a *uwekehë,* so must take care not to think[56] of the jaguar, and now she does not but still the general memory of her sleep-travel remains. She can still feel the dream-greenness and words from her husband inside her,[57] just at the edges of her vision, as she walks on.

She looks up at *Kamë,* the Sun, the round that is one of His skins.[58] It is getting higher in Its path in the sky but there is not yet enough of His sun-stuff[59] to eat into her skin with His fierceness.[60] No, when she makes this trip again when *Kamë* is in the middle of His path,[61] she will cover herself with Carla's shirt to protect her flesh, almost as fat and white as *Shapushënéshë*'s Herself,[62] which she has taken so much care to grow and protect. She is young and lovely, as beautiful as the *yanakwimpi* shell,[63] and she is joyous in this, taking pleasure in the strength of her stride. Joyous too in the sky and the earth under her and other different parts of the floodplain-*naku,* that she lightly feels go in and out of her keen awareness.[64] Softly, she sings some of the *Tineshukuma* music in the rhythm of her step, *'Eeh ha / koo ha ha'.*[65] She feels so well[66] that even when she smells, then spots, the fire burning above the forest-line near *Kumayu*'s wife's orchard[67] of *ketula*[68] fruit trees and feels it starting to enter her,[69] she simply spits[70] a few times as she walks, ridding herself of the odour-stuff of refuse, and continues on in wellness, *awëshëpai.*[71] An *urubu,* a vulture is above. *'Urubu!'* she shouts back to Carla, who does not know about the *apapanye* and their children.[72] Carla looks up at the bird and smiles. Why is she smiling? Wanakuwalu glances back and notices what she has seen before in her companion, the light in the woman's eyes dimmed,[73] and she is sure that if she stopped and looked more closely, the tiny figure of Carla that resides in the woman's eyes[74] would be fading. She will lose it if she is not careful – *Urubu* or some other *apapanye* will take it.[75] She wonders why Carla weakens like this, perhaps she is missing her lover or her family. … She will ask her, warn her about it later. And as she thinks this, she notices that a Rainbow, *Anapi,* has appeared in the sky, as though caused by the lapse, the collapsing inwards[76] of the white woman. The rainbow-serpent *Anapi* who is kept in the sky by *Kamë*[77] may come out from his house by the lake and at any time descend and eat everyone, destroying everything. For this reason[78] she decides to tell[79] Carla about the Rainbow, the terrifying story[80] of this spirit's descent and slaughter of a whole village. Carla listens closely and slows down to a halt. Again the White woman is smiling, wide-eyed, like a little girl. Does she not know, feel the danger of halting like this? Carla remains there on and on.[81] Nervousness wells in Wanakuwalu's belly; she feels a breeze on her face that could be the presence of an *apapanye*.[82] We are so vulnerable[83] just standing here but Carla shows no sign of worry, of minding, is still smiling her strange smile, gazing at the Rainbow. Mixed with fear, Wanakuwalu feels a general urge to keep going.[84] '*Ayi!*' She motions Carla onward, taking care to do so in a quiet and cheerful manner.[85]

It is a relief to be moving along again.[86] It will be all right, she will wash herself carefully in the river and be shining-clean and on her return to the village carefully[87] she will make[88] *awitsiri,* beautiful[89], slabs of manioc flour, white and perfect.[90] Swinging the steel pail she remembers the great weight it will have on her head when it is filled with water on her walk home, the pain in her neck: accept[91] it, there will be the pleasure soon of dipping into the cool water, the delicious *uwitzakyuwi* that will be made with the water brought back, *awëshëpai.*[92] The word resounds in her again, her muscles loosen, she walks on. … To one side of the path, she sees some *puyalu*[93] and some *yanumaka-itai-ituné*[94] growing. She must pick some of the roots of each plant on the way back. With the *puyalu* she will vomit[95] all morning tomorrow, which she dislikes doing. And she is afraid of the plant's owner.[96] But it is worth it;[97] her calves have been growing so round.[98] The *yanumaka-itai-ituné* will help build up little Eyúhi's legs so he begins to walk, and save her sister Kaití from going to the other side of the lake to look for it. Also, she might be able to trade[99] some of the root for the bit of the *Tineshukuma-*song[100] she has yet to learn from Kamaluku. Though she cannot see them, she imagines the spirit-owners of the plants surrounding the visible forms of the leaves.[101]

They are now almost at the river. She walks up the rise of earth and into the coolness of the forest. Immediately, she feels herself more alert.[102] She can smell hints of many presences and feels a slight prickling of her skin. Looking between the trees as she walks, she sees a trailing pile of *Uyay*

Plate 22. Diving in.

Plate 23. The River.

leaves, and envisages what the *yatama* shamans[103] can see:[104] not *Uyay* leaves but the dense undergrowth opening out to paths[105] that lead to villages of the *apapanye*. And also, deep within the forest, the original Masks of the *apapanye*, of which all other things are copies.[106] Even here, where there is less danger, the trees less dense and humans passing back and forth all the time, layering[107] the path[108] with safe humanness, still, this is the domain of the *apapanye*. Right now she and the White woman are walking beneath the house of the *apapanye* chief, *Ateshua*,[109] that is up in the branches of the great reaching *Uyay* tree. She imagines His high whistling voice. Magnificent *apapanye* spirits – tall and resplendent in their strength, with coloured and shining skin[110] – are peering to observe the human-women. The sound of star-birds,[111] the little *Tsipinyu*, can be heard and then they swoop low above their heads. Wanakuwalu looks at them perched now in trees to one side of the path, feeling revulsion. Their backs glisten black from the hair they have plucked from the heads of the souls of the human dead, in the wars between them in the sky.[112] She knows the villages of the dead are behind the blue,[113] in the glimpses of sky between the branches, and she thinks of how she will at some point walk to collect water from the Milky Way river, as she does now from the Curisevo river,[114] eat fish that are cockroaches and perhaps become a snake when she sleeps.[115]

A flickering of bright yellows is suddenly around her and these butterflies remind her of the story of the man who saw fish not butterflies,[116] and that she should not be thinking so much of what the *apapanye* spirits and the dead see – of what is beyond the skins of the world that humans perceive[117] – or she will end up caught in these visions, in the worlds of the *apapanye* and the dead. Just walk on[118] impassively,[119] through the butterflies as butterflies,[120] see now the brown river gleaming up ahead. Those *tsipinyus* are singing so much, surely they are speaking of lots of fish.[121] Maiawai must have brought home a big catch from his early-morning outing. Hopefully the ugly Kalapalo will not come looking and take a good deal of the food.[122] Salty, roasted fish and hot thick *ulepe* bread … and probably enough still left over so that tonight there will also be *wakula* stew. The food she eats will fill the hollowness she has begun to feel with the exertions and events of the morning, and make her feel solid, lustrous and calm again.[123]

Pervaded by happiness with this prospect, *Wanakuwalu* drops her pail and begins descending the steep, slippery bank to the water. In the depths of its murkiness she knows lie First Things,[124] *yeya* masks of the *apapanye* spirits pulsing with potency[125], and there are spirits moving in terrible incarnations. Though acutely alert to this, she will not stay with the thought[126] but let the water stream[127] over her skin, making her cool and clean, human; giving her beauty, making her ready[128] to move on[129] back to the village.

Cross References from
the Description to Chapters 2–5

1. Industriousness without cease, chapter 3, p. 78.
2. Social obstacles absorbed into the flow of things, chapter 3, pp. 77–78; also a general graciousness in dealings with others, chapter 5, pp. 165–66.
3. Acute awareness of surroundings all the time, chapter 3, pp. 117–18 and pp. 147–48.
4. The importance of 'smell' *(iníya),* chapter 2, pp. 36–38.
5. Danger and wildness associated with White People and the places they live, in particular cities, chapter 3, p. 88.
6. Social binding together by substance, chapter 2, pp. 39–40; absorption of outsiders into Mehinaku practices, chapter 3, pp. 77–78.
7. Close surveillance of community life, chapter 5, pp. 165–66; a general tendency to 'show-off', be a little original, chapter 5, p. 166; prestige associated with White People, chapter 2, p. 68n14.
8. Sense of substantiality of aspects of the landscape, such as light, chapter 2, pp. 40–41.
9. This is perceived as being perhaps Ahira himself (the *apapanye* spirit) or one of his copies, though plants and animals are apprehended as more likely to be copies as they are more commonly seen, chapter 2, pp. 47–48 and pp. 51–52. In seeing a creature or plant, one does not necessarily distinguish between the *apapanye*-original and its copy. This kind of perceiving without the need to decide definitively on category significance, is discussed as the 'blending of entities in consciousness', chapter 2, p. 70n44, chapter 4, pp. 129–30.
10. Fear of the presence of the *apapanye,* chapter 2, p. 43 and dealing with this by walking on, part of a general tendency of flowing,

not stopping, chapter 3, p. 76; protecting one's bodily-integrity by being 'content', thus upholding the boundaries of one's own consciousness and thus self so as not to make oneself vulnerable to the *apapanye,* chapter 3, pp. 103–4.

11. The invisible presence of the houses of certain *apapanye* villages where these *apapanye* look after particular plants, in this case, the *akãi* plant or pequi, chapter 2, pp. 47–48.

12. A flickering of consciousness that is the experience of the shifting appearances of the one category (in this case, the *apapanye's* humanoid and animal-skin aspects, chapter 2, p. 44), one of the main ways the Mehinaku make associations, chapter 4, pp. 130–31.

13. *Apapanye,* the powerful spirit beings, substantial though invisible, that are the crucial entities with which the Mehinaku live, and whose imitations make up the plants, animals and other aspects of the landscape, chapter 2, pp. 41–48.

14. Living in relation to cycles that the stars herald, chapter 3, p. 76.

15. Groups of *apapanye* nurturing certain plants, living in a village (invisible to humans) in the garden where the plants grow, chapter 2, pp. 47–48.

16. *Yerekyuki,* the notion of attracting the harm of *apapanye* by one's hunger, chapter 3, pp. 105–107.

17. Intense closeness of sociality and surveillance, chapter 5, p. 165 and p. 170.

18. The secluded groves of the orchards as associated with sexual encounters, chapter 3, p. 88.

19. The Mehinaku sense of romance, their understanding of love (just as all other emotions), as something that should be kept moderate, within the bounds of passion, chapter 5, p. 160.

20. Senses, feelings experienced as material 'things' with independent existence from the people who feel them, chapter 2, pp. 39–40.

21. The sense of being part of a whole, in this case spatially, chapter 3, p. 90 and chapter 4, p. 128.

22. The fearfulness of darkness as a substantial association, where fear has darkness as part of its substance and visa versa, chapter 4, p. 135.

23. Chapter 3, p. 82.

24. Sense of landscape in concentric circles of different orders of desire, chapter 3, pp. 87–89.

25. The *Kawëka* that were long ago taken from the women by the daring action of the men, chapter 3, pp. 110–111, and the poignant

nostalgia and pride that women still feel for the time (of union with the *apapanye*, excluding the men) when they still possessed them, chapter 5, pp. 161–163.

26. The attribute of merry daring valued by the Mehinaku, chapter 3, pp. 110–114; the shimmering balance of the ideal way of being called '*awushipai*', chapter 3, pp. 117–18.

27. The *Kawëka* Flutes spring to mind when she sees a man because of the close association of men with these flutes, chapter 5, pp. 162–163.

28. '*Kamëmululkawéné*', the Mehinaku word for 'sunset'. The Sun, *Kamë*, as a being whose house is in a village in the sky (chapter 3, p. 83).

29. Men understood by women as a fundamentally different, chapter 5, p. 159 and potentially dangerous (more like *apapanye*) category of being, chapter 5, pp. 163–64.

30. The presence and thus danger of the *Kawëka-apapanye* when the men return with the flutes (and thus the *apapanye* that accompany them everywhere) from a trip into the forest, chapter 3, p. 91.

31. Fear as substantial, as all emotions are felt to be, chapter 4, p. 135, the extreme of which are experienced as a breach of one's integrity of self, chapter 3, p. 105.

32. The breach in the integrity of self, caused by the emotion of fear, is to be made up for by right consciousness, chapter 3, p. 97, pp. 103–4.

33. The *apapanye* move more freely in and prefer darkness, chapter 2, p. 47; the encroaching of the perilous zones of darkness into the safer zones with the fall of night, chapter 3, p. 90.

34. Light/day as associated with the world in its proper form as opposed to darkness as generally associated with dissolution of boundaries of things and release of uncontrollable passions, chapter 3, pp. 95–96.

35. Her gaze turns inadvertently towards the forest because she has just been thinking about darkness and danger with which the forest is closely associated, chapter 3, p. 96.

36. In sleep the *yakulai* soul-consciousness separating from the flesh-body to travel, chapter 2, p. 56.

37. Omens and the way stories 'wrap' incidents with meaning, chapter 4, pp. 136–37.

38. The Mehinaku sorcerers who identify more with the *apapanye* than with humans, fearsome in their malevolence and their ability to cause humans harm, chapter 5, pp. 157–158.

39. The jaguar might have been a sorcerer using a jaguar's skin, or the *Yanumaka-apapanye* or both: in perceiving categories, there can be a blending of the identity of things that is not problematic for them, many possibilities of reality allowed to exist at once, chapter 4, pp. 129–30.

40. The use of the skins of animals by sorcerers, chapter 2, p. 50, chapter 5, p. 157.

41. Understanding events in terms of omens, intertwining incidence (especially ones that threaten the seamless flow of daily life) with the meaningfulness of story, and that generally the way things occur has to do with entities and forces mostly beyond human perception, chapter 4, pp. 135–137.

42. Substantiality of aspects of life such as thought, emotion, sound chapter 2, p. 39; which includes a sense of 'thingness', chapter 4, pp. 126–27.

43. Association of blood with dangerous wildness, chapter 3, pp. 95–96.

44. Sorcerers and *apapanye* are always associated with the heat of their wild passions, chapter 5, p. 157.

45. The valuing of 'flow' in all areas of life, in this case flow of the body maintained externally by sluicing with water, chapter 3, p. 75.

46. Internal cleanliness achieved by bleeding through the skin caused by scraping with the thorns of the *imya* instrument, chapter 3, p. 76.

47. 'Thinking' with the body, chapter 2, pp. 39, 56.

48. Substantiality of thought that can work like a kind of telepathy, chapter 2, p. 39; *apapanye* drawn to humans by excess of emotion, chapter 3, p. 106.

49. Extreme fear of *apapanye*, chapter 2, p. 43 and sorcerers, chapter 5, p. 158.

50. The *uwekehë* complex of reciprocal care between a human and an *apapanye*, chapter 3, pp. 97–99.

51. The working of ritual where associations (for example, between masks and their *apapanye*) are perceived as substantial links, chapter 4, pp. 140–42.

52. The way *apapanye* are drawn near in the performance of ritual and partake of the ritual meal by consuming its *iníya*, its smell, chapter 4, p. 141.

53. Protection by the *apapanye* of their human 'owner', the *uwekehë* who cares for them, chapter 3, p. 98.

54. The threat of the *apapanye*, who in their desire for humans infringe into human reality, chapter 3, pp. 83–84; with the Snake-*apapanye*

as the most commonly associated with such intrusions, chapter 3, pp. 92–93.

55. Ability of the *apapanye* to change their 'skins', chapter 2, pp. 49–50.

56. Upholding the boundaries of one's own consciousness and thus self so as not to make oneself vulnerable to the *apapanye,* chapter 3, pp. 103–4.

57. Mood, feelings and words understood as substances that gather and remain, just as other materials do, chapter 2, pp. 38–39.

58. The *apapanye*-beings may have a number of 'skins', chapter 2, pp. 44–45.

59. Sense of the substantiality of aspects of the landscape such as light, chapter 2, pp. 40–41.

60. The Sun as the supreme personification of the fierce dynamic of bold daring, chapter 3, pp. 111–112; experiencing even basic associations – such as sunlight on the skin – in terms of story. Here the sunlight is lived in terms of the many tales told of the Sun Being's aggressive exploits, chapter 4, p. 137.

61. Understanding times of the day in terms of the movement of the Sun Being, *Kamë,* chapter 3, p. 76.

62. Making one's human self in the image of the *apapanye,* and for women *Shapushënëshë* in particular, chapter 2, p. 33. Implicit in this the sense of all things as copies of archetypal originals, chapter 2, pp. 51–52, chapter 4, p. 134.

63. *Yanakwimpi* was Wanakuwalu's birth omen (understanding one's own life in the form of a story chapter 4, p. 136) foretelling that she would grow up to be as strongly, perfectly beautiful as the *yanakwimpi* (the highly prized white shell with which the Xinguanos make their jewellery), which is therefore the way she feels her own beauty.

64. The clear attentiveness of *awitsiri* experience: integration of self and place that shifts with the flow of consciousness – lightly, without attachment – so that there is an expansion in this flow and more things can be experienced at once in it, chapter 4, pp. 147–148.

65. The relation between walking and dance, chapter 3, p. 74, p. 119n1.

66. The great pleasure taken in one's own beauty and feelings of general well-being, chapter 2, pp. 32–33, chapter 3, p. 116.

67. Ownership of territories and their produce, Chapter 3, p. 91.

68. The mangaba *(Harcornia speciosa)* fruit tree that the Mehinaku plant with their treasured pequi *(Caryocar butyrosum)* trees in the orchards that surround the circle of houses, p. 17.

69. Smell as crucial sensual experience, chapter 2, pp. 36–38.
70. Ridding oneself of bad smells by spitting, chapter 2, p. 38.
71. The ideal way of being that the Mehinaku strive for, chapter 3, pp. 114–118.
72. The relationship between 'normal' animals and plants and the archetypal *apapanye* chapter 2, pp. 51–52.
73. The gaze of bright awareness made by the tension of the *awëshëpai* ideal, chapter 3, p. 117–18.
74. The way the *yakulai* soul-body is visible in the awake human flesh-body, endnotes of chapter 2, p. 56, p. 71n52.
75. Day-dreaming and otherwise not upholding a strong consciousness/boundary of selfhood as attracting *apapanye,* chapter 3, p. 81, 103–4.
76. Day-dreaming and thus not upholding a strong consciousness/boundary of selfhood as attracting *apapanye,* chapter 3, p. 81, 103–4; and associated especially with wild serpents whose appearance has to do with the ever-present threat of collapse of boundaries, chapter 3, pp. 92–95; here specifically the closing in of the world with the descent of the Rainbow Snake, chapter 3, p. 93, 95.
77. It was *Kamë,* the Sun, who established and maintains most of the fundamental boundaries of the aspects of the worlds, chapter 3, pp. 86–87.
78. The danger is that one person's breach in their sense of the consensus reality, affects the consensus reality as a whole, chapter 3, p. 99, making the whole community vulnerable to the passionate whims of *apapanye* like *Anapi,* chapter 3, p. 80, 95, therefore Wanakuwalu tells me the story to warn me of the repercussions of my weakening.
79. Understanding events and ideas in terms of *ownaki,* 'stories', chapter 4, pp. 135–37, and using them as parable chapter 4, p. 138.
80. The story of *Anapi,* Chapter 3, p. 80, p. 93.
81. Obliviousness of White people understood as a lack of awareness and sensitive care of oneself and one's relations to the environment and hence potentially destructive to these, chapter 4, p. 147.
82. The very real and near presence of the *apapanye,* chapter 2, p. 43.
83. The helpless vulnerability one feels to the *apapanye* outside the village circle, chapter 3, pp. 87–91.
84. Enjoinment to keep things going, chapter 3, p. 75.
85. Absorbing social difficulties into the flow of events, chapter 3, p. 77; the gentleness of the ideal *ketepepei* comportment chapter 5, p. 166.

86. Sense of 'flowing along' as enjoyed and valued, default sense of one's body and of one's sense of being alive in general, chapter 3, p. 76.
87. 'Care' as a crucial aspect of the beautiful *(awitsiri)* consciousness that makes beautiful things, chapter 4, pp. 146–47.
88. The value placed on continuous activity, industry, chapter 3, p. 78.
89. Making beautiful *(awitsiri)* things as a way of rectifying the effect on the state of the world from the wrong consciousness of another, with the assumption that one may determine the quality of his or her reality by the way one perceives, chapter 4, pp. 144–46; also, producing beautiful things is a source of pride, often competitive; there are different meanings of this activity, and activities in general, the purposes blending in lived experience, chapter 4, p. 131.
90. Manioc as associated with the clean body, and the whiteness of these with beauty, chapter 2, p. 35; beauty as perfection, chapter 2, p. 32.
91. Carrying water as an important activity of women, chapter 5, p. 164.
92. *Awëshëpai* 'ideal', chapter 3, pp. 114–118. In this case specifically to do with the Mehinaku 'pleasure principle': difficulty absorbed so that desires are moderately and continuously met, chapter 3, p. 85.
93. The root used to build up the round plumpness that is valued in female beauty, chapter 4, p. 143.
94. One of the various substances used to build the bodies of babies, chapter 2, p. 30, 32, in this case the root called 'Jaguar-Son walks' used by mothers to build up the babies' legs to help them learn to walk, that is, to make their legs as strong as the Sun, the son of the powerful Jaguar-*apapanye.*
95. The practice of vomiting root potions, chapter 3, pp. 75–76.
96. The relationships of risk but potential benefit entered into with *apapanye* spirits to improve the body, chapter 3, pp. 108–9.
97. The principle of 'daring', here the calculated risk of opening bodily form for the purpose of improving it, chapter 3, pp. 108–9.
98. The desire to be outstanding in some way (in this case in beauty), that is part of the *ketepepei* social ideal, chapter 5, p. 166.
99. Music considered to be a material 'thing' that can thus be traded, chapter 4, p. 126.
100. The women's song of great significance, chapter 4, p. 136, chapter 5, p. 172n21, p. 173n27.
101. The *apapanye* as keeping near, though invisibly, to the things that they 'own', chapter 2, pp. 47–48.

102. Sense that in the forest you are in the realm of the *apapanye* spirits and may encounter one at any time, and that you therefore must be especially alert and careful there, chapter 2, p. 43.
103. The *yatama,* the Mehinaku 'shamans', who are able to heal and perform other extraordinary acts in accordance with their relationships to particular *apapanye,* chapter 5, pp. 153–54.
104. The ability of the *yatama* to see into the reality of the *apapanye,* chapter 2, pp. 61–62, chapter 5, pp. 155–56.
105. The paths of the *apapanye,* normally invisible to a human perspective, chapter 3, p. 81, p. 91.
106. Concept of the *yeya,* the archetypes of all things in existence, chapter 2, p. 51.
107. Everything understood in substantiality terms, chapter 2, pp. 39–40.
108. The human-made path as a conduit of safety within non-human spaces, chapter 3, p. 91.
109. The being *Ateshua,* chapter 2, p. 46.
110. The *apapanye* as embodiments of ultimate and super-human beauty and desirability, chapter 2, p. 44, and especially to human women, between whom liaisons have always occurred since the time of their creation, chapter 3, pp. 83–85, chapter 5, pp. 161–62.
111. The birds that appear at times as stars in the sky, chapter 3, p. 80.
112. These birds as interlopers from another realm and enemies of the human dead, chapter 3, p. 80.
113. The mirrored reality of the dead beyond the visible sky, chapter 2, pp. 62–64.
114. Continuity of village life as the Mehinaku know it, even after death, chapter 3, pp. 78–79.
115. From the story of *Alatapuwana,* chapter 2, pp. 62–64.
116. The story of the lake of butterflies, chapter 2, pp. 54–55.
117. The different worlds (consensus realities) of different ways of seeing/being, chapter 2, p. 55.
118. The sense of the importance of keeping up a flowing motion, chapter 3, p. 75.
119. The protection of the state of the self by the assertion of right consciousness, chapter 3, pp. 103–4.
120. Asserting correct human perception (rather than that of the dead, the dreaming or the spirits), that is, seeing butterflies as butterflies as they are supposed to be seen in the human reality, and not as fish as they are perceived in the reality of the dead, as in the story of the lake of butterflies, chapter 2, pp. 54–55.

121. The Mehinaku believe that when these birds sing a lot they are discussing a big catch of fish.
122. Stinginess among other unpleasant emotions that can exist under the outward appearance of the generous and in general kindly social ideal of *ketepepei,* chapter 5, p. 166; these emotions include strong xenophobic feeling toward members of other Xinguano groups such as the Kalapalo in this case, chapter 5, pp. 167–68.
123. Sense of *yerekyuki,* the need to fill an emptiness that is existentially dangerous, chapter 3, pp. 105–107; also simple hunger and looking forward to the pleasure of eating.
124. The substantial archetypes of which all things of the world are copies; chapter 2, p. 51.
125. The power of the *yeya*-archetypes, chapter 2, pp. 52–53.
126. Awareness of the effect on reality of the state of one's own consciousness and thus cultivation of the optimal type, chapter 4, p. 145.
127. The valuing of 'flow' in all areas of life, in this case in terms of the cleanliness/integrity of the body maintained externally by sluicing with water, chapter 3, p. 75
128. Cultivating a certain kind of body to make a certain consciousness (flesh-body as affecting state of consciousness, chapter 2, p. 56), to keep within and help maintain human reality (chapter 2, p. 61) with its qualities of cool cleanness, chapter 2, p. 36, and to even improve that reality by making oneself and thus one's world beautiful *(awitsiri),* chapter 4, p. 146.
129. The flowing cadence valued in Mehinaku movement, chapter 3, pp. 73–74.

Bibliography

Adalbert, Prince of Prussia. 1849. *Travels in the South of Europe and Brazil, with a Voyage up the Amazon and the Xingu.* Trans. Sir Robert H. Schomburgk and John Francis Taylor. London: David Bogue.

Agostinho da Silva, Pedro. 1972. 'Information Concerning the Territorial and Demographic Situation in the Alto Xingu', *The Situation of the Indian in South America: Contributions to the Study of Inter-Ethnic Conflict in the Non-Andean Regions of South America,* ed. W. Dostal. Geneva: World Council of Churches.

———. 1974. *Kwarip: Mito e Ritual no Alto Xingu.* São Paulo: Editôra Pedagógica e Universitária Ltda.

Armstrong, David M. 1997. *A World of States of Affairs.* Cambridge: Cambridge University Press.

Atkinson, Jane Monnig. 1992. 'Shamanisms Today'. *Annual Review of Anthropology* 21: 303–330.

Bachelard, Gaston. 1969. *The Poetics of Space.* Trans. Maria Jolas. Boston: Beacon Press.

Bamberger, Joan. 1974. 'The Myth of Matriarchy: Why Men Rule in Primitive Society'. In *Woman, Culture, and Society,* ed. M. Rosaldo and L. Lamphere. Stanford, CA: Stanford University Press.

Barcelos Neto, Aristoteles. 2003. *A Arte dos Sonhos – Uma Iconografia Ameríndia.* National Ethnology Museum: Assírio & Alvim.

———. 2004. 'As Mascaras Rituais do Alto Xingu um Seculo depois de Karl von den Steinen', *Bulletin de la Societé Suisse des Americanistes* 68 (2004): 51–71.

———. 2005. *O Universo Visual dos Xamãs Wauja (Alto Xingu).* Paris: Centre de Recherches sur les Mondes Américains.

Basso, Ellen. 1973. *The Kalapalo Indians of Central Brazil.* New York, Chicago, San Francisco, Atlanta, Dallas, Montreal, Toronto, London, Sydney: Holt, Rinehart and Winston, Inc.

———. 1985. *A Musical View of the Universe: Kalapalo Myth and Ritual Performances.* Philadelphia: University of Pennsylvania Press.

————. 1987. 'The implications of a progressive theory of Dreaming'. *Dreaming: Anthropological and Psychological Interpretations,* ed. Barbara Tedlock. Cambridge: Cambridge University Press.

————. 1995. *The Last Cannibals: A South American Oral History.* Austin: University of Texas Press.

Bastos, Rafael José de Menezes. 1983. 'Sistemas Políticos de communicação e articulação social no Alto Xingu', *Anuario Antropologico,* no. 81: 43–58. Rio de Janeiro.

————. 1984–1985. 'Payemeramaraka Kamayurá: uma contribuição à etnografia do xamanismo no alto Xingu', *Revista de Antropolgia* 27–28: 139–177.

————. 1999 [1978]. *A Musicológica Kamayurá: Para Uma Antropologia da Communicaçãono Alto Xingu.* Florianópolis: Universidade Federal de Santa Catarina.

————. 2000. 'Ritual, História e Política no Alto Xingu: Observações a Partir dos Kamayurá e do Estudo da Festa da Jaguatirica'. In *Os Povos do Alto Xingu: História e Cultura,* ed. Bruna Franchetto and Michael Heckenberger. Rio de Janeiro: Editora UFJR.

————. 2005. 'A festa da jaguaritirica: o primeiro e setimo canticos. Introduçao, transcricao e comentarios', *Revista de Antropologia* 4, no. 2: 133–174.

Bateson, Gregory. 2000. [1972]. *Steps to an Ecology of Mind: Collected Essays in Anthropology, Psychiatry, Evolution, and Epistemology.* Chicago: The University of Chicago Press.

Bisilliat, Maureen. 1979. *Xingu: Tribal Territory.* St. James Place, London: William Collins Sons and Co. Ltd.

Bourdieu, Pierre. 1977. *Outline of a Theory of Practice.* Cambridge: Cambridge University Press.

Brown, Lesley, Ed. 1993 [1933]. *The New Shorter Oxford English Dictionary: On Historical Principles.* Vol. 1 and 2. Oxford: Clarendon Press.

Carneiro da Cunha, Manuela, ed. 1979. *A Construção da Pessoa nas Sociedade Indigenas Brasileiras.* Boletim de Museu Nacional. Antropologia 32. Rio de Janeiro: Museu Nacional.

————. 1992. *História dos índios no Brasil.* Sao Paulo, Cia. das Letras, FAPESP/ SMC.

Carneiro, Robert L. 1977. 'Recent Observations of Shamanism and Witchcraft among the Kuikuru Indians of Central Brazil', *Annals of the New York Academy of Science,* no. 293: 215–228. New York.

Casey, Edward, S. 1987. *Remembering: A Phenomenological Study.* (Chapter 9: 'Place-Memory').

————. 1996. "How to Get from Space to Place in a Fairly Short Stretch of Time: Phenomenological Prolegomena." In *Senses of Place.* Santa Fe, NM: School of American Research Press.

Certeau, Michel de. 2002. *The Practice of Everyday Life.* Trans. S. F. Rendall. CA: The University of California Press.

Chernela, Janet M. 1988. 'Righting History in the Northwest Amazon: Myth, Structure and History in Arapaço narrative'. In *Rethinking History and Myth: Indig-*

enous South American Perspectives of the Past, ed. J. D. Hill. Urbana and Chicago: The University of Illinois Press.

Classen, Constance. 1990. 'Sweet Colors, Fragrant Songs: Sensory Models of the Andes and the Amazon', *American Ethnologist* 17, no. 14. (Nov.): 722–735.

Collingwood, Robin George. 1992. *The Idea of History.* Oxford: Oxford University Press.

Corbin, Henry. 2000 [1964]. 'Mundus Imaginalis: Or the Imaginary and the Imaginal'. In *Working with Images.* Woodstock: Spring Publications.

Cowell, Adrian. 1990. *The Decade of Destruction.* Headway: Hodder and Stoughton.

———. 1995. *The Tribe that Hides from Man.* London: Pimlico.

Crocker, Jon Christopher. 1985. *Vital Souls: Bororo Cosmology, Natural Symbolism and Shamanism.* Tuscon: University of Arizona Press.

Davis, Shelton H. 1977. *Victims of the Miracle: Development and the Indians of Brazil.* New York: Cambridge University Press.

De Onis, Juan. 1992. *The Green Cathedral: Sustainable Development of Amazonia.* New York, Oxford: Oxford University Press.

Descola, Phillipe. 1992. 'Societies of Nature and the Nature of Society'. In *Conceptualising Society,* ed. A. Kuper. London: Routledge.

———. 1994. *In the Society of Nature: A Native Ecology in Amazonia.* Cambridge: Cambridge University Press.

———. 1996. *The Spears of Twilight: Life and Death in the Amazon Jungle.* Trans. Janet Lloyd. London: HarperCollins Publishers.

De Souza Martins, José. 1980. 'Fighting for Lands: Indians and Posseiros in Legal Amazonia'. In *Land, People and Planning in Contemporary Amazonia.* Cambridge University: Centre of Latin American Studies.

Devereux, George. 1967. *From Anxiety to Method in the Behavioural Sciences.* The Hague: Mouton.

Devisch, René. 1993. *Weaving the Threads of Life: The Khita Gyn-Eco-Logical Healing Cult Among the Yaka.* The University of Chicago Press, Chicago.

Dierchxs, Marco and Villas-Boas, Orlando. 2003. *Alto Xingu.* Porto Alegre: Editora.

Dole, Gertrude E. 1966. 'Anarchy without Chaos: Alternatives to Political Authority among the Kuikuro'. In *Political Anthropology,* ed. Marc Swartz, Victor W. Turner and Arthur Tuden. Chicago: Aldine Publishing.

———. 1973. 'Shamanism and Political Control among the Kuikuro'. In *Peoples and Cultures of Native South America,* ed. Daniel R. Gross. New York: Doubleday/ Natural History Press.

———. 1984. 'The Structure of Kuikuro Marriage'. In *Marriage Practices in Lowland South America.* Urbana and Chicago: University of Illinois Press.

———. 2000. 'Retrospectiva da História Comparativa das Culturas do Alto Xingu: Um Esboço das Origens Culturais Alto-Xinguanas'. In *Os Povos do Alto Xingu: História e Cultura,* ed. Bruna Franchetto and Michael Heckenberger. Rio de Janeiro: Editora UFJR.

Durand, Gilbert. 2000. 'Exploration of the Imaginal'. In *Working with Images.* Woodstock: Spring Publications.

Eliade, Mircea. 1964. *Shamanism: Archaic Techniques of Ecstasy.* Trans. Willard R. Trask. Princeton: Princeton University Press.

Fausto, Carlos 1999. 'Of Enemies and Pets: Warfare and Shamanism in Amazonia'. *American Ethnologist* 26 (4): 933–956.

———. 2001. *Inimigos Fiéis. História, Guerra e Xamanismo na Amazônia.* São Paulo: EDUSP.

Feld, Steven. 1996. 'Waterfalls of Song: An Acoustemology of Place Resounding in Bosavi, Papua New Guinea'. In *Senses of Place.* Santa Fe: School of American Research Press.

Fénelon Costa, Maria Heloísa. 1978. 'O Mundo dos Mehinaku: Representações Visuais, Mito e Ceremonialismo'. *Sympósio I Bienal Latino-Americana de São Paulo,* 1–4, São Paulo.

———. 1988. *O Mundo dos Mehinako e suas Representações Visuais.* Brasília. Editora UnB.

———. 1997. 'Representações Iconográficas do Corpo em Duas Sociedades Indígenas: Mehinaku e Karajá'. *Rev. do Museu de Arqueologia e Etnologia,* 7: 65–69.

Franchetto, Bruna. 1992. 'O Aparecimento dos Caraíba: para uma História Kuikuro Alto-Xinguana'. In *História dos Índios no Brasil,* ed. M. Carneiro da Cunha. São Paulo: Cia. das Letras/Fapesp/SMC.

———. 2000. 'Linguas e História no Alto Xingu'. In *Os Povos do Alto Xingu: História e Cultura,* ed. Bruna Franchetto and Michael Heckenberger. Rio de Janeiro: Editora UFJR.

———. 2000b. 'Introdução: História e Cultura Xinguana'. In *Os Povos do Alto Xingu: História e Cultura,* ed. Bruna Franchetto and Michael Heckenberger. Rio de Janeiro: Editora UFJR.

Frazer, Sir James. 1993 [1890]. *The Golden Bough: A Study in Magic and Religion.* Ware: Wordsworth Editions.

Galvão, Eduardo. 1953. *Cultura e Sistema de Parentesco dos Tribos do Alto Xingu.* Rio de Janeiro: Boletim do Museu Nacional, 4.

Geertz, Clifford. 1966. 'Religion as a Cultural System'. In *Anthropological Approaches to the Study of Religion,* ed. Michael Banton. London: Tavistock.

Gell, Alfred. 1992. *The Anthroplogy of Time: Cultural Constructions of Temporal Maps and Images.* Oxford/Providence: Berg Publishers Limited.

———. 1996. 'Reflections on a Cut Finger: Taboo in the Umeda Conception of Self'. In *Things As They Are: New Directions in Phenomenological Anthropology,* ed. Michael Jackson. Bloomington and Indianapolis: Indiana University Press.

———. 1999. 'Style and Meaning in Umeda Dance'. In *The Art of Anthropology: Essays and Diagrams,* ed. E. Hirsch. London and New Brunswick, NJ: The Athlone Press.

Goldman, Irving. 1979 [1963]. *The Cubeo: Indians of the Northwest Amazon.* Urbano, Chicago, London: University of Illinois Press.

Gow, Peter. 1991. *Of Mixed Blood: Kinship and History in Peruvian Amazonia.* Oxford: Clarendon Press.

———. 2000. 'Helpless – The Affective Preconditions of Piro Social Life'. In *Love and Anger: The Aesthetics of Conviviality in Native Amazonia.* London and New York: Routledge.

———. 2001. *An Amazonian Myth and its History.* Oxford: Oxford University Press.

Gregor, Thomas. 1970. 'Exposure and Seclusion: A Study in Institutionalized Isolation among the Mehinako Indians of Brazil'. *Ethnology,* no. 9: 234–250.

———. 1977. *Mehinaku: The Drama of Daily Life in a Brazilian Indian Village.* Chicago and London: Chicago University Press.

———. 1979. 'Secrets, Exclusion and the Dramatization of Men's Roles'. In *Brazil: Anthropological Perspectives: Essays in Honour of Charles Wagley.* New York: Columbia University Press, ed. M. L. Margolis and W. E. Carter.

———. 1981a. 'A Content Analysis of Mehinaku Dreams', *Ethos* 9, no. 4, Dreams (Winter, 1981): 353–390.

———. 1981b. '"Far, Far Away my Shadow Wandered…": The Dream Symbolism and Dream Theories of the Mehinaku Indians of Brazil', *The Journal of American Ethnology,* ed. N. E. Whitten 8, no. 4, (November): 709–720.

———. 1985. *Anxious Pleasures: The Sexual Lives of an Amazonian People.* Chicago and London: Chicago University Press.

———. 1990. 'Uneasy Peace: Intertribal Relations in Brazil's Upper Xingu'. In *The Anthropology of War,* ed. J. Haas Cambridge: Cambridge University Press.

———. 1999. 'Symbols and Rituals of Peace in Brazil's Upper Xingu'. In *The Anthropology of Peace and Nonviolence,* ed. Leslie E. Sponsel and Thomas Gregor. Boulder/ London: Lynne Rienner Publishers.

———. 2000. 'Casamento, Aliança e Paz Intertribal'. In *Os Povos do Alto Xingu: História e Cultura,* ed. Bruna Franchetto and Michael Heckenberger. Rio de Janeiro: Editora UFJR.

Griffiths, Thomas. 2001. 'Finding One's Body: Relationships between Cosmology and Work in North-West Amazonia'. In *Beyond the Visible and the Material: The Amerindianization of Society in the Work of Peter Rivière,* ed. L. M. Rival and N. L. Whitehead. Oxford: Oxford University Press.

Gross, Daniel. 1980. 'Ecology and Acculturation among Native Peoples of Central Brazil', In *Land, People and Planning in Contemporary Amazonia.* Cambridge University: Centre of Latin American Studies.

Gullestad, Marianne. 1991. 'The Transformation of the Norwegian Notion of Everyday Life'. *American Ethnologist* 18, no. 3. Representations of Europe: Transforming State, Society and Identity (August): 480–499.

Guss, David M.1989. *To Weave and Sing: Art, Symbol, and Narrative in the South American Rain Forest.* Berkeley and Los Angeles: University of California Press.

Heckenberger, Michael J., James B. Peterson, and Eduardo Goés Neves. 1999. 'Village Size and Permanence in Amazonia: Two Archaeological Examples from Brazil'. *Latin American Antiquity* 10 (4): 353–376. Society for American Archaeology.

———. 1998. 'Manioc Agriculture and Sedentarism in Amazonia: the Upper Xingu Example'. In *Antiquity,* no. 72: 633–648.

————. 2000a. 'Estrutura, História e Transfromação: a Cultura Xinguana na Longue Durée, 1000–2000 d.C.' In *Os Povos do Alto Xingu: História e Cultura,* ed. Bruna Franchetto and Michael Heckenberger. Rio de Janeiro: Editora UFJR.

————. 2000b. 'Epidemias, Índios Bravos e Brancos: Contato Cultural e Etnogênese do Alto Xingu'. In *Os Povos do Alto Xingu: História e Cultura,* ed. Bruna Franchetto and Michael Heckenberger. Rio de Janeiro: Editora UFJR.

————. 2000c. 'Introdução: História e Cultura Xinguana'. In *Os Povos do Alto Xingu: História e Cultura,* ed. Bruna Franchetto and Michael Heckenberger. Rio de Janeiro: Editora UFJR.

————. 2004. *The Ecology of Power: Culture, Place and Personhood in the Southern Amazon, A.D. 1000 – 2000.* London: Routledge.

Hemming, John. 1987. *Amazon Frontier: The Defeat of the Brazilian Indians.* London: Macmillan.

Herdt, Gilbert. 1987. 'Review: [Untitled]', *The American Journal of Sociology* 93, no. 1. (July): 230–231.

Hill, Jonathan D. 1988. 'Introduction: Myth and History'. In *Rethinking History and Myth: Indigenous South American Perspectives on the Past,* ed. Jonathan D. Hill. Urbana and Chicago: University of Illinois Press.

Hugh-Jones, Christine. 1979. *From the Milk River: Spatial and Temporal Processes in Northwest Amazonia.* Cambridge: Cambridge University Press.

Hugh-Jones, Stephen. 1979. *The Palm and the Pleiades. Initiation and Cosmology in Northwest Amazonia.* Cambridge: Cambridge University Press.

————. 1982. 'The Pleiades and Scorpius in Barasana Cosmology', *Ethnoastronomy and Archaeoastronomy in the American Tropics. Annals of the New Academy of Sciences* 385: 183–203.

————. 1989. 'Wáríbi and the White Men: history and myth in Northwest Amazonia'. *History and Ethnicity,* ed. Elizabeth Tonkin, Maryon McDonald, and Malcolm Chapman. London: Routledge.

————. 1994. 'Shamans, Prophets, Priests, and Pastors'. In *Shamans, History and the State,* ed. N. Thomas. Ann Arbor: University of Michigan Press.

Hugh-Jones, Christine and Stephen. 1996. *Evaluation of the São Paulo Medical School's Unified Health Care Program in the Xingú Indigenous Park, Brazil.* Cambridge.

Hultkrantz, Ake. 1978. 'Ecological and Phenomenological Aspects of Shamanism'. In *Shamanism in Siberia.* Budapest: Akadémiai Kiadó.

Humphrey, Caroline. 1994. 'Shamanic Practices and the State in Northern Asia: Views from the Centre and Periphery', and 'Chiefly and Shamanist Landscapes in Mongolia'. In *Shamanism, History and the State,* ed. Nicholas Thomas and Caroline Humphrey. University of Michigan Press.

Ireland, Emilienne. 1988. 'Cerebral Savage: The Whiteman as Symbol of Cleverness and Savagery in Waurá Myth'. In *Rethinking History and Myth: Indigenous South American Perspectives of the Past.* Urbana and Chicago: University of Illinois Press.

Jackson, Michael. 1996. "Introduction: Phenomenology, Radical Empiricism and Anthropological Critique." In *Things As They Are: New Directions in Phenomeno-*

logical Anthroplogy. ed. Michael Jackson. Bloomington and Indianapolis: Indiana University Press.

―――. 1989. *Paths Towards a Clearing: Radical Empiricism and Ethnographic Enquiry.* Bloomington and Indianapolis: Indiana University Press.

James, William. 1947. *Essays in Radical Empiricism.* New York. London. Toronto: Longmans, Green and Co.

Jung, Carl Gustav. 1960. *The Structure and Dynamics of the Psyche.* London: Routledge & Kegan Paul.

Jonas, Hans. 1963. *The Gnostic Religion: The Message of the Alien God and the Beginnings of Christianity.* Boston: Beacon Press.

Lévi-Strauss, Claude. 1948. "The Tribes of the Upper Xingu River." In *Handbook of South American Indians.* Vol. 3, *The Tropical Forest Tribes,* ed. J. H. Steward. Washington: Smithsonian Institute.

―――. 1963. *Structural Anthropology.* Trans. Claire Jacobsen and Brooke Grundfest Schoepf. New York & London: Basic Books Inc.

―――. 1966 [1962]. *The Savage Mind.* Chicago: University of Chicago Press.

―――. 1964. *Le Cru et le Cuit.* Paris: Plon.

―――. 1987. *Anthropology and Myth: Lectures 1951–1982,* trans. Roy Willis. Oxford: Blackwell.

―――. 1988. *The Jealous Potter.* trans. Bénédicte Chorier. Chicago and London: University of Chicago Press.

Lima, Pedro E. 1944. *Notas antropológicas sobre os índios do Xingu: Observações zoológicas e antropológicas na região dos formadores do Xingú.* Publicações Avulsas do Museu Nacional, vol. 5: 21–29.

Malinowski, Bronislaw. 1999 [1922]. *Argonauts of the Western Pacific: An Account of Native Enterprise and Adventure in the Archipelagoes of Melanesian New Guinea.* London: Routledge.

Maybury-Lewis, David. 1974. *Akwê-Shavante Society.* Clarendon: Oxford University Press.

McCallum, Cecilia. 1994. 'Ritual and the Origin of Sexuality in the Alto Xingu'. In *Sex and Violence: Issues in Representation and Experience,* ed. P. Harvey and P. Gow. London: Routledge.

Melatti, Julio Cezar. 1984. 'A Antropologia no Brasil: um Roteiro', *Boletim Informativo e Bibliografico de Ciencias Sociais* (BIB) 17: 3–52.

Menezes, Maria Lúcia Pires. 1999. *Parque Indígena do Xingu: A Construção de um território estatal.* São Paulo: Imesp-Unicamp.

―――. 2000. 'Parque do Xingu: uma História Territorial'. In *Os Povos do Alto Xingu: História e Cultura,* ed. Bruna Franchetto and Michael Heckenberger. Rio de Janeiro: Editora UFJR.

―――. 2001. 'Parque do Xingu: uma História Territorial'. In *Os Povos do Alto Xingu: História e Cultura,* ed. Bruna Franchetto and Michael Heckenberger. Rio de Janeiro: Editora UFJR.

Merleau-Ponty, Maurice. 1962. *Phenomenology of Perception.* trans. C. Smith. London: Routledge.

Monod-Becquelin, Aurore. 1987. '"Les femmes sont un bien excellent": vision des hommes, être des femmes dans le Haut Xingu', *Anthropologie et Sociétés* 11, no. 1: 121–136.

Moran, Emilio, F. 1983. 'Development and Amazonian Indians: The Aguarico Case and Some General Principles'. In *The Dilemma of Amazonian Development.* Boulder: Westview Press.

Murphy, Robert and Murphy, Yolanda. 1974. *Women of the Forest.* New York and London: Columbia University Press.

Nugent, Stephen. 1990. *Big Mouth: The Amazon Speaks.* London: Fourth Estate.

Okri, Ben. 1995. *Birds of Heaven.* London: Phoenix House.

Overing, Joanna. 1985. 'Today I shall call him "Mummy": multiple world and classificatory confusion.' In *Reason and Morality,* ed. J. Overing. London: Tavistock Publications.

———. 2000a. 'The Efficacy of Laughter: The Ludic Side of Magic within Amazonian Sociality.' In *The Anthropology of Love and Anger: The Aesthetics of Conviviality in Native Amazonia.* London and New York: Routledge.

——— and Alan Passes. 2000b. 'Introduction: Conviviality and the Opening up of Amazonian Anthropology'. In *The Anthropology of Love and Anger: The Aesthetics of Conviviality in Native Amazonia.* London and New York: Routledge.

Passes, Allen and Joanna Overing. 2000. 'Introduction: Conviviality and the Opening up of Amazonian anthropology'. In *The Anthropology of Love and Anger: The Aesthetics of Conviviality in Native Amazonia.* London and New York: Routledge.

Piot, Charles, D. 1993. 'Secrecy, Ambiguity, and the Everyday in Kabre Culture', *American Anthropologist,* New Series 95, no. 2 (June): 353–370.

Rappaport, Joanne. 1998. *The Politics of Memory: Native Historical Interpretation in the Colombian Andes.* Durham and London: Duke University Press.

Ramos, Alcida Rita. 1988b. 'Indian Voices: Contact Experienced and Expressed'. In *Rethinking History and Myth.* ed. Jonathan Hill. Urbana: University of Illinois Press.

———. 1990. 'Ethnology Brazilian Style', *Cultural Anthropology* 5, no. 4 (November): 452–472.

Reichel-Dolmatoff, Gerardo. 1971. *Amazonian Cosmos: The Sexual and Religious Symbolism of the Tukano Indians.* Chicago and London: University of Chicago Press.

———. 1975. *The Shaman and the Jaguar: A Study of Narcotic Drugs by the Indians of Colombia.* Philadelphia: Temple University Press.

Ribeiro, Darcy. 1970. *Os Indios e a Civilização.* Rio de Janeiro: Civilização Brasileira.

Riesman, Paul. 1977. *Freedom in Fulani Social Life: An Introspective Ethnography.* trans. Martha Fuller. Chicago: The University of Chicago Press.

Rivière, Peter. 1994. 'WYSINWYG in Amazonia', *JASO* 25: 255–62.

Roe, Peter. 1982. *The Cosmic Zygote: Cosmology in the Amazon Basin.* New Brunswick, NJ: Rutgers University Press.

Rosaldo, Renato. 1980. *Illongot Headhunting 1883–1974: A Study in Society and History.* Stanford, CA: Stanford University Press.

———. 1989. *Culture and Truth.* Boston: Beacon Press.

Sahlins, Marshall. 1995. *How 'Natives' Think: About Captain Cook, for Example.* Chicago and London: University of Chicago Press.

Schwartzman, Stephan. 1995. 'Epilogue to the Pimlico Edition.' *The Tribe that Hides from Man.* London: Pimlico.

Seeger, Anthony. 1981. *Nature and Society in Central Brazil: The Suya Indians of Mato Grosso.* Cambridge, MA: Harvard University Press.

Seiler-Baldinger. 1980. 'Indians and the Pioneer Font in the Northwest Amazon'. *Land People and Planning in Contemporary Amazonia.* Cambridge University: Centre of Latin American Studies.

Shirokogroff, S. M. 1935. *Psychomental Complex of the Tungus.* trans. Janet Lloyd. Peking, China: Catholic University Press; London: Kegan Paul, Trench, Trubner & Co., Ltd. Press.

Sick, Helmut. 1959. *Tukani.* London: Burke Publishing Co. Ltd.

Sobo, Elisa J. 1993. 'Bodies, Kin, and Flow: Family Planning in Rural Jamaica', *Medical Anthropology Quarterly,* New Series 7, no. 1 (March): 50–73.

Sokolowsky, Robert. 2000. *Introduction to Phenomenology.* Cambridge: Cambridge University Press.

Steinen, K, von den. 1888. 'O Rio Xingu', *Revista da Sociedade de Geographia do Rio de Janeiro* no. 4: 189–212.

———. 1940. 'Entre os Aborígenes do Brasil Central', *Revista do Arquivo Municipal.* 34–48, (Separata).

———. 1942. *O Brasil Central: Expedicão de 1884 papa a Exploração do Xingu.* trans. Catarina Canata Canabrava. São Paulo: CiaEditora Nacional. (Série Extra, vol. 3).

Taussig, Michael. 1983. *The Devil and Commodity Fetishism in South America.* Chapel Hill: The University of North Carolina Press.

Taylor, Christopher. 1988. 'The Concept of Flow in Rwandan Popular Medicine', *Social Science and Medicine* 27: 1343–1348.

Théry, Hervé. 1980. 'State and Entrepreneurs in the Development of Amazonia'. In *Land People and Planning in Contemporary Amazonia.* Cambridge University: Centre of Latin American Sudies.

Tormaid Campbell, Alan. 1999 [1995]. *Getting to Know Waiwai: An Amazonian Ethnography.* London: Routledge.

Turner, Terence. 1988. 'History, Myth and Social Consciousness among the Kayapó of Central Brazil'. In *Rethinking History and Myth: Indigenous South American Perspectives of the Past.* Urbana and Chicago: University of Illinois Press.

Tylor, Edward Burnett. 1958 [1871]. *Primitive Culture.* New York: Harper & Row.

Villas Boas, Claudio, and Orlando Villas Boas. 1974. *The Xingu: The Indians, Their Myths.* London: Souvenir Press (Educational and Academic) Limited.

———. 1995. *A Marcha para o Oeste: a Epopéia da Expedição Roncador-Xingu.* São Paulo: Editora Globo, 1994.

———. 2002. *O Xingu dos Villas Bôas.* São Paulo: Editora Metalivros.

Viveiros de Castro, Eduardo. B. 1977. *Indivíduo e Sociedade no Alto Xingu: Os Yawalapiti.* Rio de Janeiro. Dissertação de Mestrado. PPGAS/Museu Nacional/UFRJ.

————. 1987 [1979]. 'A Fabricação do Corpo na Sociedade Xinguana'. In *Sociedades Indígenas e Indigenismo no Brasil,* ed. J. P. Oliveira Filho. Rio de Janeiro: Editora UFRJ/Marco Zero.

————. 1992. *From the Enemy's Point of View: Humanity and Divinity in an Amazonian Society.* trans. Catherine V. Howard. Chicago and London: The University of Chicago Press.

————. 1998. 'Cosmological Deixis and Amerindian Perspectivism'. *Journal of the Royal Anthropological Institute (N.S.)* 4: 469–488.

————. 2001. 'GUT Feeling about Amazonia: Potential Affinity and the Construction of Sociality'. In *Beyond the Visible and the Material,* ed. L. M. Rival and N. L. Whitehead.Oxford: Oxford University Press.

————. 2002. 'Esboço de Cosmologia Yawalapiti'. In *A Inconstância da Alma Selvagem – e Outros Ensaios de Antropologia.* São Paulo: Cosac & Naify.

Wagner, Roy. 1975 [1969]. *The Invention of Culture.* Englewood Cliffs, NJ: Prentice Hall.

Wittgenstein, Ludwig. 1979 [1931]. *Remarks on Frazer's Golden Bough.* trans. A. C. Miles, rev. and ed. R. Rhees. Nottingham: Brynmill Press Ltd.

Woolf, Virginia. 2000 [1931]. *The Waves.* Hertfordshire: Wordsworth Editions Ltd.

————. 2003 [1925]. *The Common Reader.* London: Vintage Classics.

Index

metaphor, 11
and notion of 'lived metaphor', 133–34,
149n13, 181
Mehinaku, 35–36, 133–35, 185, 189
methodology, 7–10, 12, 48, 180–81
Milky Way, 51, 62, 79, 91, 189
monkeys
as food, 68n18, 122n44, 131, 138
spirit of (*Pahër*), 102, 154
Moon (*Keshë*)
ancestry of, 31–32, 35, 82, 86, 132
as creator, 31–32, 67n11, 111, 160
as personification of gentle care and
conserving dynamic, 113, 115,
124n67, 126
in sky, 76, 86, 161
Morena (*Mushuna*), 82, 88–89, 185
music, 14, 19, 74, 123n53, 172n21
and illness, 42, 98–99, 103
and joy, 104–5, 142, 186
and spirits, 42, 44, 46, 98–99, 100–3,
109, 122n51, 140–41, 163, 173n24,
186
as a 'thing', 126
See also dance, ritual
myth. *See* story
'mythical thinking', 133, 142

night, 19, 21
associations of, 133, 135 ,185
and the dead, 63, 79, 84
and sorcerers, 50, 103, 129
and spirits, 47, 80–81, 91, 103 ,129,
135, 185

Okri, Ben, 181
oldness, 14, 32, 49, 68n22, 103, 113, 131,
148
ordinary reality, 147–148
definition of, 1–2, 13
writing about, 5–7, 10–12, 132–33,
179–80, 183–89
Os Povos do Alto Xingu, 12, 22n11, 22n20,
122n43, 174n38
Overing, Joanna, 13, 149n12
on Amazonian 'social psychology', 116,
140n26, 174n32, 174n39

critique of structuralism of, 133
on interaction of worlds for Piaroa,
120n16
owls, 79
spirit of (*Mulukuhë*), 112–13, 166–67
ownership, 42, 52, 67n13, 69n40, 91,
98–99, 102, 109, 111, 126, 143, 162,
185, 187. *See also uwekehë* complex

participant observation, 8. *See also* fieldwork
peacefulness, 11, 16, 58, 114, 116–17, 158,
170, 174n43, 189
'*pegar*'. *See* daring
penis, 31, 35
perception
as substantial, 40, 57, 126–27, 135, 186
See also consciousness
pequi fruit (*akäi*), 17–18, 22n24, 24–25,
40, 47–48, 75, 81, 85, 87, 113,
123n51, 161–62, 165, 170, 172n7,
172n21, 182, 185
Perkaintye people, 92, 145
perspectivism, 14, 60
phenomenology
approach, 2–5, 8, 11, 12, 15, 21n5, 125,
139, 152, 159, 178
description, 7, 10, 177, 180
physicalism, 48, 66, 70n42, 134
plants, 25–26, 31, 38–40, 66, 183, 186
and spirits, 41, 44, 47, 52, 85, 97, 133,
145, 187
uses of, 17, 26, 31, 85, 187
See also roots, trees
Plato, 52, 70n45, 179
pregnancy, 30, 136

rainbows, 26, 80, 87, 92–93, 95–96, 187
Reichel-Dolmatoff, Gerardo, 121, 138,
171n1
river, 17, 22n21, 25, 41, 49, 53, 63, 75–76,
84, 94, 105, 120n15, 158, 165
Curisevo, 1, 6, 16, 25–26, 183–85,
187–89
Milky Way, 51, 62, 79, 91, 189
Rivière, Peter, 60
ritual, 38, 68n26, 78, 113–14, 119n1, 148,
170

Yerepëhë people, 50–51, 58, 70n43, 71n54, 86, 121n30, 131
yeya archetypes
 conceptions of, 51–53, 179, 189
 generation of copies by, 51–53, 69n40, 86, 126, 134, 140, 189
 making things in imitation of, 127–28, 134–35, 140, 189

relation of concept of 'Masters of the Animals' to, 52
spirits and their, 51–53, 70n44, 70n50, 126, 189
youth, 14, 21, 32–34, 38, 49, 54, 67n5, 68n14, 81, 84, 91–93, 102, 104, 108, 112, 137, 142, 147, 160, 166, 186

CPSIA information can be obtained
at www.ICGtesting.com
Printed in the USA
LVHW05s1551260818
588188LV00012B/897/P

9 780857 451552